SOURCES IN
WESTERN
CIVILIZATION

The Renaissance and The Reformation
1300–1600

THE

AND THE

Sources in Western Civilization

GENERAL EDITOR, *Herbert H. Rowen*

RUTGERS UNIVERSITY

RENAISSANCE
REFORMATION
1300·1600

EDITED BY

Donald Weinstein

RUTGERS UNIVERSITY

THE FREE PRESS, NEW YORK

Collier-Macmillan Limited, London

For information, address:

The Free Press
A DIVISION OF THE MACMILLAN COMPANY
The Crowell-Collier Publishing Company
60 Fifth Avenue, New York, N.Y. 10011

Collier-Macmillan Canada, Ltd., Toronto, Ontario

DESIGNED BY ANDOR BRAUN

Library of Congress Catalog Card Number: 65–11894

PREFACE

IN making this anthology I have followed the premise that a few selections long enough to convey the meaning and spirit of their originals would give more insight into the period than a large collection of short pieces torn from context. This has forced me to restrict the total number of readings and has given me some painful choices. While I have not even attempted complete coverage, I have tried to make selections which represent significant points of view and developments of the period and which offer the reader something to think about and to discuss.

In the short prefaces to each of the selections I have suggested some points to be considered, but there is much more for the reader to discover by himself.

Dates in parentheses after the name of a person indicate his life span, except in the case of rulers, where they indicate the period of reign. Dates are given only for prominent personages or for those who figure in the discussion.

I wish to thank the following people who responded to my requests for advice and help: Michael Mahoney, Janet Cox Rearick, William R. Rearick, Michael Rinehart, Traian Stoianovich, Sylvia Strauss, Warren I. Susman, my wife, Anne K. Weinstein, and the staff members of the libraries of Rutgers University, The New Brunswick Theological Seminary and "I Tatti," the Harvard University Center for Italian Renaissance Culture, Florence, Italy.

D.W.

CONTENTS

SOURCES IN WESTERN CIVILIZATION

The Renaissance and The Reformation
1300–1600

INTRODUCTION

AROUND 1300 Europe was heading into a time of troubles. After two centuries of brilliant growth the energy that had founded cities, created industries and commerce, settled new lands, and swept the Mediterranean clear of Arabs seemed to be slipping away. German colonization to the east and south came to a stop. The cloth industry of Flanders and Brabant slackened, then declined. In Italy the great banks fell victim to a financial epidemic. Trade with the East dropped off. As the great age of medieval economic expansion came to its end, competition for power and wealth became sharper. The cities, where errant serfs had found work and freedom, and enterprising merchants riches and social honors, were now becoming hells of class hatred and violence. A famine swept over Europe in 1315, hitting urban centers especially hard, while in 1347 the first wave of bubonic plague made them death traps from which people fled in terror. The Black Death wiped out perhaps a third of Europe's population. Even the boundaries of Christendom were shrinking: Russia was lost to the Mongols, and Europe's eastern bastion at Constantinople was in danger of being swamped by the Ottoman Turks.

In the face of these crises leadership faltered. The Papacy still tried to rouse Christians to a united effort by preaching its old goal of crusade against the Infidel, but few responded with enthusiasm. The Papacy itself set a sorry example of disunity and divided purpose, with its factional politics in the Curia and its use of the crusade as a weapon against its Christian rivals for power in Italy. When Clement V removed the Papal court to Avignon in 1309, many thought the Church had touched its lowest level of indignity, but worse was still to come. Two generations later Christians were confounded by the spectacle of two, then three, contestants for the Mantle of Peter, each claiming that he had been elected with divine help. The Papacy's main rivals for the leadership of Christendom had been the Hohenstaufen line of Holy Roman Emperors. But the last of the Hohenstaufens had been killed off in 1268, and their successors did not count for much in European affairs. Even when a fourteenth-century Emperor managed to wrench himself free of German politics and make his way to Rome to claim his crown, he only demonstrated his powerlessness to make it count for something. With the failure of both Empire and Papacy to provide leadership, France might have been expected to step into the vacuum, for the French monarchy in the thirteenth century had been vigorously expansionist and French culture had been the glory of Western Christendom. But in 1337 France fell into war with the English, a war that was to drag on for more than a hundred years. No one else had either the juridical authority or the power to provide an alternative to the two faltering "universal" institutions. From west to east the European princes were occupied with the more limited problems of dynastic consolidation and the internal opposition of feudalities and municipalities. Even the Hundred Years War was more a series of quarrels over a feudal succession than a war between nations rivaling each other for a leading place in the sun. The Spaniards, it is true, already were pursuing their mission of fighting for Christendom; but until the sixteenth century their vision was limited to the Iberian peninsula and the Moroccan coast. Russia, still cut off from Europe by the Mongol occupation, was a collection of dependent feudal states, while the Jagiello empire of Poland, Lithuania, Hungary, and Bohemia was held together by a dynastic tie which soon came loose.

The sense that the times had gone awry had an effect upon the way people viewed life — and death. In the fourteenth century the *memento mori,* the reminder that death awaits us all, became an important theme of Christian morality. Men as far apart as Henry Suso, the Flemish mystic, and Francesco Petrarca, the Italian poet, wrote that life's actions should be guided by the constant thought of mortality, while the *ars moriendi,* "the art of dying well," was to become one of the most popular subjects of fifteenth-century literature and book illustration. But natural calamities, depression, fear of the Infidel, and the folly and weakness of the Papacy and the Empire suggested more than the mortality of the individual: they were taken as judgments of God against mankind's wickedness, and therefore as signs that a new time was coming. Many believed that the world was old and time was running down, that Christ would soon appear again to judge the quick and the dead and put an end to earthly life. Others believed that God would not let the world go out without first giving it a foretaste of eternal bliss, that he was preparing a new millennium, when the Church would enter a new era and men would live in spiritual joy in one universal fold under one shepherd. To be sure, the Church frowned upon all such attempts to see too clearly into the dark glass of the future. It held with Saint Augustine that prophecies of the millennium referred to the present age, that no new rule would replace the rule of Rome in this life, and that the New Heaven and the New Earth of the Book of Revelation were allegories of the life beyond the grave. Nevertheless, in the thirteenth century, a new doctrine had made considerable headway against the official view. The Abbot Joachim of Fiore (? –1202) had taught that just as the Age of the Son (Christ) had succeeded the Age of the Father, so a Third Age, of the Holy Spirit, would succeed the Second, and this would be the age of peace and love, of the New Heaven and the New Earth, the millennium, when the Eternal Gospel would be revealed finally and entirely. Joachim believed that the millennium would begin in 1260, and his teaching had been carried throughout Italy and beyond, especially by Franciscan critics of conditions in the Church. How people responded we can tell from reading the chronicle of Fra Salimbene, himself a Franciscan and a Joachimite of the thirteenth century. In the year 1260, he wrote

> all men, both small and great, noble knights and men of the people, scourged themselves naked in procession through the cities . . . And this was the year wherein that age should have begun which was foretold by Abbot Joachim, who divideth the world into three estates: and they say that this last state of the world began with the Flagellants of the year 1260 who cried with God's words and not with men's.

The world did not enter a new age in 1260, but men continued to whip themselves for their sins in flagellant processions, some expecting Antichrist and the end of the world, others hoping for an Emperor Redeemer or an Angelic Pope, Poets, preachers, and chroniclers noted the conjunctions of certain planets, the floods and plagues and monstrous births, and took them as signs that the prophecies of Daniel or St. John or the Abbot Joachim were being fulfilled. Giovanni Villani, who began his chronicle in the year 1300, tells how a donkey killed a lion which had been given to the city of Florence by Pope Boniface VIII:

> This was understood as one of the many signs of great changes to come which appeared in our city at that time. Certain learned men said it pointed to the fulfillment of the prophecy of the Sibyl which says: When the ordinary beast kills the king of the beasts then the dissolution of the Church will commence.

Dante Alighieri, who wrote his *Divine Comedy* about the same time, also believed that the signs indicated a great scourge and reform.

> For what I report I plainly see, stars already nearby which are bringing an era safe from every obstacle, when a Five Hundred, Ten and Five sent by God will kill the thief and the giant who lies with her in sin.

The numbers in Dante's prediction seem to have been symbols for DUX, the reforming Emperor who would punish simony in the Church and usher in a new era. But no reforming Emperor or Angelic Pope appeared. The Avignon exile and the Great Schism pointed up the need for reform "in head" as well as "in members," but the Popes were unwilling or unable to set reform machinery in motion, while they jealously opposed the "Conciliarists" who tried to transfer the initiative from the Papacy to a general council of the Church representing all the faithful. The Popes were successful; by the mid-fifteenth century they had outmaneuvered the Conciliarists and upheld the principle of monarchical authority in the Church. But they paid a higher price for their victory than they realized. Pressure for reform mounted, and much of the criticism of clerical corruption centered on the Papacy itself. In the late fifteenth century the Popes with their magnificent courts and their power politics made an easy target. Roderigo Borgia, who reigned as Alexander VI from 1492 to 1503, became a symbol of the Church's degradation almost from the moment of his allegedly simoniacal election. Perhaps Alexander was not — apart from his private life — so bad a Pope as he was painted, but his wife and his mistress and his ambitious and showy children made good copy for scandal. Shortly afterward, during the reign of Leo X (1512–1522), another Pope with a reputation for soft living, Martin Luther launched his attack on the Roman system. While Luther aimed his main shaft at Roman theology, he also hit at the corruption of the Papacy and clergy and played upon the widespread resentment of foreign rule, thus rubbing salt into wounds that had been festering for a long time. The body of Latin Christendom broke up over the shock, and no one knew how to put it back together again. Although few were ready to discard the notion of a united body of Christendom, by 1600 it was fairly clear that this legacy of the Middle Ages would no longer hold up in the court of facts.

While Christendom seemed to be forgetting its common goals and dissolving into warring states and warring churches, the Turks mounted an offensive that carried them into the heart of Europe itself. They took Constantinople in 1453, knifed into the Balkan underbelly, tormented Venetian shipping in the Mediterranean, and even raided the coasts of Dalmatia and Italy. Under Suleiman the Magnificent they pressed up the Danube valley into Hungary, where in the battle of Mohacs in 1526 they slew the young King Louis and many of the Hungarian nobility. In 1529 they were at the gates of Vienna; Germany seemed open to them. But almost miraculously Vienna held. Nevertheless, many believed that God had only deferred His judgment. For the rest of the century the continuing Turkish menace was considered the surest sign that Antichrist was about to punish sinful Christendom.

I. THE ITALIAN RENAISSANCE

Thus, much of the anguish in life and dread of death that beset Europe around 1300 lingered on. And yet this same period was also one of recovery and new growth. The years between 1300 and 1600 were among the most vital periods of Western civilization. During this time Europeans rediscovered the wisdom and beauty in the civilizations of Greece and Rome and also discovered their own creative powers and human dignity. They penetrated Africa and Asia and opened a new hemisphere to their colonization. They created new forms of political and religious life and expanded commerce to world dimensions. They began a revolution in science which was to help them win the mastery of the world. In short, they passed from the conditions of life and thought which we call medieval to those we call modern. As always in human history, new forms came to life as old ones were passing, and, as always, the passage was painful as well as joyful; regret alternated with pride, pessimism with hope. Rarely, however, has there been a period when people were so conscious of change, because rarely have changes in so many areas of life crowded together or succeeded each other so unceasingly as in this period. That is why the waning Middle Ages saw a resurgence and confusion of apocalyptic ideas. Men still had the habit of regarding human events in the light of providential design, and since their experience was so intense they thought a great deal about the Last Judgment and yet also about an earthly paradise.

But widespread as this apocalyptic view of history was, there were some people who found it unsatisfactory as a way of understanding what was happening, and they struggled to work out a better one. Italian thinkers took the lead. In Italy the Christian and universal institutions of the Empire and Papacy had to compete with the independent-minded communes, towns which, in the late Middle Ages, had achieved political independence and a republican form of government. The communes had no place in the great theological schemata of history worked out by Augustine and Orosius centuries earlier, and their representative governments did not reflect, as the Empire and Papacy did, God's organization of the world as a pyramid topped by a monarchy. In other words, the phenomenon of the communes was a secular one, and their history stimulated men to think about the purely "natural" and human aspects of institutional development — about what causes cities to grow and to become powerful, about the nature of human capacities and achievements. The fortunes of the communes varied. Some never achieved independence; others attained it and lost it again; certain communes rose to great power at the expense of their neighbors. Already in the fourteenth century some were passing from republican government to the rule of a despot or an oligarchy. Thus, the communes presented the problem of decline as well as of growth, and providential design was not an entirely satisfactory explanation. One great example of civic growth and decline pressed on the consciousness of Italians — the example of Rome. In the Middle Ages Rome's decline was understood as part of God's plan, for the pagan world had to die before the New Rome of Christendom could be born. In the fourteenth century, however, Italian thinkers began to find a new meaning in Roman history as the outstanding example of municipal growth and decay, and they began to mine Roman authors for data which would shed light on the parallel problems of the Italian communes of their own day. Albertino Mussato (1261–1329), who tried to understand the decline of the republic of Padua and its loss of political freedom, was one of the first to attempt a new theory. Mussato combined the comments of Roman writers, notably Sallust, with Aristotelian political theory (Aristotle's *Politics* had been translated for the first time in the thirteenth century) and Arab astrological "science," to arrive at a pattern of natural, organic town development which at the same time placed much of the responsibility for the success and failure of political institutions upon the actions of men themselves. He did not break with Christian values altogether, maintaining that the unselfishness of its citizens and their service for the common good made a city strong, while greed and ambition caused it to decline; but Mussato was working toward a theory in which political development was independent of providential goals and centered on human rather than divine agency. Mussato's point of view was carried further by his younger contemporary and compatriot, known as Marsiglio of Padua (ca. 1275–ca. 1342), who concentrated, however, on the *function* of government rather than on its development [2].* Marsiglio treated government as a human institution directed toward the realization of human goals. Men organized themselves into a political community to protect their goods and meet their needs, not — at least not primarily — to serve God or to fulfill some supernatural end. Moreover, they retained the authority by which they established the state in the first place; political power rested upon the consent and represented the will of the community; it did not depend upon the sanction or will of God. No one until Machiavelli in the sixteenth century stated the secular theory of the state so clearly and forcefully as Marsiglio, although he did not make Machiavelli's separation between private Christian morality and political necessity.

While Mussato, Marsiglio, and others contributed some important new ideas of historical process and secular values, Francesco Petrarca (1304–1374) provided a whole new perspective [3]. Depressed by the Papacy's abandonment of Italy and by the tendency of Christian thought to lose itself in abstractions, Petrarch, as we usually call him, dismissed the long-held notion that Christianity had brought light into the dark world of paganism while carrying on all that was worthwhile of Roman institutions. For Petrarch the reverse was true: when pagan Rome fell the world was plunged into barbarism and shadow. He believed that the fourth century marked a sharp break in the thread of history; since then men had been living in a different age, and a worse one. Petrarch did not deny that the advent of Christianity was an incomparable blessing; he was a be-

---

* Bracketed numbers refer to the numbers of the selections presented in the text.

liever, and he tried to live according to Christian precepts. But he valued other things intensely—an elegant style of expression in speech and poetry, wisdom about human life, heroic activity, and the fame that came from achievement in these things. It seemed to Petrarch that these were the virtues which had made Rome great and were so lacking in his own time. These, in short, were the creative values of civilization. This is what he meant when he said that all history was but the praise of Rome. Petrarch did not merely carp over the deficiencies of his time nor pine for antiquity. If he had an acute sense of loss, of the historical distance that separated his own time from antiquity, he also had a faith that it was possible to revive some of the greatness of the ancients by cultivating their virtues. The best way to do this, he believed, was to study the language and writings of the ancients and try to imitate them. Thus Petrarch's new perspective of history carried with it a new program—the revival of classical antiquity. It was essentially a literary and educational program. One began by studying classical Latin—and hopefully Greek too, for Petrarch recognized how much Roman culture owed to Greece—since only by knowing the languages of the ancients as they themselves had known them could one hope to communicate with them and share their wisdom and virtues. Imitation for Petrarch was never a servile mimicry; it was not only the *form* but also the *spirit* which he strived to recapture. That spirit was the ability to shape life according to high standards of beauty and morality; it was creativity itself. In his own Latin writings Petrarch tried to prove that the classical style could be successfully imitated and that the classical writers had much to teach even Christians about the good life. He heaped scorn upon the schoolmen, the Christian theologians of the universities, for their "barbaric" Latin and their preoccupation with abstract metaphysical questions (although this was also part of the process of absorbing classical thought, a fact which Petrarch ignored). He emphasized the ethical content of classical literature and its application to the problems of evolving a personal, practical philosophy, as well as a philosophy of politics. He showed that the beauty of nature could be a stimulus to art and to reflecting upon man's relation to God. In his Italian poetry he talked about man's love for woman without shame or apology, and he sang of his love for his native land. He analyzed himself, his weaknesses, his feelings, his hopes and fears, and he wrote about them so interestingly that he founded the study of personality as a literary genre.

Petrarch was not one of the great philosophers or intellectual system builders of our civilization. By introducing the idea of a golden age of antiquity which might be restored he raised more problems than he solved. He never succeeded in reconciling, even to his own satisfaction, his commitment to Christianity with his pursuit of fame and his devotion to beauty of form and style. But his writings were full of striking insights and fruitful ideas which later men used. In this sense, and also in the sense that he made of his own life such a fascinating study, he was the first man of the Renaissance. At the base of his teaching was his new view of history, which carried with it a new appreciation of the past, a new kind of criticism of the present, and the germ of a new program for the future.

As a poet Petrarch became famous throughout Europe during his own century. Even in far-away England, first reached by Venetian galleys only in 1314, Petrarch's sonnets delighted Geoffrey Chaucer. But as a historian and educator Petrarch appealed primarily to his own countrymen. For another half-century at least, the few northerners who were interested in the new Italian learning had to come to Italy for it. This is understandable enough; Petrarch's new ideas about culture were bound up with a theory of history that exalted Rome and the superiority of the "Latins," disdained the contributions of the other European peoples to medieval civilization, and called upon Italians to resist "barbarian" debasement by reasserting their moral and intellectual, perhaps even the political leadership of their great Roman past. Besides, Petrarch's views were particularly relevant to fourteenth-century Italian society, with its urban centers, its secular interests, and its republicanism. The conflict discussed in his imaginary conversations with St. Augustine [3] was the conflict of men caught between two ideals of life, between the spiritual vision of the Heavenly City and the concrete attractions of the Earthly City. The pleasures he celebrated in his letters — friendship, literature, conversation, fame, and the quiet country life — were the pleasures of the cultivated, sophisticated men of the towns.

Nowhere were Petrarch's ideas so enthusiastically received as in Florence, the industrial and banking city-state on the Arno River. The Florentines were already proud of their cultural leadership. Florence was the city of Giotto, who had recently begun a revolution in painting, and of Dante, who used the Tuscan dialect for his *Divine Comedy.* Giovanni Boccaccio, who was not only the author of the ribald tales of the *Decameron,* but a poet and classicist and Petrarch's first disciple, settled there in 1340 and held the city's first lectureship in poetry. By the time Boccaccio died in 1375, Florence was the main center for those who had a passion for the new "humane letters.] Not that it was a withdrawn haven of the kind that Petrarch had made for himself in the valley of the Vaucluse. The city was more like a cockpit, for, from the first, humanism was polemical and required a way with language. In discussion and in writing one vaunted one's classical learning and displayed one's wit, often at the expense of others. The humanists heatedly discussed whether Petrarch was a greater poet than Dante; if it was more dignified to study law or medicine; whether a life of action was preferable to a life of contemplation; which was superior, the will or the intellect; and a hundred more questions which they believed were more vital than the *quodlibet* disputations of the theologians. When not arguing with each other the humanists made common cause against logicians and theologians who wasted philosophy on technical issues, physicians who put the cure of the body above the cultivation of the mind and refreshment of the spirit, educators who did not know good — that is, classical — Latin, and clerics who were poor examples of Christian morality. Their victims fought back, charging the humanists with ignorance of philosophy and, because of their partiality for pre-Christian writers and for the non-theological virtues, with pagan leanings. This roused the humanists to defend their activities and thereby to elaborate their theories of literature and scholarship. Boccaccio called poetry a divine gift of inspiration in the search for beauty and the communication of worthy ideas. Coluccio Salutati characterized the ancient poets as moralists who praised virtue and attacked vice with appropriate words and elegant language.

[The early enthusiasts of humanism were men of property like Roberto de' Rossi and Niccolò Niccoli, teachers like Boccaccio, and even monks like Luigi Marsigli. Soon a new type appeared, men trained as notaries and lawyers who were attracted to Florence by the double opportunity of pursuing their scholarly interests in the most stimulating environment and of employing their talents for pay, for the Florentines recognized more quickly than others the usefulness of civic servants who were also trained in classical rhetoric and literature. These were men who could frame a powerful diplomatic attack and compose an elegant public oration. In 1375 Coluccio Salutati (1331–1406) was appointed chancellor of the Florentine commune, the first of a line of famous humanists to fill the office. A chancellor, wrote the Florentine, Goro Dati, "remains all day on duty at the Palace; he writes all the letters and communiqués that are sent to the princes of the world and to all governments and private persons on behalf of the Commune." Salutati fulfilled this function of the office brilliantly. His pen was one of the Republic's most effective weapons in her struggles with the Papacy and against the greater threat of the expanding Milanese state, a service which the ruler of Milan, Giangaleazzo Visconti, ruefully acknowledged when he said that one of Salutati's letters was worth a whole troop of mounted men. But Salutati's ideas went beyond the rhetoric of diplomacy. During those years when the Florentine republic was threatened from without by Milan and from within by civil conflict which was partly due to the staggering costs of war, partly to unresolved class differences, Salutati rallied his fellow citizens by formulating the goals of resistance and unity. Florence, "the daughter of Rome," he said, was charged with the civilizing mission of the ancient Republic and if she lost her independence, not only tyranny but barbarism would be the victor. To preserve her independence abroad, Florence had to be free at home; it was unthinkable that a state which had succumbed to domestic tyranny would be fit to resist subjection from without. The key to the survival of republicanism, and therefore to independence, Salutati thought, lay in the qualities of its citizens, who must be aware of their responsibilities and prepared to fulfill them with vigorous, informed participation in the life of their city. In this Salutati carried the reassessment of medieval ideals a long way beyond Petrarch's beginnings. Where Petrarch had formulated a new idea of learning, Salutati formulated a new ideal of citizenship. Where Petrarch still regarded the scholar-poet as a lone contemplative, almost monastic in his withdrawal from the market place, from the court, even from normal family life, Salutati called upon the man of learning to be a citizen, and, conversely, upon the citizen to be an educated man.

Salutati's lead and Florence's continuing struggle for good government and independence inspired the next generation of Florentine humanists to investigate further the relations between political freedom and culture. These "civic humanists," as they have been called, argued that the pursuit of wealth and fame, far from being asocial or un-Christian, enhanced the common life and therefore had a moral function. They re-examined traditional social ideals of aristocracy, pointing out that true nobility came from the cultivation of virtue and the selfless performance of social responsibilities, rather than from "good" birth. They found something godlike in human powers, and therefore they placed artistic expression and creative thought on a level with formal worship as religious acts. Many of these ideas were put into a broad context by the Florentine chancellor Leonardo Bruni (1370–1444). Bruni wrote a history of the Florentine people to show that a great rebirth of civilization had begun with the revival of city life in the Middle Ages; thus he carried forward Petrarch's tentative formulation of a secular approach to history and the idea of a Renaissance; but he reversed Petrarch's idea of the relation between culture and politics. For Bruni, it was not literary study but political freedom that led to a revival of civilization; the life of the free city was the environment in which human society and culture flourished best. This is also why he could regard the Renaissance as a historical event, not merely, as Petrarch had, as a possibility of the future. For Bruni Italian communal life had already begun, deep in the period that Petrarch regarded as the Dark Ages.

In reality, as far as most of the Italian cities were concerned, the civic humanists were framing an epitaph rather than a program. By the fifteenth century many of the old communes had fallen under the rule of despots or had been absorbed by their more powerful neighbors — or both. Venice was the most important exception, for there republican government continued; in fact, it lasted down to the Napoleonic conquest. But Venice did not provide much inspiration for civic humanism, since it had purchased stability by creating a hereditary aristocracy and thus had shut most of its people out of participation in the political life of the republic. Even in Florence Bruni and his friends were fighting a rearguard action. Cosimo de' Medici emerged as the city's strong man by 1434, and thereafter the Medici family tightened its grip upon the government, although it kept the forms of representation, if not the substance, for another century.

However, if civic freedom did not survive in Italy, the ideas of the civic humanists did. They survived in the new ways of thinking about human history, in the humanist program of liberal education, in the new forms of political analysis, and in the ideal of free citizenship which is one of the unique values of Western civilization.

Still another major innovation of the Renaissance began in Florence. In 1397, at the Republic's invitation, a Byzantine scholar-diplomat named Manuel Chrysoloras began teaching Greek there, the first Greek to be systematically taught in the West for centuries. These lectures generated a great deal of excitement, first among humanists already in Florence, such as Leonardo Bruni, then among Italians elsewhere. By 1429 Florence was no longer dependent upon Greeks to fill the chair, and about the same time other cities began to hire teachers of Greek for their schools. Foreign students began to come to Italy to study the language of Plato and Aristotle, and by the end of the fifteenth century Greek was once more standard equipment for scholars and a part of the university curriculum in Europe. To be sure, European culture was already permeated with Greek ideas, from those in the Gospel of St. John and in the Epistles of St. Paul to those in medieval geography and astronomy. The translation of Aristotle's works in the twelfth and thirteenth centuries had injected into circulation a new dose of Hellenism which was then assimilated by Thomas Aquinas and other scholastic theologians. The Greek revival in the Italian Renaissance was, therefore, only the latest of the successive waves of Greek influence that rolled over European thought from time to time and were absorbed. Each of these waves, however, had different characteristics and effects. Renaissance Hellenism differed from earlier revivals because it was based on a restoration of the knowledge of the Greek *language,* rather than on translations and commentaries which had come, mainly, from the Arabs. This meant that the thousand-year breach between European civilization and its Hellenic foundation was put under repair. European scholars could now go directly to the source and make their own selections of what they found important in Greek thought. Moreover, where the revival of the twelfth century had been limited to Aristotle and a few scientific works, the Renaissance opened up the whole rich vein of Greek ore, and its mining operations produced incalculable wealth. Now Aristotle was no longer the only "teacher of those who know," as Dante had called him; he had rivals in Zeno, Epictetus, Galen, and, above all, Plato, most of whose works were unknown in the Middle Ages. The influence of the Platonic revival in the Renaissance was enormous. Platonism and Neoplatonism (doctrines derived from Plato's early followers rather than from Plato directly) influenced almost all subsequent philosophy and literature and even painting and sculpture. Generally speaking, Platonism, with its idea of a unified Being, stimulated new efforts to reconcile and relate the diverse phenomena of man, nature, and God, after fourteenth century scholastic thought had stressed their separateness. Some Renaissance Platonists, most notably Nicholas of Cusa (1401–1464), sought for the link through mathematical symbolism [5]; others, led by Marsilio Ficino (1433–1499), believed that man could identify himself with the universe and with God through spiritual love. Both thinkers considered themselves Christians, yet they were less interested in Christ's mediation than in a direct philosophical grasp of the great mystery. Platonism reinforced the Renaissance disposition to place man at the intellectual center of things and to exalt his role as knower and doer. On the other hand, it tended to conceive this role as contemplative, artistic, and religious, not political as the civic humanists did. This is one reason why Platonism became so popular in the second half of the fifteenth century, when men were searching for values more suited to their social environment than were the ideals of Bruni and Salutati. However, as has already been said, the older tradition of civic humanism continued as well. Certain writers, especially outside Italy, such as the Dutch humanist Desiderius Erasmus (1469–1536) and the Englishman Thomas More (1477–1536), used both the ideas of the civic humanists and of the Platonists in formulating their criticism of existing society [10].

The Greek revival not only added new-old ideas to the stock of existing knowledge, it also helped to change men's conceptions of what knowledge is and how it is attained. One of the liveliest philosophical discussions of the mid-fifteenth century was the quarrel between the champions of Plato and those of Aristotle, which Pico della Mirandola (1463–1494) hoped to resolve by showing that there was no real disagreement between the two. But some drew a different conclusion from the contradictions between the ancient authorities; they began to see that classical thought was no perfected body of wisdom that need only be appropriated by their own inferior minds, but that philosophy and science were debatable subjects open to further investigation and that modern men might have something to contribute. This turned many thinkers to consider the problems of method, for they began to see that the answers they received were partly determined by the questions they asked and the way that they proceeded in investigation. Method became a major preoccupation of Renaissance philosophy, especially at the University of Padua (where Galileo later studied) and, in the sixteenth century, at Paris, where Peter Ramus (1515–1572) claimed that he was replacing Aristotelian logic with his own, derived partly from Plato. The discussion of method bore its most important fruit in the seventeenth century, with the work of René Descartes and Francis Bacon, while it was Blaise Pascal who said that modern men were the real "ancients," since they had many more centuries of *experience* than the classical thinkers. Thus the Renaissance, which is often criticized for aspiring to nothing more than imitation of ancient models, actually produced the conditions for the emancipation of Western thought from its subservience to classical authority.

Nothing better illustrates the originality of the Renaissance than its art [6]. Classical inspiration played its part as one element in sculpture and architecture, but in painting there were almost no classical models to imitate. By the fourteenth century the Florentine Giotto (ca.1266–1337) was achieving fame for his ability to paint religious scenes which gave an illusion of reality unknown in any other painter's work. Looking at his figures one can almost forget that they are flat, like the church wall upon which they were painted, for Giotto had discovered methods of foreshortening, composition, and modeling that suggested depth and mass. His painted figures also seem to move and feel, to express deeply felt emotion. The viewer looks *into,* not merely *at* Giotto's scenes, and he feels he is participating in the action and therefore in the emotion as well. By "knocking a hole in the wall" Giotto introduced new forms into painting — not necessarily better or more beautiful ones, for earlier painting had its own genius and its own beauty, but excitingly new ones. Whether because his powerful scenes appealed to an already growing demand for more intense personal religious experience, or because he taught his contemporaries to see in a new way, Giotto established new standards of artistic taste. In Florence during the fourteenth century, his followers covered church walls with religious scenes done in his manner. Elsewhere, painters combined Giotto's new interest in foreshortening and in the expression of emotion with the more stylized forms and the delicate decoration of the Gothic to produce a Europe-wide artistic language known as "The International Style." In the second half of the fourteenth century, perhaps as a consequence of the Black Death, even the Florentines returned to the more traditional forms of religious painting, as though, like Petrarch, they felt guilty for having abandoned the old ways. But the gloom of the Black Death could not permanently obliterate the memory of Giotto or dim the excitement of experimentation. By the early fifteenth century Florentine artists had set out again on a passionate quest for new forms. The painter Masaccio (1401–1428) surpassed Giotto in representing powerful flesh-and-blood figures and discovered how to create an atmosphere around them which we feel we can almost breathe and touch. The architect Filippo Brunelleschi (1377–1446) carefully studied the forms of ancient Roman buildings to discover the secret of their beauty and applied his principles in such masterpieces as the chapel of the Pazzi family and the dome of the cathedral in Florence. The sculptor Donatello (ca.1386–1466) combined the fourteenth-century tradition of realism with the idealism of classical statues to produce figures of men who seem to declare their double origin, human yet touched with divinity.

These brilliant innovators left their successors with a host of challenging tasks which set the program of Italian art for another half-century. Everywhere in Italy there was an effort to recreate reality in paint and stone, but not in the literal, naturalistic way of the Gothic style. The Italian artists of the fifteenth century discovered that in order to convey reality they had to do more than present to the eye of the viewer perfectly reproduced separate data; they had also to present to the *mind* the illusion of life and movement within the bodies of their painted figures and the illusion of space and distance in their landscapes. In searching for the way to represent the vitality of men and animals they turned to the study of anatomy. They discovered how to suggest mass and roundness by juxtaposing light and shadow. They also learned to create perspective by the arrangement of lines, and they solved the problem of relating the foreground of a picture to its background by leading the eye along carefully planned routes and by diminishing the size of the forms. Just as Petrarch had learned to look at classical antiquity from a distance, and thereby improved his historical vision, so the Renaissance painters learned to paint a scene as though it were observed from a fixed point in space, so that each object fell into a relative position, thereby giving a more convincing impression of the whole.

Renaissance artists were anxious to create beauty as well as to convey the impression of reality, and, under the influence of classical thought, some of them — for example, Leone Battista Alberti (1404–1472) and Leonardo da Vinci (1452–1519) — considered the problem in philosophical terms. In general they concluded, with Plato, that beauty in art as in nature is the result of a harmonious relation of parts, and they tried to find the geometric shapes and arithmetic proportions which provide the greatest satisfaction. This complicated their problem of representation enormously, yet many of them faced the challenge and created works of art in which they sought to obtain beauty by the most painstaking and studied arrangement of lines, forms, and colors. Alberti tried to carry out his ideas of mathematical harmonies in his designs for buildings like the Rucellai Palace in Florence and the Church of St. Andrea in Mantua. Leonardo's *Last Supper* is a supreme example of aesthetic theory applied to painting: it captures a moment of intense excitement, when the Apostles seem to be moving in unceremonious disorder in response to Christ's statement, "one of you will betray me." Actually it is a carefully planned grouping of figures in threes, and the apparently spontaneous emotion moves from one man to another along a shrewdly plotted linear arrangement of hands and arms and bodies. A photograph of the painting turned upside down shows the complex interrelation of triangles and rectangles which contain the action within ordered limits, so that it never grows tiresome. This combination of intellectualism with a quest for beauty, and of religious inspiration with a passion for human and natural forms is one of the most striking characteristics of Renaissance art, and, in a sense, of Italian Renaissance culture in general.

If at the end of the fifteenth century not a few people still bemoaned the times and looked to the future with apprehension, many others believed that the age of darkness was over, that the times in which they lived were a new period of rebirth and vitality. Humanists, artists, and men of letters generally, had cause for optimism. The situation that Petrarch had described a hundred years before had been transformed. His call for a revival of culture had become a solid achievement in more ways than he could have foreseen. In a letter of September 12, 1492, Marsilio Ficino, the dean of Italian philosophers, rejoiced in the arrival of the golden age: liberal studies had been revived; the arts, astronomy, and Platonic studies were flourishing; and his city of Florence was the center of it all. Ficino was justified in being proud of Florence, which was still a mecca for artists and humanists; but he might have done well to look more carefully beyond the Arno and even beyond the Alps, for the Renaissance was no longer an exclusively Florentine nor even Italian movement. Not only Rome and Naples and Venice, but also London and Paris and Basel and other northern cities were becoming centers of humanistic studies in their own right, with native scholars publishing their own grammars of Greek and Latin, their own texts of classical authors, and histories of their own peoples on the Italian model. The invention of moveable type in the fifteenth century made printed books much cheaper than manuscripts, so that new ideas moved more rapidly and reached more people.

2. NORTHERN HUMANISM

While for most of the sixteenth century the current continued to flow outward from Italy, carried by travelers and books, the northern peoples shaped Italian ideas according to their own traditions and interests and grew more and more independent. At Oxford and Cambridge, for example, the reception of humanism led to a controversy over the study of Scripture. The champions of the scholastic method did not doubt that the Latin translation of the Bible made by St. Jerome in the fourth century, the Vulgate, was an accurate rendering of the original meaning of God's word. Primarily theologians, they were more interested in the doctrinal principles they could draw from Scripture by interpreting the text allegorically than in the literal meaning of the text itself. Since Western Christian theology was based mainly on interpretations from the Vulgate, to question the validity of the Vulgate text was to shake the foundations of Church doctrine. But the men who had been influenced by humanistic historical scholarship pointed out that St. Jerome's translation was itself four centuries removed from the original. While they admired Jerome's scholarship, they did not accept it uncritically; good as it might have been for its day, they were confident they could do better with their new methods of research. As for the present condition of the Vulgate, they knew that manuscript copying was never free from human error; the text must contain many corruptions. The first thing was to study the oldest Hebrew, Aramaic, and Greek manuscripts to determine what the original must have been, and then to decide what these words must have meant to the men who had first set them down. When Erasmus visited England in 1499 he was urged by John Colet (ca.1467–1519), who had already introduced humanistic methods in his Oxford lectures on St. Paul, to use his scholarship for such ends. Eventually Erasmus carried out the charge, publishing a Greek New Testament with his own Latin translation as well as critical editions of some of the early Christian thinkers. In France Jacques Lefèvre d'Étaples (ca.1455–1536) was doing the same kind of work on the Psalms and on St. Paul, while in Spain Cardinal Ximenes (1436–1517) was directing the publication of the whole Bible in all of its original languages set side by side with the official Latin translation. But textual criticism was only part of the program of these humanists. By restoring the sources of Christianity, they hoped to restore the spirit of the early Christians. They deplored the tendency of religion to become a ritual practiced by the priest for a believer who felt he was discharging his own religious responsibility by attending mass and confessing his sins. Men must seek Christianity in the Bible, where God had revealed Himself, above all where Jesus Christ had revealed the law of love. To them a true Christian was one who searched for God for himself, who loved God and his fellow man and showed it by practicing morality and charity, as well as by performing the sacramental functions. This was the theme Erasmus repeated over and over in his devotional and ethical works, a doctrine which he summarized as "the philosophy of Christ," in contrast to the technical philosophizing of the universities. It was the theme of the German Mutianus Rufus, the Spaniards Alfonso and Juan de Valdes, of the Englishman Thomas More, and many other northern humanists of the early sixteenth century. They owed much to Italian humanism which, already from Petrarch's time, had opposed an ethical Christianity to scholasticism and ritualism and had begun to evolve the methods of historical scholarship. They carried over the Italian humanist faith in education as a foundation for "the good life," and they absorbed much of the spirit of religious tolerance of the fifteenth-century Florentine Platonists. On the other hand they were generally more conservative than the Italians in their attachment to traditional Christianity. For example, for all their rationality and tolerance, neither Erasmus nor More emulated Ficino's efforts to create a "universal" religion which was as much Neoplatonic as Christian. Moreover, the piety of the northern humanists often had a mystical strain which they derived from native forerunners like Thomas à Kempis and the Brethren of the Common Life rather than from the Italian humanists. Nor had the talent of the Italian humanists run to popular satire. There is nothing in the fifteenth-century Italian humanist literature like Erasmus' *Praise of Folly*, More's *Utopia*, or the German *Letters of Obscure Men*, which, in their devastating religious and social criticism combined with delicious humor, best represent the genius of the northern humanists.

The Renaissance art of the north also combined Italian elements with native characteristics. A northern painting of the fifteenth century still has the elongated figures and vertical lines that the followers of the fourteenth-century Gothic style loved so well. A fifteenth-century statue from any of the northern countries seems in its stiffness to have just barely been liberated from the wall of a Gothic cathedral. Northern churches and public buildings of the period show none of the classical order of the Strozzi Palace in Florence or the Roman grandeur of St. Andrea, the church built by Alberti in Mantua. But the north absorbed Italian Renaissance ideas to produce an art which was not only un-Italian but brilliant in its own right. The development of Flemish painting best illustrates both the interaction and the independence of north and south. In spite of a certain influx of Italian ideas in the fourteenth century Flemish painters went their own way for another hundred years, combining native Gothic realism with a religious, even mystical devotion. To the Flemings realism meant the perception of individual objects in all their exquisite detail, just as the worshipper might admire the infinite variety of God's handiwork. The paintings of Jan van Eyck (ca.1390–1441) or Hugo van der Goes (?–1482) seem personal, intimate, filled with a naïve wonder, while those of Piero della Francesca (ca.1416–1492) convey a powerful rational clarity and those of Raphael (1483–1520) seem to follow some inner philosophic law of harmony. Fifteenth-century Flemish painting appeals to the heart and generates wonder and reverence. Fifteenth-century Italian painting speaks to the intellect and celebrates man's God-like form and his conquest of nature's laws. But toward the end of the century Italian values finally began to make headway in Flemish and German painting. Gerard David (ca.1460–1523) set his lovely northern figures in a Renaissance setting as grand as any from Italy. Classical capitals and pillars, perfect nudes and idealized faces appear in the paintings of Jan Gossaert (ca.1470–ca.1533), and Quentin Massys (1466–1530) painted profile portraits every bit as convincing as those of the Italian painters he followed. Above all others, the German Albrecht Dürer (1471–1528) captured the spirit of the

Italian Renaissance. After his return from Italy in 1494 Dürer handled perspective and form in a way he could have learned only
there. While the northern and southern paths mingled, however,
they did not unite. The northerners took what pleased them from
the Italians without giving up their own interests or abandoning
their own traditions. The literal realism, the humor, and the popular
subject matter of a late sixteenth-century painter like Peter Brueghel
(ca.1525–1569) were inspired by Flemish, not Italian life.

⟨The flow of Italian ideas northward was only one of many new
currents in motion at the turn of the sixteenth century. Independent
of Italian influence was the recovery and new growth of European
states. After more than a century of uncertainty, monarchy again
emerged as the dominant form of political leadership. In the quarter
century between the marriage of Ferdinand of Aragon and Isabella
of Castile in 1469 and the conquest of Granada, the last Moslem
kingdom in the Iberian peninsula, in 1492, Spain began to emerge
as a nation, its monarchs skillfully exploiting the crusading tradition to unite her disparate peoples. The English, divided by the civil
wars which followed hard on their defeat in France, found peace
and unity with the accession of Henry VII (1485–1509). More
than a century of brilliant Tudor rule was to follow, a wonderfully
creative period during which the English founded a national religion,
evolved their system of parliamentary monarchy, and discovered
their talent for seafaring. Even the Holy Roman Empire began to
show signs of new energy after two centuries of ineffectual existence.
Emperor Maximilian (1493–1519) lacked both the material resources and the forcefulness to achieve German unity, not to speak
of German hegemony in Europe, but he did what he could, forming
elaborate plans for an imperial federation of German states. While
he was unable to realize this aim fully, he was successful in increasing the power of the Hapsburg dynasty by making shrewd marriage
alliances with the Burgundian dukes and the Spanish royal family.
By 1526 the Hapsburg empire included Spain and its holdings over-
seas, Burgundy, Bohemia, and Hungary, as well as the imperial German crown. To the east the Muscovite princes, freed at last from the
Mongol yoke, were creating a united Russian kingdom and dream-
ing of world empire. Ivan the Great (1462–1505) dubbed himself
"sovereign of all Russia" and styled Moscow as the Third Rome, the
successor of Constantinople as the eastern capital of Christianity and
of Roman civilization. To contemporary observers, however, the

most striking case of national growth at the end of the fifteenth century was France. Victory in the Hundred Years War liberated French soil from invaders and freed the Valois kings to resume their campaign of extending their power. By defeating Duke Charles the Bold of Burgundy in 1477, King Louis XI (1461–1483) removed the last great thorn in the flesh of the French monarchy. Less than twenty years later his son Charles VIII (1483–1498) felt strong enough to pursue the old dream of establishing French power south of the Alps. His invasion of Italy in 1494 was of little benefit to his own subjects while it was a bitter awakening for the Italians, who now saw that their political disunity had cost them their independence. The "barbarians" had been able to do what they themselves could not; they had marshalled their resources, expelled foreign invaders, and begun to perform great deeds abroad. Italian thinkers of the sixteenth century, notably Niccolò Machiavelli (1469–1527) and Francesco Guicciardini (1483–1540), set themselves to find out how their people had lost control of their own political destinies. Their writings demonstrated the continuing vitality of Italian intellectual life, but also underscored the impotence of Italian political institutions. Machiavelli and his compatriots laid the basis for the up-to-date analysis of political power and statecraft [12], but it was left to men of other countries to put their theories into practice.

Politics was not the only field in which the northern Renaissance left Italy behind. Just a month after Ficino wrote his letter celebrating the great achievements of Florence, Christopher Columbus (1451–1506) landed in the Western Hemisphere [9]. Like many of the scientists and explorers who labored to find a sea route to the Indies, Columbus was an Italian who had to find employment for his talents outside his own country. The Italians lacked the political and economic organization to support sustained exploration, and they lacked the foresight to look much beyond the Mediterranean basin and the coasts of Europe. For centuries they had adapted their techniques and their ships to the problems of the Mediterranean trade, and the Mediterranean had brought them fortune. Venice, supreme among Italian maritime states by the late fifteenth century, hardly noticed the report of Columbus' first voyage, which reached her all muddled, and only gradually awoke to the serious implications of the Portuguese discovery of a route around Africa to India. At the time

Venice was totally absorbed by the Turkish challenge to her shipping in the Mediterranean.

To be sure, it is easy to overstate the effect of the discoveries upon Italian commercial activity; the Mediterranean remained a major center of trade for more than another century, and the Italians carried goods to the north in their galleys and round ships and, increasingly, in caravans toiling over the Alpine passes. The discoveries did not put an end to Italian prosperity, ruin Mediterranean commerce, or blight Italian industry. In some ways the northern boom that followed even contributed to Italian wealth in the sixteenth century. It strengthened the purchasing power and the borrowing power of the northern countries so that much of the silver of the New World and the profits of the Indian trade found their way into the pockets of Italian merchants and bankers. What the discoveries did do, however, was in the long run even more sweeping. By the 1540's enormous new wealth was being pumped into the European economy, and this wealth was primarily at the disposal of Portugal, Spain, and then, increasingly, of France, the Netherlands, and England. The northern peoples came to command resources beyond anything available to the separate Italian states — nor is it likely that Italy could have made up the difference even if she had been able to achieve national unity. With direct access to the wealth of Asia and the New World, the "New Monarchies" of the sixteenth and seventeenth centuries could finance armies and navies and bureaucracies on a new scale. Their peoples found outlets for their ambitions and energies in new enterprises of exploration, conquest, and colonization and new goals for concerted effort and national pride. The scope of European political and social as well as economic activity was now becoming not merely national but worldwide and imperial: no longer was the Mediterranean the main axis of European civilization.

3. THE REFORMATION

If Italy's central position was slipping at the end of the fifteenth century she was still the home of Mother Church. The principle of Papal absolutism had won out against the democratizing efforts of the Conciliarists earlier in the century, and, since the fall of Constantinople in 1453, no city, certainly not the upstart Moscow, could rival Rome's claim to preeminence in Christendom. Canon law, the law of the Church, governed many of the forms of daily life, the marriages and inheritances of kings as well as of peasants, for example. When the Venetians discussed the defense of Europe against the Turk, or when the Portuguese and the Spaniards wanted recognition for their spheres of power in the Far East, they looked to Rome, for was not Europe a Christian community presided over by the Pope? Was it indeed? Certainly not as regarded relations between Greek and Latin Christians. Greek prelates had come to Italy to seek help against the Turks, and the end of the schism had been proclaimed at the Council of Florence in 1439. But the so-called union was as empty as Western promises of aid; Latin and Greek continued to go their separate ways. The Papacy's victory over Conciliarism had been real in the sense that Papal monarchism in the Church had been solidly established, but at what expense for the power and prestige of the Papacy in Christendom? Pope Eugenius IV (1431-1437) had gained the support of the secular princes against the Conciliarists by signing concordats with them which guaranteed the continued jurisdiction of the princes in the affairs of their national churches. The issue of Church reform "in head and members" had been evaded because the question of reform was tied to the question of Papal power. But by refusing to place itself at the head of the reform movement Rome was encouraging the centrifugal forces in the Church. Reform-minded people — and there were many — had to look away from Rome for leadership, while by crying Roman corruption the secular princes had a powerful argument in their never-ending campaign to ease the Papacy out of local church affairs. At the beginning of the sixteenth century, then, if Christian unity under Rome was not wholly theoretical, it was becoming increasingly problematical; partly because Rome was dissipating its own reserves of prestige, partly because national and regional feeling exercised a strong pull in religion as it did in politics.

Whatever unity remained was shattered by the outbreak of the Protestant Reformation in Germany in 1517. Where before there had been an East-West schism, there now appeared dozens of churches and sects which repudiated the authority of Rome and the Papacy altogether. Where there had always been temporal interference in ecclesiastical affairs, there were now founded state churches in which the authority of the prince was frankly claimed and more or less passively accepted. The Protestant Reformation was the ultimate shock which uncovered and then widened the cracks beneath the surface of the body of European Christendom, shattering it along national and regional lines which had already existed for a long time.

The Reformation was something else besides a transfer of religious obedience from Rome to the secular capitals of Europe, something more than the breakup of Christian unity. It was also a great creative epoch in the religious life of many people. From the start Christians had always disagreed about forms of worship and about theological doctrines. There had been many movements which interpreted the fundamentals of Christian belief differently from official teaching. Some, like the Albigensian movement of the thirteenth century, had been obliterated; others had been absorbed; a few lived on, embattled, like the Hussite movement in Bohemia, or eked out an underground existence, like the Fraticelli and the Waldensians. But when Martin Luther (1483–1546) nailed his ninety-five theses to the church door in Wittenberg in 1517 he precipitated a religious revolution which had a happier fate than the others. In part this was due to the immediate support he received from his own Duke of Saxony and from other German princes. Without the protection of temporal rulers, who had their own motives for encouraging religious rebellion, Luther's movement would have gone the way of previous heresies.

Yet the brushfire spread of the new theology not only in Germany but throughout Europe, the chain reaction of increasingly radical dissent from Roman doctrine and obedience, cannot be explained merely as the result of princely protection and national feeling against Roman authority. The message of Luther and of the other Protestant Reformers "answered a savage spiritual thirst," to use the words of G. R. Elton. In its simplest and most general terms that message said that man is saved by faith alone. This was the basic text of all Protestant preaching. It meant that man cannot hope to win God's favor and thus the assurance of salvation by performing righteous acts and the sacramental rites of the Church. Only as each man reads and hears the Word of the Scriptures can he find the way of salvation, because only in the Word does God reveal Himself to man. In meditating on the meaning of Scripture man sees that he is totally unable to *win* God's favor, and he comes to understand the meaning of the Incarnation and of Christ's sacrifice. He sees that God, in assuming human form and suffering death, has performed the one act which is perfect, the only act which can satisfy His own perfect righteousness. By believing that God had done this *for him,* man not only confesses the infinite distance that separates him from God, he also unites himself with God in grateful love for the perfect gift of salvation which God has afforded him. Roman Catholic doctrine agrees that man is *justified* by God's grace, but it insists that after receiving the free gift of justification, of liberation from his heritage of sin, man must earn his salvation by good works, which include the performance of the sacraments of the Church, as well as by faith. By declaring the formula of *sola fides,* faith alone, the Reformers were also asserting that the Church was not what Rome had been saying it was for over a thousand years, that it was not an agency which mediated between man and God and had in its keeping special powers of interpretation and portions of grace. It was, so far as men could tell, the body of all those who found the Word of God in Scriptures, all those who believed that Christ had died for them. The priesthood called some men to preach and teach the Word, but this was a distinction of profession, not of religion; priest and layman were equal in the profoundest sense of all — they encountered God in the same place and in the same way.

> So it follows that there is no essential difference between the Estate of Layman, Priest, Prince, Bishop, or, as they are called, the Spiritual and the Secular Estate, other than a difference of office or function. Priests, Bishops and Pope are all equal Estates although they each have a different function, just as Priests and Monks have each their own function. This is the teaching of Saints Paul and Peter, as I said above: we are all one body of the flesh of Jesus Christ, each a member of the other. Christ does not have two bodies nor does His body have two modes of existence, a worldly and a spiritual. He is one flesh and He has one body.

Not the least important part of this quotation from Luther's *Address to the Nobility of the German Nation* is his appeal to the authority of Saints Paul and Peter. In asserting this doctrine of "the priesthood of all believers" Luther thought he was restoring the true conception of the Church, not introducing new ideas of founding a new church; *that* was God's work. Man's work was to cleave to "the good old way" as closely as he could. Like the Renaissance, the Reformation was profoundly conservative in its effort to get back to "the sources," in this case the Christian rather than the classical, of European civilization. In their preoccupation with religion the

Reformers were perhaps even more conservative than the thinkers of the Renaissance, against whose secularist tendencies the Reformers vented their spleen, but the Reformation could not have restored primitive Christianity if for no other reason than that they could not be sure what primitive Christianity had been like. Their image of "the good old way" was distorted by their rudimentary historical knowledge. Even more, their image was shaped by their own religious preoccupations, and these were of their own time and place. The God of perfect righteousness and all-exacting justice before whom Luther trembled in terror was not the God whom the early mystics embraced in contemplation nor even He whom the Thomists thought they could reach through nature and reason. He was closer to the God of the later scholastic theologians — infinite, unknowable, unattainable. The Bible Luther read was not like the Bible of the medieval exegetes, a glossary of symbolic meanings, it was the living and saving Word of God to which more and more troubled souls were already turning in a confusing world where piety and profanity were strangely mixed and the clergy offered less and less guidance. Luther found a ready response because he was in so many ways the typical German and the typical Christian of his time.

He was also unique in his time. He was one man among millions, one whose greatness of spirit would not let him accept a solution which he believed was wrong even if it meant challenging all the powers of the earth. And he was by any fair test a religious genius. In resolving his private spiritual crisis he founded a new form of Christian piety that has shaped the thought and actions of many men from his day to ours [13]. Luther's piety differed from Catholic piety in two essential respects, in its individualistic approach to God and in its conception of Christian life. While Christianity was from the first an individualistic religion, emphasizing the dignity of the individual soul and the personal responsibility of each man, medieval Catholicism treated man's relationship with God in a very complex way, by establishing the Church as the dispenser of the sacraments and the interpreter of the Word. Luther cut away almost all these functions of the Church, leaving man to confront his God supported by the Word of Scripture alone. This shifted an enormous weight of responsibility to the individual Christian, whose conscience was now actively engaged as only the consciences of unusually religious persons had been engaged before. St. Paul's question, "What think ye of Christ?" was now Everyman's to decide, and his decision would change his life. But even the man who decides for Christ lives in the world; Luther denied that man could find a more spiritual mode of existence by moving from the market place to the monastery. With faith and devotion man can make any calling as holy as any other — if he will. Even the soldier who fights with a good conscience, Luther said, fights well. Living a Christian life meant for Luther enhancing the world, not escaping from it. Thus, the dualism which had troubled Christianity since it was first touched by Greek philosophy, a dualism between the secular and the sacred, which had cut especially deep into the Renaissance consciousness from Petrarch on, was now resolved for many people. For them Luther's conception of Christian life made it possible not merely to reconcile the life of the spirit with an active life in business or politics or soldiering, but even to regard their worldly activities as their duty, the performance of which redounded to God's glory.

Radical though much of Luther's doctrine was with respect to the prevailing Catholic teaching, it might have been still more radical had he pursued all the implications of his key ideas. Notwithstanding his doctrine of the priesthood of all believers Luther clung to the idea of a Church which maintained authority over the individual by dispensing grace through baptism and the Lord's Supper and by imposing a uniform interpretation of the Word. To his mind — a mind far more conservative than it might seem at first — there could be only one interpretation of Scripture, and he was convinced that his was correct. All those who did not concur must either be wilfully wicked or still unenlightened by the Holy Spirit. Luther fervently believed that the Word would do its work in its own way; but the more he encountered opposition, both from Catholics and from other Reformers who had their own ideas of the meaning of Scripture, the more he became resigned to seeing the Word buttressed by the power of the state. Where Lutheranism prevailed, in much of Germany and in Scandinavia, state churches were established, in which the temporal power had the right and responsibility to maintain orthodoxy. The individual believer might glory in his inner, spiritual freedom, but he was to "obey the powers that be."

Other rebels against Roman Catholicism disdained Luther's passivity toward worldly power and his tolerance toward many of the traditional forms of worship. Having caught the fervor for a "free Gospel," they wished to be guided by the Word alone, no longer to submit to the sword of a state which had, perforce, other goals beside holy ones. Having taken up the torch of religious revolution they wanted to burn out every remnant of "Romanism" and "Popery," to make a "Reformation without tarrying for any," as one English enthusiast later was to put it. To their zeal they added a powerful logic: if the Church is made up of only those who have truly converted to Christ, then it must set itself apart, admitting none but those who have been called to the Truth, living by no rule but that of the Gospels. While Luther had barred the escape from the world to the monastery, these new prophets sought to reintroduce a kind of monastery into the world's midst and called upon all to enter by confessing Christ and accepting baptism as the sign of their conversion to a new life of the spirit. Adult baptism became their hallmark and "Anabaptist" [re-baptizer] their epithet, contemptuously flung at them by their enemies, who accused them of advocating two baptisms. Actually there was no single Anabaptist movement. Some who preached the spiritual, "gathered" church made common cause with social and political revolution, as Thomas Müntzer did in the German Peasants War of 1524–1525, and certain Puritan sectarians did in England in the 1640's. Some, as John of Leyden did in the city Münster, attempted to establish a society of Saints which would live under a new law of grace, emancipated from the old "natural" law of social convention [14]. Such attitudes of political revolution and of antinomianism terrified and disgusted the majority of the citizenry, Protestant and Catholic alike, who looked upon this kind of freedom as a euphemism for communism and sexual license and tended to tar all Anabaptists with the same brush. But most of the prophets of the gathered Church preached non-resistance to political authority and, indeed, non-involvement in political affairs altogether, while their sexual morals were, if anything, puritannical. The Swiss Brethren and the Mennonites were outstanding examples of this type. This did not make them loved any the more, nor did it save them from persecution to the death. Pacifism and non-cooperation seemed to most people as much a threat to social and political institutions as violent rebellion. Like the early Christians of the Roman Empire the unworldly "Separatists" were looked upon as "enemies of the human race" who must be expunged. For many years to come, until Christians learned tolerance or until men became indifferent to other men's religious opinions, the Separatists had to seek safety in the remote mountain valleys of Europe and in the wilderness of the

New World. Yet, rejected as they were, they made their influence felt in the formation of modern religious attitudes, for as advocates of unworldliness in the world and as champions of religious freedom they were the conscience of Christendom.

But Anabaptism was too exclusive, too demanding, and too disruptive of familiar ways to become a mass movement in Europe. Lutheranism, on the other hand, was too cautious and too much a product of the German political situation. The spearhead of the Protestant movement in Europe was Calvinism, which matched Anabaptism in zeal and Lutheranism in organization, while it had a dynamism all its own. In 1532 John Calvin (1509–1564), a French student of humanism and of the law, experienced "a sudden conversion," as he called it, to the new Gospel religion. Although Calvin now believed that one who had found faith was numbered among the Saints, he did not take the way of the Separatists and shun the contamination of the worldly life. Rather, he understood divine election as a mandate to establish the City of God in the world, where God's ministers were not only to preach and teach the Word but also to impose the discipline of Christian life upon the believing and the doubtful alike. Those who would not adhere must be constrained or else they would be cut off from the community by excommunication or, in extreme cases, by execution; for the community had to be safe for the Word, or else how could the Elect hear and respond? Above all, men must live in constant praise of God, who is the beginning and the end of all things. The Gospel is His law to be lived, and life must be a constant glorification of His majesty [15].

Descriptions of Calvin's theology have almost invariably centered on his doctrine of predestination. This doctrine, that before time began, for His own reasons and once for all, God chose some men for salvation and the rest for eternal damnation, has come to fascinate us as the strange product of an unusual religious mentality. As early as the seventeenth century it was the stormy rock upon which the unity of Calvinism was dashed to pieces. But predestination was neither new with Calvin nor was it the hinge of his whole thought. The problem of whether God predestines men to salvation or damnation had been treated by most Christian theologians at least since St. Augustine and had been given various answers. In understanding Calvin's thought predestination is of less importance than his idea of the overriding majesty of God and his stress upon man's experience of God through faith in Christ. Still, while we can discuss Calvin's *system* without laboring over predestination, the *spirit* of the men who became Calvinists will perplex us unless we can imagine the exultation, the sense of mission, of a man who was convinced that his faith stamped him as one of the predestined. This was the spirit that moved the Huguenots to civil war in France in 1560 and the Sea Beggars to oppose the galleons of the Most Catholic King of Spain in the Netherlands in 1566. It was the spirit of the Czechs who threw the envoys of the Holy Roman Emperor out of a high palace window in Prague in 1618, setting off the Thirty Years War. A similar zeal inspired the English Puritans to fight for the New Jerusalem as well as against royal despotism in 1642, while it sustained their Brownist brethren of the New Covenant who had begun carving a church out of New England's stubborn rock.

Indeed, Calvinist piety indirectly generated militant attitudes which Calvin himself did not envision and would not have sanctioned. Calvin did not advocate political radicalism; on the contrary he enjoined men to obey their superiors. At the same time he also told them to establish God's church against all opposition, and Calvinists in France, England, and the Netherlands took the lead in formulating doctrines of resistance to political tyranny. Neither did Calvin advocate democracy; however, a doctrine which taught its adherents that they were the elect, whatever their social class, might be used to support a democratic view of society. Calvin urged his followers to resist the temptations of wealth; but men who believed that all of life was a glorification of God and that all things were given them in stewardship for God, could learn to think of hard work as part of their God-given duty and to accept its rewards as a proof of their piety. The great sociologist, Max Weber, called this application of piety to worldly ambition "the Protestant ethic," and he believed it had been an indispensible element in the development of modern capitalism with its spirit of dedicated striving for worldly success, although Weber's critics have rightly pointed out that many other forces were involved in the transformation of Calvin's interpretation of the gospel of Christ into Andrew Carnegie's *Gospel of Wealth*.

In so many ways, then, the Reformation helped to form the attitudes of the future and direct the course of events, although like many human efforts it had some ambivalent and unintended effects. The Reformers raised up anew the idea of a Christianity free of political entanglements; but by concentrating on the inwardness of religion they made it more susceptible to control by the growing power of secular states. They hoped to restore primitive Christianity, but they actually founded new churches. Instead of the unity they sought they endowed the future with a rich variety of forms of worship and of religious life. They envisioned a piety which strives to infuse the world with spirituality, but which is liable to mistake self-righteousness for righteousness and worldly success for merit.

4. THE COUNTER-REFORMATION

Protestantism was not the only dynamic religious movement of the sixteenth century. Roman Catholicism also quickened to new vitality under the bloodletting of the Reformers. Catholics could only regard the Protestant heresy as a destructive cancer, eating away at the indivisible body of Christendom, weakening its attempt to cure itself of its other ills; but the shock of the Protestant revolt also stepped up the pace of Catholic reform and helped shape some of its major efforts. Catholic reformers infused new life into many of the old religious orders and founded new ones which were dedicated to works of charity and to serving the Church in its hour of need. An ecumenical council was called at Trent in 1545 which revamped clerical education and issued strict regulations governing the duties of priests and bishops. Some of the most earnest Catholic reformers were raised to the Cardinalate and men were elevated to the Papacy who had on the whole a more spiritual idea of their office than their immediate predecessors.

Besides reform, the Catholic leaders devoted themselves to counter-reformation — that is, the suppression of heresy and the winning back of souls who had strayed from Rome. Increasingly this second type of activity tended to dominate, although many of the Catholic reformers deplored this. Reacting against the free-wheeling discussion that prevailed earlier in the century, the Church became more suspicious of new ideas, less tolerant of criticism, more than ever attached to its own traditional ways. At Trent it was made clear that the Church was an absolute monarchy, its theology thirteenth-century Thomism, and its religion the sacramental system evolved over the preceding centuries. Largely in response to the increasing influence of fanatical Spanish Catholicism, the Papacy established the Holy Office to coordinate the work of the Inquisition. Wherever it had a free hand, the Inquisition relentlessly pursued heterodox opinion. In Italy it not only eliminated virtually all Protestant activity, it also silenced loyal Catholics who dared to utter "dangerous" thoughts. Since almost any independent thought seemed dangerous in this tense time, suspicion and fear were the order of the day. Under pressure of the Inquisition Galileo Galilei (1564–1642) recanted his assertion that the earth moved and thereby escaped with the relatively mild punishment of perpetual house arrest. But Giordano Bruno, who had written that there were many worlds besides the one we know, refused to recant and was burned alive in Rome in 1600. How many others — humanists, scientists, philosophers, and poets — were cowed into silence by the threat of a similar fate we can only speculate, but the Counter-Reformation must bear some of the responsibility for the caution and cynicism in the intellectual life of Catholic countries in the late sixteenth and seventeenth centuries.

On the other side of the account, however, are the great cultural achievements of sixteenth-century Catholics inspired by zeal for their embattled faith. Jesuit activity is a good example. In founding the Society of Jesus, Ignatius Loyola (1491–1556) had a single object in mind, to serve God by fighting for His true church. Steeped in the tradition of the Spanish reconquest, Loyola thought of the Church as engaged in a struggle for the conquest of souls, and he treated his followers as "spiritual soldiers living under martial law and discipline," who must exchange the peaceful monastic tasks of the choir office for more militant service in the world. The "Jesuits," a name first given them by their enemies, were tireless preachers, theologians, and missionaries, but also teachers, scientists, explorers, and diplomats, as their drive to win souls for the Church took them into every field of activity and every corner of the earth [16]. They brought Catholicism to India, Japan, and China and sent back Europe's first systematic knowledge of Eastern languages and civilization. They explored the rivers and forests of North America and laid out handsome cities in Renaissance proportions in Latin America. They built churches in the dynamic Baroque style and made use of Renaissance drama, recognizing that Catholicism was a religion of the senses and emotions as well as of the reason. Most of all they were educators. In their drive to win over the youth, they became the heirs of the methods of the Renaissance humanists, and their colleges were among the most progressive schools in Europe.

In such ways much of the liberal Renaissance culture which had been shut out at one door of the Counter-Reformation Church came in by another. The Church found it was impossible to gain the influence it sought without serving the interests and needs of a rapidly changing and expanding civilization. But in trying to use modern culture for its own ends it sometimes achieved unforeseen and, from its point of view, undesirable effects. Here too Jesuit activity provides examples. Descartes (1596–1650), who sapped the foundations of scholastic philosophy, and Pascal (1623–1662), the foe of Jesuit theology, were educated by the Jesuits themselves; Voltaire (1694–1778), Diderot (1713–1784), and many other eighteenth-century enemies of the Catholic Church learned to think and argue in Jesuit colleges. In broadening Europe's horizons by making it more conscious of other civilizations to the east and west the Jesuits unwittingly fostered ideas of "natural religion," toleration, and Deism, undermining the authority of the Church to which they devoted their lives. As theorists who tried to adjust religious consciences to the secular demands of politics and business the Jesuits helped attune the modern mind to rationalism and pragmatism. But such paradoxes do not alter the fact of the Jesuits' brilliant work for their faith. Their success may be described by analogy with the churches which they built. A Baroque church is a unity of opposites; it provides an intensely sensual setting for the sacramental drama of the Mass. With its bold lines, brilliant color, and magnificent decoration it celebrates the power and glory of the Church Visible engaged in savings souls with God's invisible grace. In the same way the Jesuits united spirituality and worldliness, mysticism and science, humility and power, and the energy that resulted was creative for life as well as for art.

5. SCIENCE

If European civilization did not entirely follow the direction plotted for it either by the humanists or by the religious reformers this was because there was no single way to cope with all the forces determining its course. Religion was a major concern for many people in the sixteenth century, but so were the growing opportunities for making and spending money, for improving one's status, and for grasping, or serving those who grasped, the new concentrations of political power. Reformation faith had to compete with Renaissance tolerance, with the Erasmian ideal of moderation, even, in some cases, with indifference to things eternal. The very debates of the Reformation raised the question of how men could know what was true. Michel de Montaigne (1533–1592) answered that he could not know, therefore he must accept on faith what the Church taught, while for the rest he resolved to live his life according to reason and convenience without bothering too much [20]. But of all the forces which competed with religion for a hold on men's minds, none was to be more influential than science, which, in the sixteenth century, stood on the threshold of a revolutionary era. The rational and systematic investigation of the operations of natural phenomena, which we call science, began millennia earlier, in Mesopotamia and Egypt. The Greeks had made brilliant advances and so did the Arabs. From the twelfth century on European Christians began to assimilate ancient science and mathematics, first through translations and commentaries from the Arabic, and then, in the Renaissance, directly from the classical texts. At least as early as the fourteenth century Europeans began to develop scientific ideas of their own. At the University of Paris Jean Buridan (ca.1295–1358) and Nicholas of Oresme (ca.1323–1382) conceived of natural bodies as moving by some "impetus" in the body itself and not, as Aristotle had taught, by a motion imparted to it through the medium of air which in turn received it from the Universal Mover. The impetus theory was defective, but it was a step toward the conception of nature as a mechanical system unaffected by hidden Intelligences and independent of a Prime Mover and therefore subject to observation, measurement, and prediction. There were many other such steps in the fourteenth and fifteenth centuries, both of a conceptual and a specific kind, for example: the advances in scientific method made by William of Occam and by the Experimentalists of the University of Padua, Oresme's arguments for the earth's rotation and against its central position in the universe, Leonardo da Vinci's insistence that nature must be approached through "number" and his formulation, albeit imperfect, of a law of freely falling bodies. But other considerations pressed down upon these scientists, obscuring and limiting their progress. One source of confusion was the still awesome authority of Aristotelianism, which opposed mechanism with the idea of a universe made up of forms and intelligences of graded quality, and opposed mathematical experimentation with syllogistic logic. Another was the power of Christian belief. Oresme, for example, offered his arguments for the earth's rotation only "in fun," for he did not dare to contradict seriously the accepted religious teaching which was based on the evidence of Scripture. Still another obstacle to science was occultism. Occultism (magic, astrology, alchemy) had invaded Christian Europe with new force in the twelfth century through the books of Avicenna, Albumasar, and other Arab thinkers. It was nourished on the Neoplatonic theory that beneath the varying material appearances of the world is a single directing Mind, a spiritual substance which diffuses itself through all the levels of being. Since man shares some part of the universal Mind with all the rest of being, he is able to understand the world by penetrating behind the material appearances of things. He can enter into harmony with his environment and thus gain a certain amount of control over it and over his own destiny. Occultism thus offered men a comprehensive view of the world and a promise of power, but by blurring the distinction between experiment and magic, between natural forces and hidden spirits, and between prediction and divination, it confused the real scientific issues and clouded the practical goals of nature investigation well into the seventeenth century.

With all these difficulties, it is not remarkable that progress toward a self-consistent and self-correcting natural science was irregular and uncertain, nor that science was plagued by false starts and blind alleys. Often the same man will seem to us to have been at one time a serious thinker and at another a quack, but this is because we are now more confident of the distinction between science and pseudo-science. Pico della Mirandola mounted an offensive against astrology, but he also believed that he had found the key to all knowledge in Cabala, a system of Jewish number magic. Paracelsus (1493–1541) was a self-dramatizing charlatan but he had a love of research and an elevated conception of the art of healing [17]. Even Nicholas Copernicus (1473–1543), often heralded as the founder of a scientific revolution because of his theory of heliocentric astronomy, mixed Neoplatonic arguments with empirical ones. He was as much concerned to improve the symmetry and harmony of the Ptolemaic theory and to exalt the "nobility" of the sun as to describe what actually takes place in the sky.

But the Copernican theory *was* revolutionary, despite its archaic trappings. Only after Copernicus had overturned Ptolemaic geocentrism would Johannes Kepler (1571–1630), Galileo, and Isaac Newton (1642–1727) be able to work out a mathematical and mechanical description of the universe, and extricate science from Aristotelian metaphysics, religious dogmatism, and occultism. When Luther heard of Copernicus' theory he exclaimed, "This fool wishes to reverse the entire science of astronomy; but Sacred Scripture tells us that Joshua commanded the sun to stand still, and not the earth." That might have been a crushing refutation once but no longer; the heliocentric theory continued to make headway. If Galileo later recanted the theory of the earth's motion it was clear to all that he did so not to preserve the authority of Scripture but to save his skin. The real loser was religious dogmatism, which showed itself to be so vulnerable as to need the fires of the Inquisition to protect it. For the most part the scientists had no intention of invading the province of Christianity, but they could not help doing so since Christianity had taken all creation for its province. With science coming to view the universe, including the earth, as an infinite number of bodies moving in an infinite space by force of a mutual attraction, a head-on collision with the Christian doctrines of Creation, Providence, and the nature and destiny of man was inevitable. It came in the late seventeenth century, producing what has been called "the crisis of the European conscience." Since that time European civilization has, largely through its supremacy in science, become a world civilization, and wherever its influence is felt this crisis, generated by competing systems of value and divergent views of reality, has been felt too.

1

Dante Advocates World Government

IT MAY HAVE BEEN as early as 1309 that Dante set to work upon his treatise in which he supported the Holy Roman Empire as the best hope of Christendom. Disgusted with Papal politicking and dismayed by the endless conflicts of the Italian states, Dante supported the efforts of Henry VII to revive the Empire as a world power. Since the claims of universal empire were already being ignored by the temporal princes, by the Italian city states, and by the Popes, by the time De Monarchia appeared it was less a program for the future than a statement of a lost cause. Nevertheless, it illustrates the reasoning of a great fourteenth-century thinker who had mastered scholastic philosophy and logic and had also read deeply in the available classics. By carefully analyzing Dante's method of argument and examining his values, we can better understand what was new and what was traditional in the thought of others who came after him.

Dante Alighieri (1265–1321), On World Government ("De Monarchia")

Book one, that mankind needs unity and peace

I

The knowledge of a single temporal government over mankind is most important and least explored.] All men whose higher nature has endowed them with a love of truth, obviously have the greatest interest in working for posterity, so that in return for the patrimony provided for them by their predecessors' labors they may make provision for the patrimony of future generations. Certainly a

From Dante Alighieri, ON WORLD GOVERNMENT OR DE MONARCHIA (New York, 1949), pp. 1–7, 11–15, 34, 59–61. Translation by Herbert W. Schneider. Reprinted by permission of The Liberal Arts Press.

man who has received public instruction would be far from performing his duty if he showed no concern for the public weal, for he would not be a "tree by the streams of waters, bearing his fruit in due season," but rather an erosive whirlpool always sucking in and never returning what it devours. Therefore, as I have often reminded myself of these things and wish not to be charged with burying my talent, I endeavor not only to grow in public usefulness but also to bear fruit by publishing truths that have not been attempted by others. For what fruit is there in proving once more a theorem in Euclid, or in trying to show man his true happiness, which Aristotle has already shown, or in defending old age as Cicero did? Fruitless and positively tiresome are such superfluous "works."

Among the truths that remain hidden, though useful, the knowledge of the temporal government of the world is most useful and most unknown, but since this knowledge is not directly gainful it has been neglected by all. I therefore propose to drag it from its hiding place, in order that my alertness may be useful to the world and may bring me the glory of being the first to win this great prize. It is a difficult task I attempt and beyond my powers, but I rely not on my own ability; I trust in that giver of light who gives abundantly to all and reproaches none.

2

Since this theory is a practical science, its first principle is the goal of human civilization, which must be one and the same for all particular civilizations.] First, we must see what is meant by the temporal government of the world, both its kind and its aim. By the temporal government of the world or universal empire we mean a single government over all men in time, that is, over and in all things which can be measured by time. On this subject there are three chief questions to be examined: first, we must ask and inquire whether such a government is necessary for the good of the world; secondly, whether the Roman people has a right to assume such an office; and thirdly, whether the authority of this government comes directly from God or through some servant or vicar of God. . . .

3

This goal is proved to be the realization of man's ability to grow in intelligence.] Accordingly we must now see what the whole of human civilization aims at; with this aim before us more than half our work is done, as the Philosopher says in his *Nichomachean Ethics*. And as evidence for what we seek we ought to note that just as nature makes the thumb for one purpose, the whole hand for another, the arm for still another, and the whole man for a purpose different from all these, so an individual man has one purpose, a family another, a neighborhood another, a city another, a state another, and finally there is another for all of mankind, established by the Eternal God's art, which is nature. This goal it is that we are now seeking as the guiding principle of our inquiry. We should know, in this connection, that God and nature make nothing in vain, and that whatever is produced serves some function. For the intention of any act of creation, if it is really creative, is not merely to produce the existence of something but to produce the proper functioning of that existence. Hence a proper functioning does not exist for the sake of the being which functions, but rather the being exists for the sake of its function. There is therefore some proper function for the whole of mankind as an organized multitude which can not be achieved by any single man, or family, or neighborhood, or city, or state. What that may be would be plain if we could see what the basic capacity of the whole of humanity is. Now I would say that no capacity which several different species have in common can be the basic power of any one of them. For in that case the basic capacity, which characterizes a species, would be the same for several species, which is impossible. Accordingly man's basic power is not mere being, for he shares being with the elements; nor is it to be compounded, for this is found in minerals, too; nor is it to be alive, for so are plants; nor is it to be sensitive, for other animals share this power; but it is to be sensitive to intellectual growth, for this trait is not found in beings either above or below man. For though there are angelic beings that share intellect with man, they do not have intellectual growth, since their very being is to be intellect and nothing else and hence they are intellectual continuously, otherwise they would not be changeless. Therefore, it is clear that man's basic capacity is to have a potentiality or power for being intellectual. And since this power can not be completely actualized in a single man or in any of the particular communities of men above mentioned, there must be a multitude in mankind through whom this whole power can be actualized; just as there must be a multitude of created beings to manifest adequately the whole power of prime matter, otherwise there would have to be a power distinct from prime matter, which is impossible. With this judgment Averroes agrees in his commentary on *Dè Anima*. This intellectual power, of which I am speaking, is directed not only toward universals or species, but also by a sort of extension toward particulars. Hence it is commonly said that the speculative intellect becomes practical by extension, and acquires thus the aims of action and production. I distinguish between matters of action which are governed by political prudence, and matters of production which are governed by the arts; but all of them are extensions of theoretical intellect, which is the best function for which the Primal Goodness brought mankind into being. Now we have already thrown light on that saying in the *Politics* — that the intellectually vigorous naturally govern others.

4

The best means toward this end is universal peace.] I have now made clear enough that the proper work of mankind taken as a whole is to exercise continually its entire capacity for intellectual growth, first, in theoretical matters, and, secondarily, as an extension of theory, in practice. And since the part is a sample of the whole, and since individual men find that they grow in prudence and wisdom when they can sit quietly, it is evident that mankind, too, is most free and easy to carry on its work when it enjoys the quiet and tranquility of peace. Man's work is almost divine ("Thou hast made him a little lower than the angels") and it is clear that of all the things that have been ordained for our happiness, the greatest is universal peace. Hence there rang out to the shepherds from on high the good news, not of riches, nor pleasures, nor honors, nor long life, nor health, nor strength, nor beauty, but peace. For the heavenly host proclaimed "glory to God in the highest and on earth peace to men of good will." Hence, too, "Peace be with you" was the salutation of Him who is the Salvation of Men; for it was fitting that the Supreme Saviour should give voice to the supreme salutation. His disciples took care to make this salutation customary, and so did Paul in his salutations, as must be evident to all.

What I have now said makes clear what is that better, that best way by following which mankind may achieve its proper work, and consequently it is also clear what way we must directly take to attain that final goal set for all our work, which is universal peace. Let this, then, be our principle underlying all our subsequent arguments, as I said, and let it serve as a standard set before us by which to test the truth of whatever we shall try to prove.

5

To achieve this state of universal well-being a single world-government is necessary.] There are three chief questions, as I said in the beginning, which must be raised and discussed concerning the temporal government of the world, more commonly called empire, and these three I propose, as I said, to take up in order. And so the first question is, whether a single temporal world-government is necessary for the world's well-being. There exists no weight of argument or of authority against this necessity and there are very strong and clear arguments for it. The first argument, which enjoys the authority of the Philosopher, is in his *Politics,* where this venerable authority states that whenever several things are united into one thing, one of them must regulate and rule, the others must be regulated and ruled. This seems credible not only on the strength of the glorious name of its author, but also for inductive reasons. Consider, for example, an individual man; we see this truth exhibited in him, for while all his energies are directed toward happiness, he could not attain it did not his intellectual power rule and guide the others. Or consider a household whose aim it is to prepare the members of the family to live well; one alone must regulate and rule, whom we call father of the family, or else there is someone who takes his place. So says our Philosopher: "Every home is ruled by the eldest." It is his duty, as Homer says, to govern all and give laws to others. Hence the proverbial curse: "May you have an equal in your home!" Or consider a neighborhood, whose aim is to provide mutual aid in persons and things. Someone must govern the others, either someone appointed by the others or some outstanding member whom the others consent to follow, otherwise the community will not only fail to furnish the mutual aid for which it exists, but, as sometimes happens when several strive for pre-eminence, the whole neighborhood is destroyed. Likewise a city, whose aim is to live well and self-sufficiently, must have a single government, whether the city have a just or corrupt constitution. Otherwise not only does civil life fail to reach its goal, but the city ceases to be what it was. Or take finally a state or kingdom, whose aim is the same as that of a city, save that it takes more responsibility for peace — there must be a single government which both rules and governs; otherwise the end of the state is lost sight of, or the state itself falls to pieces, according to the infallible truth: "Every kingdom directed against itself shall be laid waste." If, therefore, these things are true among individuals and particular communities which have a unified goal, what we proposed above must be true. Since it appears that the whole of mankind is ordained to one end, as we proved above, it should therefore have a single rule and government, and this power should be called the Monarch or Emperor. And thus it is plain that for the well-being of the world there must be a single world-rule or empire.

*   *   *

I I

The world-government is apt to be least greedy and most just.] Moreover, the world is best ordered when justice is its greatest power. Thus Virgil, seeking to praise an age which seemed to be arising in his day, sang in his *Bucolics:*

Iam redit et Virgo, redeunt Saturnia regna.[1]

By "Virgo" he meant justice, sometimes called "the starry." By "Saturnia regna" he meant the best ages, sometimes called "the golden." Justice has greatest power under a unitary government; therefore the best order of the world demands world-government or empire. The minor premise will become evident if we recall that justice is by its nature a kind of rightness or straight rule without deviation, and therefore, like whiteness, justice in the abstract is not susceptible of degrees. . . . And as to its *action,* justice suffers from the limitations of human ability; for since justice is a virtue affecting others, how can a person act justly when he lacks the ability of giving to each his due? Whence it follows that the more powerful a just man is, the more adequate can justice be in its action.

And so, on the basis of this proposition, we may argue as follows: justice is most powerful in the world when it resides in the most willing and able being; the only being of this nature is the world-governor. Therefore, justice is the most powerful in the world when it resides solely in the world-governor. This compound syllogism is in the second figure necessarily negative, thus:

All B is A		All B is A
Only C is A	or	No non—C is A
Only C is B		No non—C is B

The major premise is evident from the foregoing. The minor is justified as follows: first, respecting *volition,* then, respecting *ability.* As evidence for the first we must note that greed is the extreme opposite of justice, as Aristotle says in the Fifth Book of his *Nichomachean Ethics.* Take away greed completely and nothing opposed to justice remains in the will. Hence the opinion of the Philosopher, that whatever can be decided by law should not be left to a judge, is based on the fear of greed, which readily twists the minds of men. Now where there is nothing left to desire, greed is impossible, for passions cannot exist when their objects are destroyed. But a universal ruler has nothing that he might desire, for his jurisdiction is bounded only by the ocean, which is true of no other ruler whose realm is bounded by those of others, as, for example, the King of Castile's is bounded by the King of Aragon's. Hence it follows that the world-ruler is the purest among mortal wills in which justice may reside. . . .

12

Human freedom consists in being ruled by reason and in living for the goal of mankind. Such freedom is possible only under world-government.] Mankind is at its best when it is most free. This will be clear if we grasp the principle of liberty. We must realize that the basic principle of our freedom is freedom to choose, which saying many have on their lips but few in their minds. For they go only so far as to say freedom of choice is freedom of will in judging. This is true, but they do not understand its import. They talk as our logicians do, who for their exercises in logic constantly use certain propositions, such as "A triangle has three angles equal to two right angles." And so I must explain that judgment lies between apprehension and appetition; for, first a thing is apprehended, then, being apprehended, is judged to be good or bad, and lastly, being judged, is either sought or rejected. Therefore, if the judgment completely dominates the appetite and is in no way prejudiced by appetite, it is free; but if the appetite somehow antecedes the judgment and influences it, the judgment can not be free, since it does not move itself, but is led captive by another. For this reason, the lower animals can not have free judgment, since their appetites always get ahead of their judgments. This also explains why intellectual beings whose wills are immutable and those spirits who have departed this life in grace do not lose their freedom of judgment, though their wills are fixed, but retain and exercise it perfectly.

If we grasp this principle, we can again appreciate why this liberty, the principle of all our liberty, is God's greatest gift to human nature (as I said in the "Paradiso"),[2] for in this life it makes us happy as men, and in another it makes us happy as gods. If all this is true, who can deny that mankind lives best when it makes the most use of this principle?

But to live under a world-ruler is to be most free. To understand this we must know to be free means to exist for one's own sake, not for another's, as the Philosopher puts it in his *De Simpliciter Ente*.[3] For whatever exists for the sake of another is under a necessity derived from that for which it exists, as a road is necessarily determined by its goal. Now it is only under the reign of a world-ruler that mankind exists for itself and not for another, since then only is there a check on perverted forms of government such as democracies, oligarchies and tyrannies, which carry mankind into slavery, as anyone can see who runs down the list of them all, whereas those only govern who are kings, aristocrats (called "the best"), and champions of the people's liberty. Hence the world-ruler, who has the greatest love for men, as I have explained, desires that all men be made good, which is impossible among perverted politicians. Thus the Philosopher says in his *Politics* that "under a perverted form of government a good man is a bad citizen, while under a right form a good man and a good citizen are identical." In this way right forms of government aim at liberty, that is, men live for their own sake. For citizens do not live for their representatives nor peoples for their kings, but on the contrary, representatives exist for citizens and kings for peoples. As a social order is established not for the sake of the laws, but the laws for its sake, so they who live according to law are ordered not for the sake of the legislator but rather he for them. This is the way the Philosopher puts it in his books on this subject that have come down to us. Hence it is clear that though in matters of policy representatives and kings are the rulers of others, in matters of aims they are the servants of others, and most of all the world-ruler, who should be regarded as the servant of all. Hence we must be well aware that world-government is itself governed by a pre-established end in establishing its laws. Therefore mankind lives best when it lives under a single ruler; and it follows that a single world-government is necessary for the world's well-being.

*   *   *

Book two, that Roman world-rule was acquired by right

13

That universal government is most apt to be reasonable.] ... So I maintain that if the Roman Empire did not exist *de jure*, Christ's birth implies an injustice. The consequence is false, therefore the contradictory of the antecedent is true, for of contradictory propositions one is true and the other false. It is needless to prove the falsity of the consequent to the faithful, for anyone who is faithful will admit the falsity of that proposition. If not, he is unfaithful. And if he is not of the faith, he will have no interest in this proof. The argument runs as follows: Anyone who voluntarily submits to an edict, proves by his deed that he regards the edict as just, for since deeds are more powerful arguments than words (as the Philosopher says toward the end of the *Nicomachean Ethics*), his act was a better evidence than if he had approved it in words. But Christ, as his scribe Luke testifies, willed to be born of the Virgin Mary under an edict of Roman authority in order that he, the Son of God, made man, might register in that extraordinary register of mankind as a man; thus he recognized its legality. Of course, a more devout way of putting this would be that by a divine decision the edict was given by Caesar, in order that he who had been awaited for ages to appear in the society of mortals might associate himself with mortals. Therefore Christ signified by his coming that the edict given by Augustus, under the authority of the Romans, was just. And since the issuing of an edict justly implies the jurisdiction of its author, Christ recognized Caesar's jurisdiction, for a just edict must be issued *de jure*.

*   *   *

Book three, that temporal world-rule came direct from God and not from the Papacy

16

God alone rules man toward his twofold goal and chooses rulers for each.] Though in the preceding chapter we have proved, by showing the improper implications of its contrary, that the imperial authority cannot be caused by papal authority, we have not yet proved, except by implication, that this authority comes immediately from God. By implication, if it does not depend on the vicar of God, it depends on God himself. But for a perfect demonstration of our proposition it is necessary to prove that the emperor or world-government derives its powers immediately from the ruler of the universe, God.

Our knowledge of this truth depends on the fact that man alone of all beings occupies a place mid-way between the corruptible and the incorruptible. Hence he has been rightly likened by philosophers to the horizon, which is between two hemispheres. Man has two essential parts, soul and body; considered from the point of view of one part, the body, he is corruptible; from the other, the soul, incorruptible. Of the soul the Philosopher has well stated the incorruptibility when he says, "By this alone, since it is eternal, man has achieved separation from the perishable." Accordingly, if man is a kind of mean between the corruptible and the incorruptible, like every mean, he partakes of the nature of the extremes. And since every nature is arranged to seek its proper and final goal, it follows that man exists for a double purpose. And since he alone among beings partakes of both corruptibility and incorruptibility, he alone among beings belongs in two final orders — one of which is his goal as a corruptible being, the other as incorruptible.

Twofold, therefore, are the ends which unerring Providence has ordained for man: the bliss of this life, which consists in the functioning of his own powers, and which is typified by the earthly Paradise; and the bliss of eternal life, which consists in the enjoyment of that divine vision to which he cannot attain by his own powers, except they be aided by the divine light, and this state is made intelligible by the celestial Paradise. These two states of bliss, like two different goals, man must reach by different ways. For we come to the first as we follow the philosophical teachings, applying them according to our moral and intellectual capacities; and we come to the second as we follow the spiritual teachings which transcend human reason according to our theological capacities, faith, hope and charity. Though these two goals and their ways are made plain to us, the one by human reason, which as it is used by the philosophers makes all these things known to us, the other by the Holy Spirit, which through the prophets, through the holy writers, through Jesus Christ the Son of God coeternal with the Spirit, and through his disciples, has revealed to us whatever supernatural truths we need, yet man's greed would keep them from us were not men like horses in their animal vagaries kept on the road by bit and rein. Thus the reins of man are held by a double driver according to man's twofold end; one is the supreme pontiff, who guides mankind with revelations to life eternal, and the other is the emperor, who guides mankind with philosophical instructions to temporal happiness. And since none or very few (and these with difficulty) can reach this goal, unless a free mankind enjoys the tranquility of peace and the waves of distracting greed are stilled, this must be the constant aim of him who guides the globe and whom we call Roman Prince, in order that on this threshing floor of life mortals may exist free and in peace.

And inasmuch as the condition of our globe depends on the order inherent in the revolving heavens, it is needful to have the useful teachings of liberty and peace adapted to times and places by one supervisor, to whom the total state of the heavens is visible at once; and He alone is such a being who in his providence sees to it that all things are ordered as he himself has preordained. If this be the case, God alone elects, he alone establishes governments, for he has none above him. From this follows another conclusion, that those who now or in former times are called Electors should not bear this title, but should be called heralds of the divine Providence. It sometimes happens that those to whom the dignity is granted of proclaiming the divine election fail to agree. This is because some or all of them may have their vision clouded by the fogs of greed, so that they cannot look into the face of the divine dispensation.

It is now clear that the authority for temporal world-government must come directly, without intermediary, from the universal Fount of authority, which, though it flows pure from a single spring, spills over into many channels out of the abundance of its goodness. And so I see that I have reached the mark set before us. For the truth is now unfolded concerning the basic questions in our inquiry, whether for the world's well-being a single government must be established over it, and whether the Roman people has a right to its imperial power, and whether, lastly, the authority for world-government comes directly from God or through some other. However, the truth concerning this last question must not be interpreted so strictly as to imply that the Roman government is in no way subject to the Roman pontificate, for in some ways our mortal happiness is ordered for the sake of immortal happiness. Caesar therefore owes to Peter the piety which a first-born son owes to his father. And so, in the light of paternal grace, this government will better enlighten our globe, over which it rules through Him alone who is the ruler of all things spiritual and temporal.

NOTES

1. "At last the Virgin and the Saturnian Kingdoms are returning."
2. This is probably a gloss.
3. *Metaphysics* I.

A Secular Theory of the State

To REFUTE the claim that Popes were endowed with plenitudo potestatis, the fullness of power that overrode all other authorities, temporal as well as spiritual, Marsiglio of Padua undertook an investigation into the origins, nature, and functions of civil government. In 1324 he published The Defender of Peace, greatest of the fourteenth-century treatises which, for better or worse, began the divorce between political theory and theology. Marsiglio had little of Dante's religious outlook, although the two men were contemporary. His historical-naturalistic method is strikingly different from Dante's syllogistic reasoning. His conceptions of law, of the legislator, of citizenship, and of the function of the ruler all contained important innovations, so that some scholars have regarded him as the founder of "modern" notions of legislation, democracy, and sovereignty.

Marsiglio of Padua (ca. 1275–ca. 1342), The Defender of Peace

Chapter iii, on the origin of the civil community

*   *   *

2] HOWEVER, before discussing the state and its species or kinds, since the state is the perfect community we must first trace the origin of civil communities and of their regimes and modes of living. From the imperfect kinds, men have advanced to perfect communities, regimes, and modes of living in them. For from the less to the more perfect is always the path of nature and of its imitator, art. And men do not think that they have scientific knowl-

From Alan Gewirth, ed., MARSILIUS OF PADUA, 2 vols. (New York, 1951, 1956), II, pp. 10–16, 44–48, 56–58. Reprinted by permission of Columbia University Press.

edge of each thing unless they "know its first causes and first principles down to the elements."

3] Following this method, then, we must note that civil communities had small beginnings in diverse regions and times, and growing gradually came at length to completion, just as we said happens in every process of nature or of art. For the first and smallest combination of human beings, wherefrom the other combinations emerged, was that of male and female, as the foremost of the philosophers says in the *Politics,* Book I, Chapter I, and as appears more fully from his *Economics.* From this combination there were generated other humans, who first occupied one household; from these, more combinations of the same kind were formed, and so great was the procreation of children that a single household did not suffice for them, but many households had to be made. A number of these households was called a village or hamlet, and this was the first community, as is also written in the above-cited treatise.

*   *   *

5] These communities having gradually increased, men's experience became greater, more perfect arts and rules and ways of living were discovered, and also the parts of communities were more fully differentiated. Finally, the things which are necessary for living and for living well were brought to full development by men's reason and experience, and there was established the perfect community, called the state, with the differentiation of its parts, to the discussion of which we shall now proceed.

Let this much suffice, then, concerning the rise of the civil community.

Chapter iv, on the final cause of the state and of its civil requirements, and the differentiation in general of its parts

The state, according to Aristotle in the *Politics,* Book I, Chapter I, is "the perfect community having the full limit of self-sufficiency, which came into existence for the sake of living, but exists for the sake of living well." This phrase of Aristotle — "came into existence for the sake of living, but exists for the sake of living well" — signifies the perfect final cause of the state, since those who live a civil life not only live, which beasts or slaves do too, but live well, having leisure for those liberal functions in which are exercised the virtues of both the practical and the theoretic soul.

* * *

4] But since among men thus assembled there arise disputes and quarrels which, if not regulated by a norm of justice, would cause men to fight and separate and thus finally would bring about the destruction of the state, there had to be established in this association a standard of justice and a guardian or maker thereof. And since this guardian has to restrain excessive wrongdoers as well as other individuals both within and outside the state who disturb or attempt to oppress the community, the state had to have within it something by which to resist these. Again, since the community needs various conveniences, repairs and protection of certain common things, and different things in time of peace and in time of war, it was necessary that there be in the community men to take care of such matters, in order that the common necessity might be relieved when it was expedient or needful. But beside the things which we have so far mentioned, which relieve only the necessities of the present life, there is something else which men associated in a civil community need for the status of the future world promised to the human race through God's supernatural revelation, and which is useful also for the status of the present life. This is the worship and honoring of God, and the giving of thanks both for benefits received in this world and for those to be received in the future one. For the teaching of these things and for the directing of men in them, the state had to designate certain teachers. The nature and qualities of all these and the other matters mentioned above will be treated in detail in the subsequent discussions.

5] Men, then, were assembled for the sake of the sufficient life, being able to seek out for themselves the necessaries enumerated above, and exchanging them with one another. This assemblage, thus perfect and having the limit of self-sufficiency, is called the state, whose final cause as well as that of its many parts has already been indicated by us in some measure, and will be more fully distinguished below. For since diverse things are necessary to men who desire a sufficient life, things which cannot be supplied by men of one order or office, there had to be diverse orders or offices of men in this association, exercising or supplying such diverse things which men need for sufficiency of life. But these diverse orders or offices of men are none other than the many and distinct parts of the state. . . .

Chapter v, on the differentiation of the parts of the state, and the necessity of their separate existence for an end discoverable by man

We have now completely listed the parts of the state, in whose perfect action and intercommunication, without external impediment, we have said that the tranquillity of the state consists. But we must now continue our discussion of them, since the fuller determination of these parts, with respect both to their functions or ends and to their other appropriate causes, will make more manifest the causes of tranquillity and of its opposite. Let us say, then, that the parts or offices of the state are of six kinds, as Aristotle said in the *Politics,* Book VII, Chapter 7: the agricultural, the artisan, the military, the financial, the priestly, and the judicial or deliberative. Three of these, the priestly, the warrior, and the judicial, are in the strict sense parts of the state, and in civil communities they are usually called the honorable class (*honorabilitatem*). The others are called parts only in the broad sense of the term, because they are offices necessary to the state according to the doctrine of Aristotle in the *Politics,* Book VII, Chapter 7. And the multitude belonging to these offices are usually called the common mass (*vulgaris*). These, then, are the more familiar parts of the city or state, to which all the others can appropriately be reduced.

2] Although the necessity of these parts has been indicated in the preceding chapter, we wish to indicate it again more distinctly, assuming this proposition as having been previously demonstrated from what is self-evident, namely, that the state is a community established for the sake of the living and living well of the men in it. Of this "living" we have previously distinguished two kinds: one, the life or living of this world, that is, earthly; the other, the life or living of the other or future world. From these kinds of living, desired by man as ends, we shall indicate the necessity for the differentiation of the parts of the civil community. The first kind of human living, the earthly, is sometimes taken to mean the being of living things, as in Book II of the treatise *On the Soul:* "For living things, living is their being"; in which sense life is nothing other than soul. At other times, "living" is taken to mean the act, the action or passion, of the soul or of life. Again, each of these meanings is used in two ways, with reference either to the numerically same being or to the similar being, which is said to be that of the species. And although each of these kinds of living, both as proper to man and as common to him and to the other animate things, depends upon natural causes, yet we are not at present considering it insofar as it comes from these causes; the natural science of plants and animals deals with this. Rather, our present concern is with these causes insofar as they receive fulfillment "through art and reason," whereby "the human race lives."

* * *

9] Which of the temperate governments is better, monarchy or one of the other two species, aristocracy or polity; and again, which of the monarchies is better, the elected or the non-elected; and moreover, which of the elected monarchies, that established with hereditary succession ensuing or that in which one man alone is named without such succession; which in turn is divided into the further alternatives of whether it is better to name the ruler for a whole lifetime, either of himself alone or of some of his successors also, or only for some determinate period, such as one or two years, more or less—in all these questions there is room for inquiry and reasonable doubt. It must be held without doubt, however, in accordance with the truth and the manifest view of Aristotle, that election is the more certain standard of government, as will be more fully shown in Chapters XII, XVI, and XVII of this discourse.

10] We must not overlook, however, that different multitudes in different times and places are inclined toward different kinds of polity and government, as Aristotle says in the *Politics,* Book III, Chapter 9. Legislators and institutors of governments must hearken to this fact. For just as not every man is inclined toward the best discipline or study, whereupon it is appropriate that he be directed toward the acquisition not of that discipline but of some other good one for which he is more fitted, so too a multitude in some time or place may perhaps not be inclined to accept the best kind of government, and therefore recourse must first be had to that kind of temperate government which is more appropriate to it. For example, before the monarchy of Julius Caesar, the Roman people were for a long time unwilling to accept any definite monarch, either with hereditary succession or even one who was named only for his own lifetime. The reason for this was perhaps that there was a large number of heroic men worthy of rulership among them, both families and individuals.

* * *

Chapter xii, on the demonstrable efficient cause of human laws, and also on that cause which cannot be proved by demonstration: which is to inquire into the legislator. Whence it appears also that whatever is established by election derives its authority from election alone apart from another confirmation

* * *

2] Let us say, to begin with, that it can pertain to any citizen to discover the law taken materially and in its third sense, as the science of civil justice and benefit. Such inquiry, however, can be carried on more appropriately and be completed better by those men who are able to have leisure, who are older and experienced in practical affairs, and who are called "prudent men," than by the mechanics who must bend all their efforts to acquiring the necessities of life. But it must be remembered that the true knowledge or discovery of the just and the beneficial, and of their opposites, is not law taken in its last and most proper sense, whereby it is the measure of human civil acts, unless there is given a coercive command as to its observance, or it is made by way of such a command, by some one through whose authority its transgressors must and can be punished. Hence, we must now say to whom belongs the authority to make such a command and to punish its transgressors. This, indeed, is to inquire into the legislator or the maker of the law.

3] Let us say, then, in accordance with the truth and the counsel of Aristotle in the *Politics,* Book III, Chapter 6, that the legislator, or the primary and proper efficient cause of the law, is the people or the whole body of citizens, or the weightier part thereof, through its election or will expressed by words in the general assembly of the citizens, commanding or determining that something be done or omitted with regard to human civil acts, under a temporal pain or punishment. By the "weightier part" I mean to take into consideration the quantity and the quality of the persons in that community over which the law is made. The aforesaid whole body of citizens or the weightier part thereof is the legislator regardless of whether it makes the law directly by itself or entrusts the making of it to some person or persons, who are not and cannot be the legislator in the absolute sense, but only in a relative sense and for a particular time and in accordance with the authority of the primary legislator. And I say further that the laws and anything else established through election must receive their necessary approval by that same primary authority and no other, whatever be the case with regard to certain ceremonies or solemnities, which are required not for the being of the matters elected but for their well-being, since the election would be no less valid even if these ceremonies were not performed. Moreover, by the same authority must the laws and other things established through election undergo addition, subtraction, complete change, interpretation, or suspension, insofar as the exigencies of time or place or other circumstances make any such action opportune for the common benefit. And by the same authority, also, must the laws be promulgated or proclaimed after their enactment, so that no citizen or alien who is delinquent in observing them may be excused because of ignorance.

4] A citizen I define in accordance with Aristotle in the *Politics,* Book III, Chapters 1, 3, and 7, as one who participates in the civil community in the government or the deliberative or judicial function according to his rank. By this definition, children, slaves, aliens, and women are distinguished from citizens, although in different ways. For the sons of citizens are citizens in proximate potentiality, lacking only in years. The weightier part of the citizens should be viewed in accordance with the honorable custom of polities, or else it should be determined in accordance with the doctrine of Aristotle in the *Politics,* Book VI, Chapter 2.

5] Having thus defined the citizen and the weightier part of the citizens, let us return to our proposed objective, namely, to demonstrate that the human authority to make laws belongs only to the whole body of the citizens or to the weightier part thereof. Our first proof is as follows. The absolutely primary human authority to make or establish human laws belongs only to those men from whom alone the best laws can emerge. But these are the whole body of the citizens, or the weightier part thereof, which represents that whole body; since it is difficult or impossible for all persons to agree upon one decision, because some men have a deformed nature, disagreeing with the common decision through singular malice or ignorance. The common benefit should not, however, be impeded or neglected because of the unreasonable protest or opposition of these men. The authority to make or establish laws, therefore, belongs only to the whole body of the citizens or to the weightier part thereof.

The first proposition of this demonstration is very close to self-evident, although its force and its ultimate certainty can be grasped from Chapter V of this discourse. The second proposition, that the best law is made only through the hearing and command of the entire multitude, I prove by assuming with Aristotle in the *Politics*, Book III, Chapter 7, that the best law is that which is made for the common benefit of the citizens. As Aristotle said: "That is presumably right," that is, in the laws, "which is for the common benefit of the state and the citizens." But that this is best achieved only by the whole body of the citizens or by the weightier part thereof, which is assumed to be the same thing, I show as follows: That at which the entire body of the citizens aims intellectually and emotionally is more certainly judged as to its truth and more diligently noted as to its common utility. For a defect in some proposed law can be better noted by the greater number than by any part thereof, since every whole, or at least every corporeal whole, is greater in mass and in virtue than any part of it taken separately. Moreover, the common utility of a law is better noted by the entire multitude, because no one knowingly harms himself. Anyone can look to see whether a proposed law leans toward the benefit of one or a few persons more than of the others or of the community, and can protest against it. Such, however, would not be the case were the law made by one or a few persons, considering their own private benefit rather than that of the community. This position is also supported by the arguments which we advanced in Chapter XI of this discourse with regard to the necessity of having laws.

6] Another argument to the principal conclusion is as follows. The authority to make the law belongs only to those men whose making of it will cause the law to be better observed or observed at all. Only the whole body of the citizens are such men. To them, therefore, belongs the authority to make the law. The first proposition of this demonstration is very close to self-evident, for a law would be useless unless it were observed. Hence Aristotle said in the *Politics*, Book IV, Chapter 6: "Laws are not well ordered when they are well made but not obeyed." He also said in Book VI, Chapter 5: "Nothing is accomplished by forming opinions about justice and not carrying them out." The second proposition I prove as follows. That law is better observed by every citizen which each one seems to have imposed upon himself. But such is the law which is made through the hearing and command of the entire multitude of the citizens. The first proposition of this prosyllogism is almost self-evident; for since "the state is a community of free men," as is written in the *Politics*, Book III, Chapter 4, every citizen must be free, and not undergo another's despotism, that is, slavish dominion. But this would not be the case if one or a few of the citizens by their own authority made the law over the whole body of citizens. For those who thus made the law would be despots over the others, and hence such a law, however good it was, would be endured only with reluctance, or not at all, by the rest of the citizens, the more ample part. Having suffered contempt, they would protest against it, and not having been called upon to make it, they would not observe it. On the other hand, a law made by the hearing or consent of the whole multitude, even though it were less useful, would be readily observed and endured by every one of the citizens, because then each would seem to have set the law upon himself, and hence would have no protest against it, but would rather tolerate it with equanimity. The second proposition of the first syllogism I also prove in another way, as follows. The power to cause the laws to be observed belongs only to those men to whom belongs coercive force over the transgressors of the laws. But these men are the whole body of citizens or the weightier part thereof. Therefore, to them alone belongs the authority to make the laws.

7] The principal conclusion is also proved as follows. That practical matter whose proper establishment is of greatest importance for the common sufficiency of the citizens in this life, and whose poor establishment threatens harm for the community, must be established only by the whole body of the citizens. But such a matter is the law. Therefore, the establishment of the law pertains only to the whole body of the citizens. The major premise of this demonstration is almost self-evident, and is grounded in the immediate truths which were set forth in Chapters IV and V of this discourse. For men came together to the civil community in order to attain what was beneficial for sufficiency of life, and to avoid the opposite. Those matters, therefore, which can affect the benefit and harm of all ought to be known and heard by all, in order that they may be able to attain the beneficial and to avoid the opposite. Such matters are the laws, as was assumed in the minor premise. For in the laws being rightly made consists a large part of the whole common sufficiency of men, while under bad laws there arise unbearable slavery, oppression, and misery of the citizens, the final result of which is that the polity is destroyed.

8] Again, and this is an abbreviation and summary of the previous demonstrations: The authority to make laws belongs only to the whole body of the citizens, as we have said, or else it belongs to one or a few men. But it cannot belong to one man alone for the reasons given in Chapter XI and in the first demonstration adduced in the present chapter; for through ignorance or malice or both, this one man could make a bad law, looking more to his own private benefit than to that of the community, so that the law would be tyrannical. For the same reason, the authority to make laws cannot belong to a few; for they too could sin, as above, in making the law for the benefit of a certain few and not for the common benefit, as can be seen in oligarchies. The authority to make the laws belongs, therefore, to the whole body of citizens or to the weightier part thereof, for precisely the opposite reason. For since all the citizens must be measured by the law according to due proportion, and no one knowingly harms or wishes injustice to himself, it follows that all or most wish a law conducing to the common benefit of the citizens.

*   *   *

Chapter xiv, on the qualities or dispositions of the perfect ruler, that it may be known what kind of person should be named to the rulership. Whence there appears also the appropriate matter or subject of human laws

*   *   *

2] The man who is to be a perfect ruler should have two intrinsic habits which cannot exist separately, namely, prudence and moral virtue, especially justice. Prudence is required in order that his understanding may be guided in ruling. As it is said in the *Poli-*

tics, Book III, Chapter 2: "Prudence alone is the virtue proper to a ruler, for it seems appropriate that the other virtues be common to rulers and subjects." The other habit, moral virtue, especially justice, is required in order that the ruler's emotion be right. As Aristotle says in the fourth book of the *Ethics,* the treatise on justice: "The ruler is the guardian of justice."

3] Prudence, then, is necessary for the man who is to be a ruler because it makes him magnificently capable for his proper function, the judgment of matters of civil benefit and justice. For in those civil human acts where the act itself or its manner is not determined by law, the ruler is guided by prudence in his judgment of the act or its manner or both, as well as in his execution of the judgment, whereas without prudence he might err. To take an example from Sallust's *Catiline,* when the accomplices of Catiline, powerful Roman citizens, conspired against the republic and hence were liable to the death penalty, if Cicero the consul had punished them according to the law in the customary time, place, and manner, there would very likely have arisen civil war destructive of the polity because of the sedition which these conspirators had incited among the people against the consul and the other rulers. Cicero, the consul or ruler of the city, avoided this danger through his prudence; for he handed the accused men over to the executioners and commanded that they be killed in the prison which perhaps for this reason is called "Tullian."

*   *   *

5] For these reasons it was necessary to entrust to the discretion (*arbitrio*) of rulers the judgment of certain aspects of men's civil acts, that is, those aspects which were not determined in themselves, or as to some manner or circumstance, by law. For in those aspects which have been determined by law, the ruler's duty is to follow that legal determination. This was the view of Aristotle in the *Politics,* Book III, Chapter 6: "The ruler, whether one man or many, must have the supreme authority in those cases concerning which the laws cannot speak with certainty, because it is difficult for laws universally to determine about all things." . . .

6] Also necessary to the ruler is moral goodness, that is, virtue, especially justice; for if the ruler be perverted in moral character, the polity will be greatly harmed, however much it be formed by laws. For we have already said that it is difficult or impossible to determine all things at once by laws, but some matters must be entrusted to the discretion of the ruler; and in these matters he can harm the polity if he be of perverted emotion. This was also the view of Aristotle in the *Politics,* Book II, Chapter 8: "Men who are dominant in important matters do much harm if they are villainous," that is, morally vicious; "and they have already harmed the Chalcedonian state." And since they are preserved from this by moral virtue, especially justice, it is therefore appropriate, if we may call "appropriate" what is necessary, that no one who is to be a ruler lack moral virtue, especially justice.

7] It is also appropriate that the future ruler have a certain virtue called equity (*epieikeiam*) by which the judge is guided, especially with respect to his emotions, in those cases where the law is deficient. As Aristotle said in the fourth book of the *Ethics,* the treatise on justice: "This is the nature of equity, that it is a rectification of the law when it fails because of this particular." This, I think, is what the jurists mean by "fairness" (*aequitas*). For it is a benign interpretation or moderation of the law in some case which the law comprehends under rigorous universality, and in which the law is said to be deficient because it does not except that case from the universality of the standard rule, although it would have done so either entirely or with some moderation if it had foreseen its occurence.

Also, together with these virtues the future ruler is required to have outstanding love or benevolence for the polity and the citizens. For this love the ruler's actions will be directed with solicitude and goodness toward the benefit of the community and of the individuals in it. . . .

3

Petrarch on the Two Kinds of Immortality

FRANCESCO PETRARCA, better known by the Latinized form, Petrarch, was born in the Tuscan city of Arezzo of parents who were political exiles from Florence. His father sent him to the universities of Montpellier and Bologna to study law, but as soon as Petrarch could he gave his full time to poetry and to classical studies, fields in which he became teacher to his age. In these imaginary dialogues with St. Augustine which he wrote when he was about forty, Petrarch shows himself torn between the desire for two different kinds of immortality, one of the soul, the other of worldly fame. He seems to concur in St. Augustine's unflattering description of the human condition and to agree that man can improve his situation only if he seeks virtue rather than glory; yet there is irony in Petrarch's promise to devote himself to his spiritual welfare as soon as he has attended to the "crowd of important affairs" which is pressing for his attention. One wonders whether he finally gave up the view he expresses in his first speech below.

Francesco Petrarca (1304–1374), The Secret, or The Soul's Conflict with Passion

Dialogue the third

* * *

S. AUGUSTINE] ... But let us take for granted (what is quite impossible) that the duration of life will be long and assured: still, do you not find it is the height of madness to squander the best years and the best parts of your existence on pleasing only the eyes of others and tickling other men's ears, and to keep the last and

From Francesco Petrarca, THE SECRET, OR THE SOUL'S CONFLICT WITH PASSION (London, 1911), pp. 175–192. Translation by William H. Draper. Reprinted by permission of Chatto and Windus.

worst — the years that are almost good for nothing — that bring nothing but distaste for life and then its end — to keep these, I say, for God and yourself, as though the welfare of your soul were the last thing you cared for?

Even supposing the time were certain, is it not reversing the true order to put off the best to the last?

PETRARCH]   I do not think my way of looking at it is so unreasonable as you imagine. My principle is that, as concerning the glory which we may hope for here below, it is right for us to seek while we are here below. One may expect to enjoy that other more radiant glory in heaven, when we shall have there arrived, and when one will have no more care or wish for the glory of earth. Therefore, as I think, it is in the true order that mortal men should first care for mortal things; and that to things transitory things eternal should succeed; because to pass from those to these is to go forward in most certain accordance with what is ordained for us, although no way is open for us to pass back again from eternity to time.

S. AUGUSTINE]   O man, little in yourself, and of little wisdom! Do you, then, dream that you shall enjoy every pleasure in heaven and earth, and everything will turn out fortunate and prosperous for you always and everywhere? But that delusion has betrayed thousands of men thousands of times, and has sunk into hell a countless host of souls. Thinking to have one foot on earth and one in heaven, they could neither stand here below nor mount on high. Therefore they fell miserably, and the moving breeze swept them suddenly away, some in the flower of their age, and some when they were in midst of their years and all their business.

And do you suppose what has befallen so many others may not befall you? Alas! if (which may God forefend!) in the midst of all your plans and projects you should be cut off — what grief, what shame, what remorse (then too late!) that you should have grasped at all and lost all!

PETRARCH]   May the Most High in His mercy save me from that misery!

S. AUGUSTINE]   Though Divine Mercy may deliver a man from his folly, yet it will not excuse it. Presume not upon this mercy overmuch. For if God abhors those who lose hope, He also laughs at those who in false hope put their trust. I was sorry when I heard fall from your lips that phrase about despising what you called the old story of the philosophers on this matter. Is it, then, an old story, pray, by figures of geometry, to show how small is all the earth, and to prove it but an island of little length and width? Is it an old story to divide the earth into five zones, the largest of which, lying in the centre, is burned by the heat of the sun, and the two utmost, to right and left, are a prey to binding frost and eternal snow, which leave not a corner where man can dwell; but those other two, between the middle and two utmost zones, are inhabited by man? Is it an old story that this habitable part is divided again into two parts, whereof one is placed under your feet, guarded by a vast sea, and the other is left you to inhabit everywhere, or, according to some authorities, is again in two parts subdivided, with but one part habitable and the other surrounded by the winding intricacies of the Northern Ocean, preventing all access to it? As to that part under your feet, called the antipodes, you are aware that for a long time the most learned men have been of two opinions whether it is inhabited or not: for myself, I have set forth my opinion in the book called *The City of God,* which you have doubtless read. Is it also an old story that your habitable part, already so restricted, is yet further diminished to such an extent by seas, marshes, forests, sand and deserts, that the little corner left you, of which you are so proud, is brought down to almost nothing? And, finally, is it an old story to point out to you that on this narrow strip, where you dwell, there are divers kinds of life, different religions which oppose one another, different languages and customs, which render it impossible to make the fame of your name go far?

But if these things are to you nought but fables, so, to me, all I had promised myself of your future greatness must be a fable also; for I had thought, hitherto, that no man had more knowledge of these things than you yourself. To say nothing of the conceptions of Cicero and Virgil and other systems of knowledge, physical or poetic, of which you seemed to have a competent knowledge, I knew that not long since, in your *Africa,* you had expressed the very same opinions in these pretty lines—

> "The Universe itself is but an isle
> Confined in narrow bounds, small and begirt
> By Ocean's flowing waves." (*Africa,* ii. 361, 363.)

You have added other developments later on, and now that I know you think them all fables, I am astonished you have put them forth with such hardihood.

What shall I say now of the brief existence of human fame, the short, short span of time, when you know too well how small and recent even the oldest memory of man is if compared to eternity? I spare to call to your mind those opinions of the men of old, laid up in Plato's *Timaeus* and in the sixth book of Cicero's *Republic*, where it is foretold what floods and conflagrations shall be coming not seldom on the earth. To many men such things have seemed probable; but they wear a different aspect to those who, like yourself, have come to know the true religion.

And besides these, how many other things there are that militate against, I do not say the eternity, but even the survival of one's name. First there is the death of those with whom one has passed one's life; and that forgetfulness which is the common bane of old age: then there is the rising fame, ever growing greater, of new men; which always, by its freshness, is somewhat derogatory to that of those who went before, and seems to mount up higher just in so far as it can depress this other down. Then you must add, also, that persistent envy which ever dogs the steps of those who embark on any glorious enterprise; and the hatred of Truth itself, and the fact that the very life of men of genius is odious to the crowd. Think, too, how fickle is the judgment of the multitude. And alas for the sepulchres of the dead! to shatter which ——

> "The wild fig's barren branch is strong enough,"

as Juvenal has told us.

In your own *Africa* you call this, elegantly enough, "a second death"; and if I may here address to you the same words you have put in the mouth of another ——

> "The animated bust and storied urn
>   Shall fall, and with them fall thy memory,
>   And thou, my son, thus taste a second death."

Lo, then, how excellent, how undying that glory must be which the fall of one poor stone can bring to nought!

And, then, consider the perishing of books wherein your name has been written, either by your own hand or another's. Even though that perishing may appear so much more delayed as books outlast monuments, nevertheless it is sooner or later inevitable; for, as is the case with everything else, there are countless natural or

fortuitous calamities to which books are ever exposed. And even
if they escape all these, they, like us, grow old and die ——

> "For whatsoever mortal hand has made,
>   With its vain labour, shall be mortal too,"

if one may be allowed, for choice, to refute your childish error by
your own words.

What need to say more? I shall never cease to bring to your
recollection lines of your own making which only too truly fit the
case.

> "When your books perish you shall perish too;
>   This is the third death, still to be endured."

And now you know what I think about glory.

* * *

PETRARCH] . . . What you have been saying — so far from
seeming to me like old stories — has stirred in me a new desire to get
rid of my old delusions. For albeit that these things were known
to me long ago, and that I have heard them oftentimes repeated,
since, as Terence puts it ——

> "Everything that one can say
>   Has all been said before,"

nevertheless the stateliness of phrase, the orderly narration, the authority of him who speaks, cannot but move me deeply.

But I have yet a last request to make, which is that you will give
me your definite judgment on this point. Is it your wish that I
should put all my studies on one side and renounce every ambition,
or would you advise some middle course?

S. AUGUSTINE] I will never advise you to live without
ambition; but I would always urge you to put virtue before glory.
You know that glory is in a sense the shadow of virtue. And therefore, just as it is impossible that your body should not cast a shadow
if the sun is shining, so it is impossible also in the light of God
Himself that virtues should exist and not make their glory to appear. Whoever, then, would take true glory away must of necessity
take away virtue also; and when that is gone man's life is left bare,
and only resembles that of the brute beasts that follow headlong
their appetite, which to them is their only law. Here, therefore, is

the rule for you to live by — follow after virtue, and let glory take care of itself; and as for this, as someone said of Cato, the less you seek it the more you will find it. I must once more allow myself to invoke your own witness ——

> "Thou shalt do well from Honour's self to flee,
> For then shall Honour follow after thee."

Do you not recognize the verse? It is your own. One would surely think that man a fool who at midday should run here and there in the blaze of the sun, wearing himself out to see his shadow and point it out to others; now the man shows no more sense or reason who, amid the anxieties of life, takes huge trouble, first one way, then another, to spread his own glory abroad.

What then? Let a man march steadily to the goal set before him, his shadow will follow him step by step: let him so act that he shall make virtue his prize, and lo! glory also shall be found at his side. I speak of that glory which is virtue's true companion; as for that which comes by other means, whether from bodily grace or mere cleverness, in the countless ways men have invented, it does not seem to me worthy of the name. And so, in regard to yourself, while you are wearing your strength out by such great labours in writing books, if you will allow me to say so, you are shooting wide of the mark. For you are spending all your efforts on things that concern others, and neglecting those that are your own; and so, through this vain hope of glory, the time, so precious, though you know it not, is passing away.

PETRARCH] What must I do, then? Abandon my unfinished works? Or would it be better to hasten them on, and, if God gives me grace, put the finishing touches to them? If I were once rid of these cares I would go forward, with a mind more free, to greater things; for hardly could I bear the thought of leaving half completed a work so fine and rich in promise of success.

S. AUGUSTINE] Which foot you mean to hobble on, I do not know. You seem inclined to leave yourself derelict, rather than your books.

As for me, I shall do my duty, with what success depends on you; but at least I shall have satisfied my conscience. Throw to the winds these great loads of histories; the deeds of the Romans have been celebrated quite enough by others, and are known by their own fame. Get out of Africa and leave it to its possessors. You will add

nothing to the glory of your Scipio or to your own. He can be exalted to no higher pinnacle, but you may bring down his reputation,
and with it your own. Therefore leave all this on one side, and now
at length take possession of yourself; and to come back to our start-
ing point, let me urge you to enter upon the meditation of your
last end, which comes on step by step without your being aware.
Tear off the veil; disperse the shadows; look only on that which is
coming; with eyes and mind give all your attention there: let
nought else distract you. Heaven, Earth, the Sea — these all suffer
change. What can man, the frailest of all creatures, hope for? The
seasons fulfill their courses and change; nothing remains as it was.
If you think you shall remain, you are deceived. For, as Horace
beautifully says ——

> "The losses of the Changing Heaven,
> The changing moons repair;
> But we, when we have gone below,
> And our rich land no longer know,
> And hear no more its rivers flow,
> Are nought but dust and air."

Therefore, as often as you watch the fruits of summer follow the
flowers of spring, and the pleasant cool of autumn succeed the
summer heat, and winter's snow come after autumn's vintage, say
to yourself: "The seasons pass, yet they will come again; but I am
going, never again to return." As often as you behold at sunset the
shadows of the mountains lengthening on the plain, say to yourself: "Now life is sinking fast; the shadow of death begins to over-
spread the scene; yonder sun tomorrow will again be rising the
same, but this day of mine will never come back."

Who shall count the glories of the midnight sky, which, though
it be the time that men of evil heart choose for their misdoing, yet
is it to men of good heart the holiest of all times? Well, take care
you be not less watchful than that admiral of the Trojan fleet; for
the seas you sail upon are no more safe than his; rise up at the mid
hour of night, and

> "All the stars, that in the silent sky
> Roll on their way, observe with careful heed."

As you see them hasten to their setting in the west, think how you
also are moving with them; and that as for your abiding you have no

hope, saving only in Him who knows no change and suffers no decline. Moreover, when you meet with those whom you knew but yesterday as children, and see them now growing up in stature to their manhood, stage by stage, remember how you in like manner, in the same lapse of time, are going down the hill, and at greater speed, by that law in nature under which things that are heavy tend to fall.

When your eyes behold some ancient building, let your first thought be, Where are those who wrought it with their hands? and when you see new ones, ask, Where, soon, the builders of them will be also? If you chance to see the trees of some orchard, remember how often it falls out that one plants it and another plucks the fruit; for many a time the saying in the *Georgics* comes to pass——

> "One plants the tree, but ah, the slow-grown shade
> His grandchild will enjoy."

And when you look with pleased wonder at some swiftly flowing stream, then, that I bring no other poet's thought, keep ever in mind this one of your own——

> "No river hurries with more rapid flight
> Than Life's swift current."

Neither let multitude of days or the artificial divisions of time deceive your judgment; for man's whole existence, let it be never so prolonged, is but as one day, and that not a day entire.

Have oftentimes before your eyes one similitude of Aristotle's, whom I know to be a favourite of yours; and his words I am sure you never read or hear without feeling them deeply. You will find it reported by Cicero in the *Tusculan Orations,* and in words possibly even more clear and impressive than the original. Here is what he says, or very nearly so, for at the moment I have not his book at hand——

"Aristotle tells us that on the banks of the river Hypanis, which on one side of Europe empties itself into the Euxine Sea, there exists a race of little animals who only live one day. Any one of them that dies at sunrise dies young; he that dies at noon is middle-aged; and should one live till sunset, he dies in old age: and especially is this so about the time of the solstice. If you compare the time of man's life with eternity, it will seem no longer than theirs." So far I give you Cicero; but what he says seems to me so beyond all cavil that now for a long time the saying has passed from the tongue of philosophers into common speech. Every day you hear even ignorant and unlearned men, if they chance to see a little child, make use of some expression like this — "Well, well, it's early morning with him yet"; if they see a man they will say, "Oh, it's high noon with him now," or "He's well in the middle of his day"; if they see one old and broken down they will remark, "Ah! he's getting toward evening and the going down of the sun."

Ponder well on these things, my very dear son, and on others akin to them, which will, I doubt not, flock into your thoughts, as these on the spur of the moment have come into mine. And one more thing I beseech you to have in mind: look at the graves of those older, perhaps, than you, but whom nevertheless you have known; look diligently, and then rest assured that the same dwelling-place, the same house, is for you also made ready. Thither are all of us travelling on; that is our last home. You who now, perchance, are proud and think that your springtime has not quite departed, and are for trampling others underfoot, you in turn shall underfoot be trampled. Think over all this; consider it by day and by night; not merely as a man of sober mind and remembering what nature he is of, but as becomes a man of wisdom, and so holding it all fast, as one who remembers it is written

"A wise man's life is all one preparation for death."

This saying will teach you to think little of what concerns earthly things, and set before your eyes a better path of life on which to enter. You will be asking me what is that kind of life, and by what ways you can approach it? And I shall reply that now you have no need of long advice or counsel. Listen only to that Holy Spirit who is ever calling, and in urgent words saying, "Here is the way to your native country, your true home."

You know what He would bring to mind; what paths for your feet, what dangers to avoid. If you would be safe and free obey His voice. There is no need for long deliberations. The nature of your danger calls for action, not words. The enemy is pressing you from behind, and hastening to the charge in front; the walls of the citadel, where you are besieged, already tremble. There is no time for hesitation. Of what use is it to make sweet songs for the ears of others, if you listen not to them yourself? . . .

PETRARCH] Ah! would that you had told me all this before I had surrendered myself over to these studies!

S. AUGUSTINE] I have told you, many a time and oft. From the moment when I saw you first take up your pen, I foresaw how short life would be, and how uncertain: how certain, too, and how long the toil. I saw the work would be great and the fruit little, and I warned you of all these things. But your ears were filled with the plaudits of the public, which, to my astonishment, took you captive, although you talked as if you despised them. But as we have now been conferring together long enough, I beg that if any of my counsels have seemed good to you, you will not allow them to come to nothing for want of energy or recollection; and if, on the other hand, I have sometimes been too rough, I pray you take it not amiss.

PETRARCH] Indeed I owe you a deep debt of gratitude, as for many other things, so, especially, for this three days' colloquy; for you have cleansed my darkened sight and scattered the thick clouds of error in which I was involved. And how shall I express my thankfulness to Her also, the Spirit of Truth, who, unwearied by our much talking, has waited upon us to the end? Had She turned away her face from us we should have wandered in darkness: your discourse had then contained no sure truth, neither would my understanding have embraced it. And now, as She and you have your dwelling-place in heaven, and I must still abide on earth, and, as you see, am greatly perplexed and troubled, not knowing for how long this must be, I implore you, of your goodness, not to forsake me, in spite of that great distance which separates me from such as you; for without you, O best of fathers, my life would be but one long sadness, and without Her I could not live at all.

S. AUGUSTINE] You may count your prayer already granted, if you will only to yourself be true: for how shall anyone be constant to him who is inconstant to himself?

PETRARCH] I will be true to myself, so far as in me lies. I will pull myself together and collect my scattered wits, and make a great endeavour to possess my soul in patience. But even while we speak, a crowd of important affairs, though only of the world, is waiting my attention.

S. AUGUSTINE] For the common herd of men these may be what to them seem more important; but in reality there is nothing of more importance, and nothing ought to be esteemed of so much worth. For, of other trains of thought, you may reckon them to be not essential for the soul, but the end of life will prove that these we have been engaged in are of eternal necessity.

PETRARCH] I confess they are so. And I now return to attend to those other concerns only in order that, when they are discharged, I may come back to these.

I am not ignorant that, as you said a few minutes before, it would be much safer for me to attend only to the care of my soul, to relinquish altogether every bypath and follow the straight path of the way of salvation. But I have not strength to resist that old bent for study altogether.

S. AUGUSTINE] We are falling into our old controversy. Want of will you call want of power. Well, so it must be, if it cannot be otherwise. I pray God that He will go with you where you go, and that He will order your steps, even though they wander, into the way of truth.

PETRARCH] O may it indeed be as you have prayed! May God lead me safe and whole out of so many crooked ways; that I may follow the Voice that calls me; that I may raise up no cloud of dust before my eyes; and, with my mind calmed down and at peace, I may hear the world grow still and silent, and the winds of adversity die away.

4

A Humanist's Program of Liberal Studies

PIER PAOLO VERGERIO was associated with the humanist Vittorino da Feltre in the latter's famous school in Padua. He was also a professor of logic in Padua and in Florence. He wrote his treatise on education around 1404 for the son of Padua's ruler, and it became so popular that it went through forty editions before 1600. Vergerio's urging of both the social and the intellectual aspects of education, his concern for the psychology of learning, and his combination of physical with mental development are typical elements of the humanist pedagogical tradition. His insistence on the relation between education and freedom link him to the developing civic humanist movement in Florence.

Pier Paolo Vergerio (1370–1444), The Qualities of a Free Man ("De Ingenuis Moribus")

P. P. Vergerius to Ubertinus of Carrara

* * *

3] WE CALL THOSE STUDIES *liberal* which are worthy of a free man; those studies by which we attain and practise virtue and wisdom; that education which calls forth, trains and develops those highest gifts of body and of mind which ennoble men, and which are rightly judged to rank next in dignity to virtue only. For to a vulgar temper gain and pleasure are the one aim of existence, to a lofty nature, moral worth and fame. It is, then, of the highest

From William H. Woodward, ed., VITTORINO DA FELTRE AND OTHER HUMANIST EDUCATORS (Cambridge, 1921), pp. 102–110, 112–114. Reprinted by permission of Cambridge University Press.

importance that even from infancy this aim, this effort, should constantly be kept alive in growing minds. For I may affirm with fullest conviction that we shall not have attained wisdom in our later years unless in our earliest we have sincerely entered on its search. Nor may we for a moment admit, with the unthinking crowd, that those who give early promise fail in subsequent fulfilment. This may, partly from physical causes, happen in exceptional cases. But there is no doubt that nature has endowed some children with so keen, so ready an intelligence, that without serious effort they attain to a notable power of reasoning and conversing upon grave and lofty subjects, and by aid of right guidance and sound learning reach in manhood the highest distinction. On the other hand, children of modest powers demand even more attention, that their natural defects may be supplied by art. But all alike must in those early years,

'Dum faciles animi iuvenum, dum mobilis aetas,'

whilst the mind is supple, be inured to the toil and effort of learning. Not that education, in the broad sense, is exclusively the concern of youth. Did not Cato think it honourable to learn Greek in later life? Did not Socrates, greatest of philosophers, compel his aged fingers to the lute?

Our youth of to-day, it is to be feared, is backward to learn; studies are accounted irksome. Boys hardly weaned begin to claim their own way, at a time when every art should be employed to bring them under control and attract them to grave studies. The Master must judge how far he can rely upon emulation, rewards, encouragement; how far he must have recourse to sterner measures. Too much leniency is objectionable; so also is too great severity, for we must avoid all that terrifies a boy. In certain temperaments — those in which a dark complexion denotes a quiet but strong personality — restraint must be cautiously applied. Boys of this type are mostly highly gifted and can bear a gentle hand. Not seldom it happens that a finely tempered nature is thwarted by circumstances, such as poverty at home, which compels a promising youth to forsake learning for trade: though, on the other hand, poverty is less dangerous to lofty instincts than great wealth. Or again, parents encourage their sons to follow a career traditional in their family, which may divert them from liberal studies: and the customary pursuits of the city in which we dwell exercise a decided influence on our choice. So that we may say that a perfectly unbiassed decision in these matters is seldom possible, except to certain select natures, who by favour of the gods, as the poets have it, are unconsciously brought to choose the right path in life. The myth of Hercules, who, in the solitude of his wanderings, learned to accept the strenuous life and to reject the way of self-indulgence, and so attain the highest, is the significant setting of this profound truth. For us it is the best that can befall, that either the circumstances of our life, or the guidance and exhortations of those in charge of us, should mould our natures whilst they are still plastic.

In your own case, Ubertinus, you had before you the choice of training in Arms or in Letters. Either holds a place of distinction amongst the pursuits which appeal to men of noble spirit; either leads to fame and honour in the world. It would have been natural that you, the scion of a House ennobled by its prowess in arms, should have been content to accept your father's permission to devote yourself wholly to that discipline. But to your great credit you elected to become proficient in both alike: to add to the career of arms traditional in your family, an equal success in that other great discipline of mind and character, the study of Literature.

There was courage in your choice. For we cannot deny that there is still a horde — as I must call them — of people who, like Licinius the Emperor, denounce learning and the Arts as a danger to the State and hateful in themselves. In reality the very opposite is the truth. However, as we look back upon history we cannot deny that learning by no means expels wickedness, but may be indeed an additional instrument for evil in the hands of the corrupt. To a man of virtuous instincts knowledge is a help and an adornment; to a Claudius or a Nero it was a means of refinement in cruelty or in folly.

*   *   *

Indeed the power which good books have of diverting our thoughts from unworthy or distressing themes is another support to my argument for the study of letters. Add to this their helpfulness on those occasions when we find ourselves alone, without companions and without preoccupations — what can we do better than gather our books around us? In them we see unfolded before us vast stores of knowledge, for our delight, it may be, or for our inspiration. In them are contained the records of the great achievements of men; the wonders of Nature; the works of Providence in the past, the key to her secrets of the future. And, most important of all, this

Knowledge is not liable to decay. With a picture, an inscription, a coin, books share a kind of immortality. In all these memory is, as it were, made permanent; although, in its freedom from accidental risks, Literature surpasses every other form of record.

Literature indeed exhibits not facts alone, but thoughts, and their expression. Provided such thoughts be worthy, and worthily expressed, we feel assured that they will not die: although I do not think that thoughts without style will be likely to attract much notice or secure a sure survival. What greater charm can life offer than this power of making the past, the present, and even the future, our own by means of literature? How bright a household is the family of books! we may cry, with Cicero. In their company is no noise, no greed, no self-will: at a word they speak to you, at a word they are still: to all our requests their response is ever ready and to the point. Books indeed are a higher — a wider, more tenacious — memory, a store-house which is the common property of us all.

I attach great weight to the duty of handing down this priceless treasure to our sons unimpaired by any carelessness on our part. How many are the gaps which the ignorance of past ages has wilfully caused in the long and noble roll of writers! Books — in part or in their entirety — have been allowed to perish. What remains of others is often sorely corrupt, mutilated, or imperfect. It is hard that no slight portion of the history of Rome is only to be known through the labours of one writing in the Greek language: it is still worse that this same noble tongue, once well nigh the daily speech of our race, as familiar as the Latin language itself, is on the point of perishing even amongst its own sons, and to us Italians is already utterly lost, unless we except one or two who in our time are tardily endeavouring to rescue something — if it be only a mere echo of it — from oblivion.

We come now to the consideration of the various subjects which may rightly be included under the name of 'Liberal Studies.' Amongst these I accord the first place to History, on grounds both of its attractiveness and of its utility, qualities which appeal equally to the scholar and to the statesman. Next in importance ranks Moral Philosophy, which indeed is, in a peculiar sense, a 'Liberal Art,' in that its purpose is to teach men the secret of true freedom. History, then, gives us the concrete examples of the precepts inculcated by philosophy. The one shews what men should do, the other what men have said and done in the past, and what practical lessons we may draw therefrom for the present day. I would indicate as the third main branch of study, Eloquence, which indeed holds a place of distinction amongst the refined Arts. By philosophy we learn the essential truth of things, which by eloquence we so exhibit in orderly adornment as to bring conviction to differing minds. And history provides the light of experience — a cumulative wisdom fit to supplement the force of reason and the persuasion of eloquence. For we allow that soundness of judgment, wisdom of speech, integrity of conduct are the marks of a truly liberal temper.

We are told that the Greeks devised for their sons a course of training in four subjects: letters, gymnastic, music and drawing. Now, of these drawing has no place amongst our liberal studies; except in so far as it is identical with writing, (which is in reality one side of the art of Drawing), it belongs to the Painter's profession: the Greeks, as an art-loving people, attached to it an exceptional value.

The Art of Letters, however, rests upon a different footing. It is a study adapted to all times and to all circumstances, to the investigation of fresh knowledge or to the re-casting and application of old. Hence the importance of grammar and of the rules of composition must be recognised at the outset, as the foundation on which the whole study of Literature must rest: and closely associated with these rudiments, the art of Disputation or Logical argument. The function of this is to enable us to discern fallacy from truth in discussion. Logic, indeed, as setting forth the true method of learning, is the guide to the acquisition of knowledge in whatever subject. Rhetoric comes next, and is strictly speaking the formal study by which we attain the art of eloquence; which, as we have just stated, takes the third place amongst the studies specially important in public life. It is now, indeed, fallen from its old renown and is well nigh a lost art. In the Law-Court, in the Council, in the popular Assembly, in exposition, in persuasion, in debate, eloquence finds no place now-a-days: speed, brevity, homeliness are the only qualities desired. Oratory, in which our forefathers gained so great glory for themselves and for their language, is despised: but our youth, if they would earn the repute of true education, must emulate their ancestors in this accomplishment.

After Eloquence we place Poetry and the Poetic Art, which though not without their value in daily life and as an aid to oratory, have nevertheless their main concern for the leisure side of existence.

As to Music, the Greeks refused the title of 'Educated' to anyone who could not sing or play. Socrates set an example to the Athenian youth, by himself learning to play in his old age; urging the pursuit of music not as a sensuous indulgence, but as an aid to the inner harmony of the soul. In so far as it is taught as a healthy recreation for the moral and spiritual nature, music is a truly liberal art, and, both as regards its theory and its practice, should find a place in education.

Arithmetic, which treats of the properties of numbers, Geometry, which treats of the properties of dimensions, lines, surfaces, and solid bodies, are weighty studies because they possess a peculiar element of certainty. The science of the Stars, their motions, magnitudes and distances, lifts us into the clear calm of the upper air. There we may contemplate the fixed stars, or the conjunctions of the planets, and predict the eclipses of the sun and the moon. The knowledge of Nature — animate and inanimate — the laws and the properties of things in heaven and in earth, their causes, mutations and effects, especially the explanation of their wonders (as they are popularly supposed) by the unravelling of their causes — this is a most delightful, and at the same time most profitable, study for youth. With these may be joined investigations concerning the weights of bodies, and those relative to the subject which mathematicians call 'Perspective.'

I may here glance for a moment at the three great professional Disciplines: Medicine, Law, Theology. Medicine, which is applied science, has undoubtedly much that makes it attractive to a student. But it cannot be described as a Liberal study. Law, which is based upon moral philosophy, is undoubtedly held in high respect. Regarding Law as a subject of study, such respect is entirely deserved: but Law as practised becomes a mere trade. Theology, on the other hand, treats of themes removed from our senses, and attainable only by pure intelligence.

4] The principal 'Disciplines' have now been reviewed. It must not be supposed that a liberal education requires acquaintance with them all: for a thorough mastery of even one of them might fairly be the achievement of a lifetime. Most of us, too, must learn to be content with modest capacity as with modest fortune. Perhaps we do wisely to pursue that study which we find most suited to our intelligence and our tastes, though it is true that we cannot rightly understand one subject unless we can perceive its relation to the rest.

The choice of studies will depend to some extent upon the character of individual minds. For whilst one boy seizes rapidly the point of which he is in search and states it ably, another, working far more slowly, has yet the sounder judgment and so detects the weak spot in his rival's conclusions. The former, perhaps, will succeed in poetry, or in the abstract sciences; the latter in real studies and practical pursuits. Or a boy may be apt in thinking, but slow in expressing himself; to him the study of Rhetoric and Logic will be of much value. Where the power of talk alone is remarkable I hardly know what advice to give. Some minds are strong on the side of memory: these should be apt for history. But it is of importance to remember that in comparison with intelligence memory is of little worth, though intelligence without memory is, so far as education is concerned, of none at all. For we are not able to give evidence that we know a thing unless we can reproduce it.

Again, some minds have peculiar power in dealing with abstract truths, but are defective on the side of the particular and the concrete, and so make good progress in mathematics and in metaphysic. Those of just opposite temper are apt in Natural Science and in practical affairs. And the natural bent should be recognized and followed in education. Let the boy of limited capacity work only at that subject in which he shews he can attain some result.

Respecting the general place of liberal studies, we remember that Aristotle would not have them absorb the entire interests of life: for he kept steadily in view the nature of man as a citizen, an active member of the State. For the man who has surrendered himself absolutely to the attractions of Letters or of speculative thought follows, perhaps, a self-regarding end and is useless as a citizen or as prince.

*　　*　　*

5] In what I have written thus far upon the choice of studies I have had regard more particularly to those whose temperament inclines them to Learning rather than to War. But where an active frame is conjoined to a vigorous intellect a true education will aim at the efficient training of both — the Reason, that it may wisely control, the Body, that it may promptly obey. So that if we be involved in arms we may be found ready to defend our rights or to strike a blow for honour or power. Especially must the education of a Prince accord a high place to instruction in the art of war, not less than to training

in the arts of peace. Alexander the Great, himself a prince conspicu-
ous in arms, and also a constant student of Homer, preferred to every
other line of the Poet that one in which he speaks of Agamemnon
as a great king *because* a valiant warrior, holding him thus typical
of every true ruler of men.

Now war involves physical endurance as well as military skill. So
that from his earliest years a boy must be gradually inured to priva-
tions and grave exertion, to enable him to bear strain and hardship
when he reaches manhood. The institutions of Minos and Lycurgus
ordained that the youth of Crete and Sparta should be exercised in
activity and courage by feats of strength, or dangers of the field; in
endurance by bearing heat and cold, hunger and thirst. For as luxury
enervates mind and body alike, so exertion fortifies both. Nor could
I find, even in antiquity, a more significant example than that of
your own father Francesco, who always declared that this stedfastness
under hardship and bodily strain was the quality of which he felt
most proud. Endeavour to shew yourself a worthy son in this most
important quality. This physical power, also, is accompanied by a
contempt of death and by a consequent invincible courage. For all
ought to regard life as of less moment than noble action. If we hold
it our first duty to live honourably and bravely, whether in peace
or war, we shall not over-rate the blessing of long life, as so many
do. If death comes we shall meet it manfully, and, if need be, go to
welcome it cheerfully. Even if it seem to come untimely, we shall
still have had our opportunities. Scipio Africanus, the hero of the
Second Punic War, hardly more than a boy at the time, had at the
battle of the Ticino the glory of saving his father under the very
feet of the enemy. Aemilius Lepidus is another instance of conspicu-
ous bravery rewarded by the highest distinction of his fellow citizens.
Nor have you yourself been backward in the field, as you shewed
lately at Brescia against the German hordes, winning there the
highest admiration of friend and foe alike.

So, I repeat, it is of greatest importance that boys should be
trained from childhood in feats of courage and endurance. The
Lacedaemonian discipline was indeed severe. The boys were trained
to be of such a temper that in their contests they could not yield
nor confess themselves vanquished; the severest tests produced no
cry of pain, though blood might flow and consciousness itself give
way. The result was that all antiquity rehearses the deathless courage
of the Spartans in the field; their arms were to them part of their

very selves, to be cast away, or laid down, only with their lives. What else than this same early and most diligent training could have enabled the Romans to shew themselves so valiant, so enduring, in the campaigns they fought? Wherefore, whether a boy be trained in Arms or in Letters (for these are the two chief liberal Arts and fittest therefore for a prince), so soon as he be able to use his limbs let him be trained to Arms: so soon as he can rightly speak let him be trained to Letters. Further, it will be easy and it will be of great benefit to a boy to alternate the study of letters wih bodily exercises: and, indeed, at whatever age he may be, the same practice is to be commended. Theodosius, we are told, spent the day in martial exercises, or in the business of the state; the evening he devoted to books. . . .

5

The Theology of Learned Ignorance

NICHOLAS KRYPFFS, or Krebs, usually called by the Latinized name of his birthplace, Cues, in Germany, was educated in the universities of Heidelberg and Padua. He had a distinguished career in the Church, first as a Conciliarist and then as a supporter of Papal absolutism and was made a cardinal by the humanist Pope Nicholas V in 1448. In the history of thought Cusanus represents the fifteenth-century Neoplatonic reaction against Aristotelian scholasticism. A sudden illumination, he tells us, fused the two elements of Neoplatonism and mysticism into his doctrine of "learned ignorance." Although his ideas are difficult, a careful reader can recreate for himself that sudden illumination of the dilemma of the finite mind struggling with the problem of the infinite. It is interesting to consider whether such ideas contributed towards the religious climate which later fostered Protestantism.

Nicholas Cusanus (1401–1464), Of Learned Ignorance, Book I

Chapter i, how knowledge is ignorance

WE SEE THAT God has implanted in all things a natural desire to exist with the fullest measure of existence that is compatible with their particular nature. To this end they are endowed with suitable faculties and activities; and by means of these there is in them a discernment that is natural and in keeping with the purpose of their knowledge, which ensures their natural inclination serving its purpose and being able to reach its fulfilment in that object towards which it is attracted by the weight of its own nature. If at times this does not happen, it is necessarily the result of an accident, as when sickness deceives taste or conjecture upsets calculation. That

From Nicholas Cusanus, OF LEARNED IGNORANCE (London, 1954), pp. 7–12, 25–28, 59–61. Translation by Germain Heron. Reprinted by permission of Routledge and Kegan Paul Ltd.

is the explanation of the sound untrammelled intellect's desire for truth, which, by its natural discursive movement, it ceaselessly seeks in all things; and once it takes possession of the object of its natural desire, we say it knows the truth; for, without any hesitation, we call that true, which no sound mind can refuse to embrace. In every enquiry men judge of the uncertain by comparing it with an object presupposed certain, and their judgment is always approximative; every enquiry is, therefore, comparative and uses the method of analogy. When there is comparatively little distance from the object of enquiry back to the object regarded as certain, a judgment is easily formed; when many intermediaries are required, the task becomes difficult. We are familiar enough with this in mathematics, in which the reducing of the first propositions to the well-known first principles is easier, whereas the more remote propositions give rise to more difficulty, because it is only by means of the first propositions that these can be led back to the first principles. Every enquiry, therefore, consists in a relation of comparison that is easy or difficult to draw; for this reason the infinite as infinite is unknown, since it is away and above all comparison. Now, while proportion expresses an agreement in some one thing, it expresses at the same time a distinction, so that it cannot be understood without number. Number, in consequence, includes all things that are capable of comparison. It is not then in quantity only that number produces proportion; it produces it in all things that are capable of agreement and difference in any way at all, whether substantially or accidentally. That is why Pythagoras was so insistent on maintaining that in virtue of numbers all things were understood.

It so far surpasses human reason, however, to know the precision of the combinations in material things and how exactly the known has to be adapted to the unknown that Socrates thought he knew nothing save his own ignorance, whilst Solomon, the Wise, affirmed that in all things there are difficulties which beggar explanation in words; and we have it from another, who was divinely inspired, that wisdom and the locality of the understanding lie hidden from the eyes of all the living. If this is so — and even the most profound Aristotle in his First Philosophy affirms it to be true of the things most evident to us in nature — then in presence of such difficulty we may be compared to owls trying to look at the sun; but since the natural desire in us for knowledge is not without a purpose, its immediate object is our own ignorance. If we can fully realize this desire, we will acquire learned ignorance. Nothing could be more beneficial for even the most zealous searcher for knowledge than his being in fact most learned in that very ignorance which is peculiarly his own; and the better a man will have known his own ignorance, the greater his learning will be. It is in bearing this in mind that I have undertaken the task of writing a few words on learned ignorance.

Chapter ii, preliminary explanation of all that follows

As I am about to deal with ignorance as the greatest learning, I consider it necessary to determine the precise meaning of the maximum or greatest. We speak of a thing being the greatest or maximum when nothing greater than it can exist. But to one being alone does plenitude belong, with the result that unity, which is also being, and the maximum are identical; for if such a unity is itself in every way and entirely without restriction then it is clear that there is nothing to be placed in opposition to it, since it is the absolute maximum. Consequently, the absolute maximum is one and it is all; all things are in it because it is the maximum. Moreover, it is in all things for this reason that the minimum at once coincides with it, since there is nothing that can be placed in opposition to it. Because it is absolute, it is in actuality all possible being, limiting all things and receiving no limitation from any. In the First Book I will endeavour to study this maximum, who without any doubt is believed to be the God of all nations. It is a study that is above reason and cannot be conducted on the lines of human comprehension; and for my guide I will take him alone who dwells in light inaccessible.

In the second place, just as we have the absolute maximum, which is the absolute entity by which all things are what they are, so we have from it the universal unity of being which is called the maximum effect of the absolute. In consequence, its existence as the universe is finite, and its unity, which could not be absolute, is the relative unity of a plurality. Though this maximum embraces all things in its universal unity, so that all that comes from the absolute is in it and it in all, yet it could not subsist outside the plurality in which it is contained, for this restriction is inseparably bound up with its existence. Of this maximum, which is the universe, I will have something further to say in the second book.

In the third place, we shall see that there is still one more manner in which to consider the maximum. Since the subsistence in plurality of the universe is necessarily finite, we shall study the plurality itself of things in order to discover the one maximum in which the universe finds especially and most completely its actual and ultimate subsistence. This maximum in the universe is united with the absolute, for the absolute is the ultimate term of all; and as this maximum, which is at once relative and absolute, is the most perfect realization of the purpose of the universe and entirely beyond our reach, my comments on it will be added in accordance with the inspiration of Jesus himself; in fact, this maximum bears the ever blessed name of Jesus.

An understanding of this matter will be attained rather by our rising above the literal sense of the words, than by insisting upon their natural properties, for these natural properties cannot be effectively adapted to such intellectual mysteries. For the reader we must even use drawings as illustrations, but he must rise above these in leaving aside what is sensible in them in order to arrive unimpeded at what is purely intelligible. In pursuing this method I have eagerly tried, by the avoidance of all difficulties of expressions, to make it as clear as possible to the average mind that the foundation for learned ignorance is the fact that absolute truth is beyond our grasp.

Chapter iii, absolute truth is beyond our grasp

From the self-evident fact that there is no gradation for infinite to finite, it is clear that the simple maximum is not to be found where we meet degrees of more and less; for such degrees are finite, whereas the simple maximum is necessarily infinite. It is manifest, therefore, that when anything other than the simple maximum itself is given, it will always be possible to find something greater. Equality, we find, is a matter of degree: with things that are alike one is more equal to this than to that, in-so-far as they belong, or do not belong, to the same genus or species, or in-so-far as they are, or are not, related in time, place or influence. For that reason it is evident that two or more things cannot be so alike and equal that an infinite number of similar objects cannot still be found. No matter, then, how equal the measure and the thing measured are, they will remain for ever different.

A finite intellect, therefore, cannot by means of comparison reach the absolute truth of things. Being by nature indivisible, truth excludes 'more' or 'less', so that nothing but truth itself can be the exact measure of truth: for instance, that which is not a circle cannot be the measure of a circle, for the nature of a circle is one and indivisible. In consequence, our intellect, which is not the truth, never grasps the truth with such precision that it could not be comprehended with infinitely greater precision. The relationship of our intellect to the truth is like that of a polygon to a circle; the resemblance to the circle grows with the multiplication of the angles of the polygon; but apart from its being reduced to identity with the circle, no multiplication, even if it were infinite, of its angles will make the polygon equal the circle.

It is clear, therefore, that all we know of the truth is that the absolute truth, such as it is, is beyond our reach. The truth, which can be neither more nor less than it is, is the most absolute necessity, while, in contrast with it, our intellect is possibility. Therefore, the quiddity of things, which is ontological truth, is unattainable in its entirety; and though it has been the objective of all philosophers, by none has it been found as it really is. The more profoundly we learn this lesson of ignorance, the closer we draw to truth itself.

* * *

Chapter xi, mathematics are a very great help in the understanding of different divine truths

All our greatest philosophers and theologians unanimously assert that the visible universe is a faithful reflection of the invisible, and that from creatures we can rise to a knowledge of the Creator, "in a mirror and in a dark manner", as it were. The fundamental reason for the use of symbolism in the study of spiritual things, which in themselves are beyond our reach, has already been given. Though we neither perceive it nor understand it, we know for a fact that all things stand in some sort of relation to one another; that, in virtue of this inter-relation, all the individuals constitute one universe and that in the one Absolute the multiplicity of beings is unity itself. Every image is an approximate reproduction of the exemplar; yet, apart from the Absolute image or the Exemplar itself in unity of nature, no image will so faithfully or precisely reproduce the exemplar, as to rule out the possibility of an infinity of more faithful and precise images, as we have already made clear.

When we use an image and try to reach analogically what is as yet unknown, there must be no doubt at all about the image; for it is only by way of postulates and things certain that we can arrive at the unknown. But in all things sensible material possibility abounds which explains their being in a continual state of flux. Our knowledge of things is not acquired by completely disregarding their material conditions, without which no image of them could be formed; nor is it wholly subject to their possible variations; but the more we abstract from sensible conditions, the more certain and solid our knowledge is. Mathematics is an example of such abstract knowledge. That explains why philosophers so readily turned to mathematics for examples of the things which the intellect had to investigate; and none of the masters of old, when solving a difficulty, used other than mathematical illustrations, so that Boethius, the most learned of Romans, went so far as to say that knowledge of things divine was impossible without some knowledge of mathematics.

Was not the key to all truth to be found in numbers, according to Pythagoras, who was the first to be called a philosopher and who was the first philosopher in fact? In so far as they have followed him, the Platonists and the chief of our own philosophers, like Augustine and later Boethius, have not hesitated to assert that number was the essential exemplar in the mind of the Creator of all things to be created. Aristotle, who, by disagreeing with the Platonists, seemed to desire to be an exception to the rule, found it impossible in his Metaphysics to explain the specific differences otherwise than by a comparison with numbers; and when he wishes to show that in nature one form is in another, he is forced to turn to mathematical figures for an illustration: 'Just as the triangle is in the tetragon, so is the lower form contained in the higher'; and he has innumerable examples of this kind that there is no need to mention. It was also to mathematics that Aurelius Augustine, the Platonist, turned for assistance in dealing with such questions as the quantity of the soul and its immortality and other lofty subjects. Boethius had such high regard for this method that he constantly affirmed that all truth was contained in numbers and magnitude. And if you would have me be more concise, — was it not solely by the mathematical demonstration of the Pythagoreans and the Peripatetics that the Epicureans' teaching about the atoms in the void was refuted — a teaching that at once involved the denial of God's existence and the collapse of all truth? And the principle taken for granted by Epicurus was that there could be found ultimately in all things simple indivisible atoms.

Following in the way of the Ancients, we are in complete agreement with them in saying that, since there is no other approach to a knowledge of things divine than that of symbols, we cannot do better than use mathematical signs on account of their indestructible certitude.

Chapter xii, the way in which mathematical signs should be used for our purpose

It is now evident from what we have said that no object that we know or of which we have any idea, can be the Absolute Maximum; and since it is by way of symbols that we intend to conduct our search of it, we must, therefore, look for something more than a simple comparison. In mathematics, in fact, we are always dealing with finite things, for if they were not finite we could form no idea of them at all. If then we want to reach the Absolute Maximum through the finite, we must, in the first place, study finite, mathematical figures as they are, namely a mixture of potency and act; then we must attribute the respective perfections to the corresponding infinite figures, and finally we must, in a much more sublime way, attribute the perfections of the infinite figures to the simple Infinite, which cannot possibly be expressed by any figure. Then, whilst we are groping in the dark, our ignorance will enlighten us in an incomprehensible fashion and enable us to form a more correct and truer notion of the Absolute.

By this method, and guided by Infinite Truth, we note the difference of expressions used by saintly men and brilliant intellects who gave themselves to the study of figures. St. Anselm, for instance, compared Absolute Truth to infinite straightness; following him, we will take the straight line as our figure of straightness. Some very learned men have drawn a comparison between the Most Holy Trinity and a triangle whose three angles are right angles; such a triangle could be called infinite, since its sides, as we shall see, must be infinite; we will also follow this opinion. Others, striving to depict the infinite unity, have said God is an infinite circle; and there are those who have likened God to an infinite sphere from their considerations of His most perfect act of existence. We shall show that all these views are correct and that they all form only one opinion.

* * *

Chapter xxvi, negative theology

The worship of God, who is to be adored in spirit and truth, necessarily rests on dogmatic assertions about Him; for that reason the cult in every religion is necessarily developed by affirmative theology: God is adored as one and three, as The Most Wise, The Most Good, The Light Inaccessible, The Life, The Truth and so on; and worship always is regulated by a faith which is acquired more surely through learned ignorance. By faith, for example, it is acknowledged that He who is adored as one is one and all; that He who is worshipped as Light Inaccessible, is not light that is material, the opposite of which is darkness, but light absolutely simple and infinite in which darkness is infinite light; that He who is infinite light itself shines always in the darkness of our ignorance, but the darkness cannot comprehend the Light. Negative Theology, in consequence, is so indispensable to affirmative theology that without it God would be adored, not as the Infinite but rather as a creature, which is idolatry, or giving to an image what is due to Truth alone. It will be useful, then, to add a few words on negative theology.

Sacred ignorance has taught us that God is ineffable, because He is infinitely greater than anything that words can express. So true is this that it is by the process of elimination and the use of negative propositions that we come nearer the truth about Him. For that reason the most noble Denis would not have Him called Truth or Intellect or Light or any name that man can utter; and in this he was followed by Rabbi Salomon and all the wise. According to this negative theology, therefore, He is neither Father nor Son nor Holy Ghost; one word alone may be used of Him: Infinite. Infinity, as such, does not engender, is not engendered and does not proceed, — which called from Hilary of Poitiers, whilst distinguishing the Persons, these subtle words: 'In aeterno infinitas, species in imagine, usus in munere.' His meaning is that all we see in eternity is infinity; and, while it is true that infinity is eternity, yet infinity is a negative and for that reason it cannot be conceived as a principle of generation. Eternity, on the other hand, clearly can be so conceived, for eternity is an affirmation of infinite unity or of the infinite present, and is, therefore, a principle that does not proceed from any other. 'Species in imagine' expresses the principle that proceeds from a principle and 'usus in munere' signifies procession from both.

All that is clear enough from what we have already said. We know, in fact, that eternity is infinity, and that both of these belong to the Father in the same way. Yet considered in one way eternity is an attribute of the Father but not of the Son nor of the Holy Ghost, whereas infinity belongs to all the persons equally. Considered from the point of view of unity, infinity is the Father, from the point of view of equality of unity it is the Son, from the point of view of the connection it is the Holy Ghost; but when considered, not from any of these points of view, but absolutely in itself infinity says nothing of Father, Son and Holy Ghost, nor does it say anything of unity or plurality in God. And according to negative theology infinity is all we discover in God. Yet the fact is that infinity, as well as eternity, is each of the Three Persons and conversely each of the Persons is infinity and eternity. As far as negative theology is concerned, then, we must conclude that God cannot be known in this life or in the life to come. God alone knows Himself. He is as incomprehensible to creatures as infinite light is to darkness.

From this it is clear how in theology negative propositions are true and affirmative ones inadequate; and that of the negative ones those are truer which eliminate greater imperfections from the infinitely Perfect. It is truer, for example, to deny that God is a stone than to deny that He is life or intelligence, — truer to deny that He is intemperate than to deny that He is virtuous. In affirmative propositions the contrary holds good: it is truer to assert that God is intelligence and life than to assert that He is earth, stone or anything material.

All these points, which must now be abundantly clear, leave us with the conclusion that, in a way we cannot comprehend, absolute truth enlightens the darkness of our ignorance. That, then, is the learned ignorance for which we have been searching. We have shown how the sole approach to the Maximum — the Triune God of infinite Goodness — passes through the stages of that ignorance which is learning, and how, in consequence, amidst all our gropings, we can always praise Him, the Incomprehensible, for His revelation of Himself to us.

May He be blessed above all for ever.

6

A Renaissance History of Art

THE FIRST TO HOLD that a rebirth of civilization had succeeded a Middle Age of darkness were the writers of the Renaissance itself. By the sixteenth century it was a commonplace that the arts too had emerged from a state of medieval decadence. Giorgio Vasari, himself a painter and architect working mainly in Florence, decided to write the history of this rebirth through the lives of the men who had brought it about. The result was his one masterpiece. Since the first edition of Vasari's Lives appeared in 1550, it has been an indispensable sourcebook of information not only about Renaissance artists and their works but also about Renaissance ideas of art.

Giorgio Vasari (1511–1574), Lives of the Most Eminent Painters, Sculptors, and Architects

Introduction to the lives

IT IS WITHOUT DOUBT a fixed opinion, common to almost all writers, that the arts of sculpture and painting were first discovered by the nations of Egypt, although there are some who attribute the first rude attempts in marble, and the first statues and relievi, to the Chaldeans, while they accord the invention of the pencil, and of colouring, to the Greeks. But I am myself convinced, that design, which is the foundation of both these arts, nay, rather the very soul of each, comprising and nourishing within itself all the essential parts of both, existed in its highest perfection from the first moment of creation, when the Most High having formed the great body of the world, and adorned the heavens with their re-

From Mrs. Jonathan Foster, trans., LIVES OF THE MOST EMINENT PAINTERS, SCULPTORS AND ARCHITECTS, 5 vols. (London, 1898–1914), I, pp. 9–12, 20–24, 26–27, 31–33, 304–307; II, pp. 357–365. Reprinted by permission of G. Bell and Sons Ltd.

splendent lights, descended by his spirit, through the limpidity of the air, and penetrating the solid mass of earth, created man; and thus unveiled, with the beauties of creation, the first form of sculpture and of painting. For from this man, as from a true model, were copied by slow degrees (we may not venture to affirm the contrary), statues and sculptures: the difficulties of varied attitude, — the flowing lines of contour — and in the first paintings, whatever these may have been, the softness, harmony, and that concord in discord, whence result light and shade. The first model, therefore, from which the first image of man arose, was a mass of earth; and not without significance, since the Divine Architect of time and nature, Himself all-perfect, designed to instruct us by the imperfection of the material, in the true method of attaining perfection, by repeatedly diminishing and adding to; as the best sculptors and painters are wont to do, for by perpetually taking from or adding to their models they conduct their work, from its first imperfect sketch, to that finish of perfection which they desire to attain. The Creator further adorned his model with the most vivid colours, and these same colours, being afterwards drawn by the painter from the mines of earth, enable him to imitate whatsoever object he may require for his picture. It is true, that we cannot with certainty declare what was accomplished in these arts and towards the imitation of so beautiful a model, by the men who lived before the deluge, although we are fully justified in believing that they produced works of every kind, both in sculpture and painting, since Belus, son of the proud Nimrod, about two hundred years after the deluge, caused the statue to be made, which, at a later period, gave birth to idolatry. His renowned daughter-in-law, moreover, Semiramis, queen of Babylon, when building that city, not only placed various figures of animals, drawn and coloured from nature, among the ornaments of her edifices, but added statues of herself and of her husband Ninus, with figures in bronze, representing her father-in-law, her mother-in-law, and the mother of the latter, calling them, as Diodorus relates, by the names of the Greeks, Jupiter, Juno, and Ops (which as yet were not in use). And it was probably from these statues that the Chaldeans learned to form the images of their gods, since we know, that a hundred and fifty years later, Rachael daughter of Laban, when flying from Mesopotamia with Jacob, her husband, stole the idols of her father, as is plainly set forth in the book of Genesis.

Nor were the Chaldeans the only people who devoted themselves to sculpture and painting; the Egyptians also laboured with great zeal in these arts, as is proved by the wondrous sepulchre of that ancient monarch, Osimandyas, described at length by Diodorus, and, as may be clearly inferred from the severe law enacted by Moses at the departure from Egypt, namely, that no image whatever should be raised to God, under pain of death. . . .

It was from the works seen before the deluge, then, that the pride of man acquired the art of constructing statues of all those to whom they desired to attribute immortal fame; and the Greeks, who account for the origin of art in various methods, declare, according to Diodorus, that the Ethiopians constructed the first statues, affirming, that from them the Egyptians acquired the art, and that the Greeks derived it from the Egyptians. That sculpture and painting had attained their perfection in Homer's time, is rendered obvious by the manner in which that divine poet speaks of the shield of Achilles, and which he sets before our eyes with so much art, that it is rather sculptured and painted, than merely described. Lactantius Firmianus attributes the discovery to Prometheus, who moulded the human form of clay, after the example of the Almighty himself, and the art of sculpture is thus affirmed to have come from him.

* * *

We find, then, that the art of sculpture was zealously cultivated by the Greeks, among whom many excellent artists appeared; those great masters, the Athenian Phidias, with Praxiteles and Polycletus, were of the number, while Lysippus and Pyrgoteles, worked successfully in intaglio, and Pygmalion produced admirable reliefs in ivory — nay, of him it was affirmed, that his prayers obtained life and soul for the statue of a virgin which he had formed. Painting was in like manner honoured, and those who practised it successfully were rewarded among the ancient Greeks and Romans; this is proved by their according the rights of citizenship, and the most exalted dignities, to such as attained high distinction in these arts, both of which flourished so greatly. . . .

The rise of art in Rome must have taken place at a late epoch, if it be true, as we find asserted, that among her first statues was the bronze figure of Ceres, formed from the spoils of Spurius Cassius, who was deliberately put to death by his own father, for having aspired to become king. And although the arts of sculpture and painting continued to be practised to the close of the reign of the twelve

Cæsars, yet they did not maintain themselves in that degree of excellence and perfection which they had previously displayed; so that, in all the buildings erected by the emperors, one after another, the arts may be gradually seen to decline, until all perfection of the art of design was ultimately lost. To the truth of this assertion, the works in sculpture and architecture; executed in Rome under Constantine, bear ample testimony, more particularly the triumphal arch, raised to him by the Roman people, near the Colosseum, where we perceive that, for the want of good masters, they not only availed themselves of sculptures executed in the time of Trajan, but also of the spoils brought to Rome from other parts of the empire.

* * *

But as fortune, when she has raised either persons or things to the summit of her wheel, very frequently casts them to the lowest point, whether in repentance or for her sport, so it chanced that, after these things, the barbarous nations of the world arose, in divers places, in rebellion against the Romans; whence there ensued, in no long time, not only the decline of that great empire, but the utter ruin of the whole, and more especially of Rome herself, when all the best artists, sculptors, painters, and architects, were in like manner totally ruined, being submerged and buried, together with the arts themselves, beneath the miserable slaughters and ruins of that much renowned city. Painting and sculpture were the first to suffer, as arts ministering rather to pleasure than utility; while architecture, being requisite to the comfort and safety of life, was still maintained, although not in its earlier excellence. Indeed, had it not been that sculpture and painting still placed before the eyes of the existing generation, the representations of those whom they were accustomed to honour, and to whom they gave an immortality, the very memory, both of one and the other, would have been soon extinguished. . . .

But infinitely more ruinous than all other enemies to the arts above named, was the fervent zeal of the new Christian religion, which, after long and sanguinary combats, had finally overcome and annihilated the ancient creeds of the pagan world, by the frequency of miracles exhibited, and by the earnest sincerity of the means adopted; and ardently devoted, with all diligence, to the extirpation of error, nay, to the removal of even the slightest temptation to heresy, it not only destroyed all the wondrous statues, paintings, sculptures, mosaics, and other ornaments of the false pagan deities, but at the same time extinguished the very memory, in casting down the honours, of numberless excellent ancients, to whom statues and other monuments had been erected, in public places, for their virtues, by the most virtuous times of antiquity. Nay, more than this, to build the churches of the Christian faith, this zeal not only destroyed the most renowned temples of the heathens, but, for the richer ornament of St. Peter's, and in addition to the many spoils previously bestowed on that building, the tomb of Adrian, now called the castle of St. Angelo, was deprived of its marble columns, to employ them for this church, many other buildings being in like manner despoiled, and which we now see wholly devastated. And although the Christian religion did not effect this from hatred to these works of art, but solely for the purpose of abasing and bringing into contempt the gods of the Gentiles, yet the result of this too ardent zeal did not fail to bring such total ruin over the noble arts, that their very form and existence was lost. . . . No trace, no vestige of excellence in art, now remained; the men who followed immediately on these unhappy times, proceeded in a rude and uncultivated manner in all things, but more especially in painting and sculpture; yet, impelled by nature, and refined, to a certain degree, by the air they breathed, they set themselves to work, not according to the rules of art, which they no longer possessed, but each according to the quality of his own talent.

The arts of design — being reduced to this state during and after the domination of the Lombards in Italy — continued to deteriorate in all that was attempted, so that nothing could be worse, or evince less knowledge of art, than the works of that period; and we have proof of this, among other things, in certain figures which are over the door of the portico of St. Peter's, at Rome; they are in the Greek manner, and represent certain holy fathers who had disputed for the Christian Church before some of the councils. . . . It is to the masters of those times that we owe the fantastic images and absurd figures still to be seen in many old works. And a similar inferiority is perceptible in architecture, for it was necessary to build; but all good methods and correct forms being lost by the death of good artists and the destruction of their works, those who devoted themselves to that employment were in no condition to give either correct proportion or grace of any kind to their designs. Then arose new architects, and they, after the manner of their barbarous nations, erected the buildings in that style which we now call Gothic, and raising edifices that, to use moderns, are rather to the discredit than glory of the builders, until at a later period there appeared better artists, who returned, in some measure, to the purer style of the antique; and this may be seen in most of the old (but not antique) churches throughout Italy, which were built in the manner just alluded to by these last-named artists. . . .

In Florence, meanwhile, the practice of architecture began to display some little improvement, and the Church of Sant' Apostolo, built by Charlemagne, was in a very beautiful manner, although small: the shafts of the columns, though formed of separate pieces, are extremely graceful and well-proportioned; the capitals, likewise, with the arches and vaulting of the two small naves, furnish proof that some good artist had still remained in Tuscany, or had once again arisen in the land. In fine, the architecture of this church, is such, that Filippo di Ser Brunellesco did not disdain to use it as his model in building the Church of Santo Spirito, and that of San Lorenzo, in the same city. A similar progress may be remarked in the Church of St. Mark, at Venice, (to say nothing of San Giorgio Maggiore, built by Giovanni Morosini, in the year 978,) which was commenced under the Doge Giustiniano and Giovanni Particiaco, next to San Teodosio, when the body of the Evangelist was sent from Alexandria to Venice. . . . All these buildings, as well as the vestiges of those that are ruined, bear testimony to the fact, that architecture still maintained itself in life, though grievously degenerated and departing widely from the excellent manner of the antique. And of this we find further proof in many old palaces, constructed in Florence after the ruin of Fiesole, in the Tuscan fashion, but in a very barbarous and ill-proportioned manner, as witness those doors and windows of immoderate length, and the aspect of those acute pieces in the vaulting of their arches, which were peculiar to the foreign architects of those times.

In the year 1013, we nevertheless perceive, that the art had regained somewhat of her ancient vigour; and this we infer, from the rebuilding of that most beautiful church San Miniato sul Monte, constructed in the time of Messer Alibrando, citizen and bishop of Florence; for to say nothing of the marble ornaments by which it is embellished, both within and without, the façade gives us clear proof that the Tuscan architects here made efforts to imitate the fine proportions and pure taste of the antique in columns, arches, cornices, doors, and windows, correcting and improving their perceptions by the study of that most ancient temple, the church of San Giovanni, in their own city. At the same period, painting, which had been little less than totally extinguished, was seen to be slowly regaining life, as may be proved by the mosaic executed in the principal chapel of this same church of San Miniato.

From this commencement, then, the arts of design began to make progress in Tuscany by slow degrees, advancing gradually towards a better state of things as we see from the first steps taken by the Pisans towards the construction of their cathedral, in 1016; for in those days it was a great undertaking to erect a church of such a character, having five naves, and being almost entirely covered with marble both within and without. . . . It was only by slow degrees that those who came after, being aided in some places by the subtlety of the air around them, could begin to raise themselves from these depths; when, towards 1250, Heaven, moved to pity by the noble spirits which the Tuscan soil was producing every day, restored them to their primitive condition. It is true that those who lived in the times succeeding the ruin of Rome, had seen remnants of arches, colossi, statues, pillars, storied columns, and other works of art, not wholly destroyed by the fires and other devastations; yet they had not known how to avail themselves of this aid, nor had they derived any benefit from it, until the time specified above. When the minds then awakened, becoming capable of distinguishing the good from the worthless, and abandoning old methods, returned to the imitation of the antique, with all the force of their genius, and all the power of their industry.

But that my readers may the better comprehend what it is that I call "old", and what "antique", I add that the antique are worke executed before the time of Constantine, in Corinth, Athens, Rome, and other far-famed cities, down to the times of Nero, Vespasian, Trajan, Adrian, and Antonine; "old" are such as were executed from the days of St. Silvester, downwards by a certain residue of the Greeks, whose profession was rather that of dyeing than painting. For the greater part of the excellent earlier artists being extirpated in those times of war, there remained, as I have said, nothing to these Greeks ("old", but not "antique") save only the first rude outlines on a ground of colour, as is made sufficiently manifest by a crowd of mosaics executed throughout Italy by these Greeks, and which may be seen in any old church of whatsoever city you please, through all the land. The cathedral of Pisa and St. Mark of Venice, and other places, will furnish examples. Thus, in this manner, they executed many pictures;

figures with senseless eyes, outstretched hands, standing on the points of their feet, similar to those that may still be seen in San Miniato, outside Florence, between the doors which lead to the sacristy and the convent. . . .

Thus much I have thought it advisable to say respecting the first commencement of sculpture and painting, and may perhaps have spoken at greater length than was here needful; but this I have done, not so much because I was carried on by my love of art, as because I desire to be useful and serviceable to the whole body of artists, for they, having here seen the manner in which art proceeded from small beginnings, until she attained the highest summit, and next how she was precipitated from that exalted position into the deepest debasement; and considering that it is the nature of art, as of human existence, to receive birth, to progress, to become old, and to die, may thus more perfectly comprehend and follow the progress of her second birth to the high perfection which she has once more attained in these our days.

*   *   *

Introduction to the second part

. . . Do we not clearly see to what extent architecture had been ameliorated, from the Greek Buschetto — to begin with one of the most distinguished masters — to the German Arnolfo, and to Giotto? For our perfect conviction of this truth, we need only to glance at the fabrics of the earlier period: the pilasters, the columns, the bases, the capitals, and the cornices, with their ill-formed members, as we see them, for example, in Santa Maria del Fiore, in Florence; in the exterior incrustations of San Giovanni; at San Miniato al Monte; in the cathedral of Fiesole; the Duomo of Milan; the church of San Vitale at Ravenna; that of Santa Maria Maggiore in Rome; and the Duomo Vecchio, outside the city of Arezzo; wherein, with the exception of those few fragments from the antique, which remain in different parts, there is nothing which deserves to be called good, whether as regards arrangement or execution. But, by the masters above named, architecture was, without doubt, greatly ameliorated, and the art made considerable progress under their influence, since they brought the various parts to more correct proportion, and not only erected their buildings in a manner which imparted strength and durability, but also added the grace of ornament to certain parts of them. It is, indeed, true that their decorations were complicated, confused, and very far from perfection, so that they could scarcely be said to contribute in any great measure to the beauty of the fabric. In the columns, for example, the measure and proportion required by the rules of art were not observed, nor were the orders distinguished, whether Doric, Corinthian, Ionic, or Tuscan; all were mingled together, after a rule of their own, which was no rule at all, and were constructed of excessive thickness, or exceedingly slender, as seemed good in their eyes. Their inventions were partly confused notions of their own, partly as irregular adaptations of the ancient relics with which they were acquainted. Their plans were derived in part from good sources, but partly also from their own caprices; insomuch, that when the walls were raised, they sometimes presented a very different form from that of their so-called model. But, notwithstanding all this, whoever compares the labours of that period with those of an earlier day, will see that they had materially improved in all respects, even though there should still be found many particulars wherein the critics of our times find cause for dissatisfaction; as, for example, the small oratories constructed of brick, covered over with stucco, at San Giovanni Laterano, in Rome.

The same remarks may be applied to sculpture, which, at the first moment of its revival, had some remains of excellence. Being once freed from the rude Byzantine manner, which was, indeed, so coarse that the works produced in it displayed more of the roughness of the raw material, than of the genius of the artist; those statues of theirs being wholly destitute of flexibility, attitude, or movement of any kind, and their draperies entirely without folds, so that they could scarcely be called statues — all this became gradually ameliorated, and when Giotto had improved the art of design, the figures of marble and stone improved also: those of Andrea Pisano, of his son Nino, and of his other disciples, were greatly superior to the statues that had preceded them; less rigid and stiff, displaying some approach to grace of attitude, and in all respects better. . . . There was, in short, a commencement of effort to reach the better path, but defects still remained in great numbers on every point; the art of design had not yet attained its perfection, nor were there many good models for the artists of those times to imitate. All these impediments and difficulties considered, the masters of those days, and who have been placed by me in the first period, deserve all the praise and credit that can be awarded to their works, since it must not be forgotten that they had received no aid from those who preceded them, but had to find their way by their own efforts. Every beginning, moreover, however insignificant and humble in itself, is always to be accounted worthy of no small praise.

Nor had painting much better fortune during those times; but the devotion of the people called it more frequently into use, and it had more artists employed; by consequence, the progress made by it was more obvious than that of the two sister arts. Thus we have seen that the Greek, or Byzantine manner, first attacked by Cimabue, was afterwards entirely extinguished by the aid of Giotto, and there arose a new one, which I would fain call the manner of Giotto, since it was discovered by him, continued by his disciples, and finally honoured and imitated by all. By Giotto and his disciples, the hard angular lines by which every figure was girt and bound, the senseless and spiritless eyes, the long pointed feet planted upright on their extremities, the sharp formless hands, the absence of shadow, and every other monstrosity of those Byzantine painters, were done away with, as I have said; the heads received a better grace, and more softness of colour. Giotto himself, in particular, gave more easy attitudes to his figures; he made some approach to vivacity and spirit in his heads, and folded his draperies, which have more resemblance to reality than those of his predecessors; he discovered, to a certain extent, the necessity of foreshortening the figure, and began to give some intimation of the passions and affections, so that fear, hope, anger, and love were, in some sort, expressed by his faces. The early manner had been most harsh and rugged; that of Giotto became softer, more harmonious, and — if he did not give his eyes the limpidity and beauty of life, if he did not impart to them the speaking movement of reality, let the difficulties he had to encounter plead his excuse for this, as well as for the want of ease and flow in the hair and beards: or if his hands have not the articulations and muscles of nature, if his rude figures want the reality of life, let it be remembered that Giotto had never seen the works of any better master than he was himself. And let all reflect on the rectitude of judgment displayed by this artist in his paintings, at a time when art was in so poor a state; on the large amount of ability by which alone he could have produced the results secured; for none will deny that his figures perform the parts assigned to them, or that in all his works are found proofs of a just — if not a perfect — judgment, in matters pertaining to his art. . . .

Introduction to the third part

... But to the end that the character of the amelioration effected by the above-mentioned artists, the masters of the second period, namely, may be more clearly understood, it may not be out of place to describe, in few words, the five distinctive properties, or characteristics, which I have just enumerated, and briefly to declare the origin of that truly good manner, which, surpassing that of the older period, has contributed to render the modern era so glorious. To begin with the first-mentioned, therefore: the Rule in architecture was the process of measuring works of antiquity, and considering the plans and ground-work of ancient edifices in the construction of modern buildings. Order was the division of one mode from another, to the end that each might have the parts appropriate to itself, and that the Doric, Ionic, Corinthian, and Tuscan might no longer be mingled and interchanged. Proportion was the universal law prevailing in architecture as in sculpture, which demanded that all bodies should be exact and correct in form with all the members justly and duly organized: this was equally enforced in painting. Design was the imitation of the most beautiful parts of nature in all figures, whether sculptured or painted, and this requires that the hand and mind of the artist should be capable of reproducing, with the utmost truth and exactitude, on paper, panel, or such other level surface as may be used, whatever the eye beholds — a remark that also applies to works of relief in sculpture. Finally, Manner attained its highest perfection from the practice of frequently copying the most beautiful objects, and of afterwards combining the most perfect, whether the hand, head, torso, or leg, and joining them together to make one figure, invested with every beauty in its highest perfection: to do this in every figure for all the works executed, is what is called fine manner. These things neither Giotto, nor any other of the early masters, treated of in the first period, had done, although they had discovered the sources of all the difficulties in art, and even attained to a superficial knowledge thereof: thus their drawing was more correct, and made a closer approach to nature than had previously been seen; they displayed more harmony in colouring, and a better disposition of their figures in historical composition, with many other qualities of which we have sufficiently discoursed. The masters of the second period, although they effected very important ameliorations in art, as to all the characteristics described above, were yet not so far advanced as to be capable of conducting it to its ultimate perfection; there was yet wanting to their rule a certain freedom which, without being exactly of the rule is directed by the rule, and is capable of existing without causing confusion or disturbing the order, which last demanded a rich variety in invention, ever ready for all points, with a certain perception of beauty, even in the most trifling accessories, which amply secures the order and adds a higher degree of ornament. In proportion, there was still wanting that rectitude of judgment which, without measurement, should give to every figure, in its due relation, a grace exceeding measurement. In drawing, the highest eminence had not been attained; for although the arm was made round and the leg straight, there was yet not that judicious treatment of the muscles, nor that graceful facility, which holds the medium between suffering them to be seen but not displaying them, which is apparent in the life: the masters, on the contrary, had, in this respect, something crude and excoriated in their practice, producing an effect that was displeasing to the eye and which gave hardness to the manner. This last wanted the grace which imparts lightness and softness to all forms, more particularly to those of women and children, which should be represented with as much truth to nature as those of men, but with a roundness and fulness, never bordering on coarseness, as may sometimes happen in nature, but which in the drawing should be refined and ennobled by the judgment of the artist. Variety and beauty in the vestments were also wanting, with many other rich and multiform fancies. The charm of colouring, namely, the diversity of buildings, the distance and changeful character of landscape; for although many did begin — as, for example, Andrea Verrocchio, Antonio del Pollaiuolo, and many still later — to give more study to their figures, to improve the drawing, and to increase their similitude to nature; they had, nevertheless, not succeeded fully, although they had attained to greater firmness, and were proceeding in a direction tending towards the right path. That this last assertion is true may be seen even by a comparison with the antique, as is proved by the figure of Marsyas, of which Andrea Verrocchio executed the legs and arms for the palace of the Medici, in Florence: but there is still wanting a certain delicacy of finish, and that ultimate charm of perfection in the feet, hands, hair, and beard, which alone can fully satisfy the cultivated judgment and the refined taste of the master in art; even though the limbs are, upon the whole, in just accord with the part of the antique statue still remaining, and although there is without doubt a certain harmony in the proportions.

Had these masters attained to that minuteness of finish which constitutes the perfection and bloom of art, they would also have displayed power and boldness in their works, when the result would have been a lightness, beauty, and grace which are not now to be found, although we perceive proofs of diligent endeavour, but which are, nevertheless, always secured to beautiful figures by the highest efforts of art, whether in sculpture or painting. Nor could this last perfection — this certain somewhat thus wanting — be readily obtained, seeing that, from much study, the manner derives a sort of dryness, when it is from study alone that men are labouring to force that highest finish. But to those who came after, success was rendered possible, from the time when they beheld those works of ancient art, which Pliny enumerates as among the most justly celebrated drawn forth from the recesses of the earth for their benefit. The Laocoon namely, the Hercules, the mighty Torso of the Belvedere, with the Venus, the Cleopatra, the Apollo, and many others, in which softness and power are alike visible, which display roundness and fulness justly restrained, and which, reproducing the most perfect beauty of nature, with attitudes and movements wholly free from distortion, but turning or bending gracefully in certain parts, exhibit everywhere the flexibility and ease of nature, with the most attractive grace. These statues caused the disappearance of that hard, dry sharpness of manner which had been still left in art, by the too anxious study of Piero della Francesco, Lazzaro Vasari, Alesso Baldovinetti, Andrea dal Castagno, Pesello, Ercole Ferrarese, Giovan Bellini, Cosimo Roselli, the Abbot of San Clemente, Domenico Ghirlandajo, Sandro Botticelli, Andrea Mantegna, Filippo Lippi, and Luca Signorelli.

These masters had laboured by unremitting effort to produce the impossible in art, more especially in foreshortenings or in objects displeasing to the sight, and which, as they were difficult in the execution, so are they unattractive to those who behold them. It is true that the greater part of their works were well drawn and free from errors, but there were wanting to them that certainty and firmness of handling, that harmony in the colouring, which may be perceived in the works of Francia, of Bologna, and of Pietro Perugino, but are never to be found in those of which we have now been speaking. When the last-mentioned masters commenced this new treatment, people rushed like madmen to behold that unwonted and life-like beauty, believing then that it would be absolutely impossible ever to do better; but the error of this judgment was clearly demonstrated soon after by the works of Leonardo da Vinci, with whom began that third manner, which we will agree to call the modern; for, in addition to the power and boldness of his drawing, and to say nothing of the exactitude with which he copied the most minute particulars of nature exactly as they are, he displays perfect rule, improved order, correct proportion, just design, and a most divine grace; abounding in resource, and deeply versed in art, he may be truly said to have imparted to his figures, not beauty only, but life and movement.

After Leonardo there followed, even though somewhat distantly, Giorgione da Castel Franco, whose pictures are painted with much delicacy, and who gave extreme force and animation to his works by a certain depth of shadow, very judiciously managed; nor are the works of Fra Bartolommeo di San Marco less worthy of commendation, for the force, relief, and softness imparted to them by the master. But above all is to be distinguished the most graceful Raffaello da Urbino, who, examining and studying the works both of the earlier and later masters, took from all their best qualities, and, uniting these, enriched the domain of art with paintings of that faultless perfection anciently exhibited by the figures of Apelles and Zeuxis; nay, we might even say more perchance, could the works of Raffaello be compared or placed together with any by those masters; nature herself was surpassed by the colours of Raphael, and his invention was so easy and original, that the historical pieces of his composition are similar to legible writings, as all may perceive who examine them: in his works, the buildings, with their sites and all surrounding them, are as the places themselves, and whether treating our own people or strangers, the features, dresses, and every other peculiarity were at pleasure represented, with equal ease. To the countenances of his figures Raphael imparted the most perfect grace and truth; to the young as to the old, to men as to women; each and all have their appropriate character, for the modest he reserved an expression of modesty, to the licentious he imparted a look of licentiousness; his children charm us, now by the exquisite beauty of the eyes and expression, now by the spirit of their movement and the grace of their attitudes; his draperies are neither too rich and ample, nor too simple and meagre in their folds, still less are they complicated or confused, but all are so arranged and ordered in such a manner, that they appear to be indeed what they represent.

*   *   *

But he who bears the palm from all, whether of the living or the dead; he who transcends and eclipses every other, is the divine Michelagnolo Buonarotti, who takes the first place, not in one of these arts only, but in all three. This master surpasses and excels not only all those artists who have well nigh surpassed nature herself, but even all the most famous masters of antiquity, who did, beyond all doubt, vanquish her most gloriously: he alone has triumphed over the later as over the earlier, and even over nature herself, which one could scarcely imagine to be capable of exhibiting any thing, however extraordinary, however difficult, that he would not, by the force of his most divine genius, and by the power of his art, design, judgment, diligence, and grace, very far surpass and excel; nor does this remark apply to painting and the use of colours only, wherein are, nevertheless, comprised all corporeal forms, all bodies, direct or curved, palpable or impalpable, visible or invisible, but to the exceeding roundness and relief of his statues also. Fostered by the power of his art, and cultivated by his labours, the beautiful and fruitful plant has already put forth many and most noble branches, which have not only filled the world with the most delicious fruits, in unwonted profusion, but have also brought these three noble arts to so admirable a degree of perfection, that we may safely affirm the statues of this master to be, in all their parts, more beautiful than the antique. If the heads, hands, arms, or feet of the one be placed in comparison with those of the other, there will be found in those of the modern a more exact rectitude of principle, a grace more entirely graceful, a much more absolute perfection, in short, while there is also in the manner, a certain facility in the conquering of difficulties, than which it is impossible even to imagine any thing better; and what is here said applies equally to his paintings, for if it were possible to place these face to face with those of the most famous Greeks and Romans, thus brought into comparison, they would still further increase in value, and be esteemed to surpass those of the ancients in as great a degree as his sculptures excel all the antique.

But if the most renowned masters of old times, who, stimulated as they were by excessive rewards, produced their works amidst all the delights that fortune can bestow, obtain so large a share of our admiration, how much more highly should we not celebrate and extol even to the heavens, those most wonderful artists, who not only without reward, but in miserable poverty, bring forth fruits so precious? It is therefore to be believed and may be affirmed, that if, in this our day, the due remuneration were accorded to upright effort, there would be still greater and much better works executed than were ever produced by the ancients. But since artists have now rather to combat with, and struggle against poverty, than to strive after, and labour for fame, so is their genius miserably crushed and buried, nor does this state of things permit them (reproach and shame to those who could bring the remedy, but who give themselves no trouble concerning the matter), to make their true value adequately known. . . .

7

Principalities and Powers

SOME OF OUR BEST descriptions of late fifteenth-century princes come from the pen of Commines, the Flemish gentleman who was counselor to Louis XI, ambassador to the Italians for Charles VIII, and a fine historian as well. By the late fifteenth century the territorial state was emerging as the most serious alternative to feudal regionalism and Europe's kings were achieving wealth and power on a scale unknown to their medieval forebears. But the brow that wore the crown was not often serene: the ruler who was strong enough to withstand noble conspiracies, court intrigues, and rival claims to his territory had still to conquer himself; it was so easy for a king to indulge his private appetites and to put his ambitions for glory above the welfare of his kingdom. Commines is often described as a man who understood the realities of politics. Here we see that he was something of a moralist as well.

Phillippe de Commines (ca. 1445–ca. 1511), Memoires

Chapter xii, a digression concerning the miseries of mankind, especially of princes, by the example of those who reigned in the author's time, and chiefly of King Louis

SMALL HOPES and comfort ought poor and inferior people to have in this world, considering what so great a king suffered and underwent, and how he was at last forced to leave all, and could not, with all his care and diligence, protract his life one single hour. I knew him, and was entertained in his service in the flower of his age, and at the height of his prosperity, yet I never saw him free from labour and care. Of all diversions he loved hunting and hawking in their seasons; but his chief delight was in dogs. As for ladies, he never

From Andrew R. Scoble, ed. and trans., THE MEMOIRES OF PHILIPPE DE COMMINES, LORD OF ARGENTON, 2 vols. (London, 1912), II, pp. 80–92. Reprinted by permission of G. Bell and Sons Ltd.

meddled with any in my time; for about the time of my coming to
his court he lost a son, at whose death he was extremely afflicted, and
he made a vow to God in my presence never to have intercourse with
any other woman but the queen; and though this was no more than
what he was bound to do by the canons of the church, yet it was
much that his self-command should be so great, that he should be
able to persevere in his resolution so firmly, considering that the
queen (though an excellent princess in other respects) was not a person in whom a man could take any great delight.

In hunting, his eagerness and pain were equal to his pleasure, for
his chase was the stag, which he always ran down. He rose very early
in the morning, rode sometimes a great distance, and would not leave
his sport, let the weather be never so bad; and when he came home
at night he was often very weary, and generally in a violent passion
with some of his courtiers or huntsmen; for hunting is a sport not always to be managed according to the master's direction; yet, in the
opinion of most people, he understood it as well as any prince of his
time. He was continually at these sports, lodging in the country vil-
lages to which his recreations led him, till he was interrupted by business; for during the most part of the summer there was constantly
war between him and Charles Duke of Burgundy, and in the winter
they made truces.

He was also involved in some trouble about the county of Rous-
sillon, with John, King of Arragon, father of Peter of Castile, who
at present is King of Spain; for though both of them were poor, and
already at variance with their subjects in Barcelona and elsewhere,
and though the son had nothing but the expectation of succeeding to
the throne of Don Henry of Castile, his wife's brother (which fell to
him afterwards), yet they made considerable resistance; for that
province being entirely devoted to their interest, and they being universally beloved by the people, they gave our king abundance of
trouble, and the war lasted till his death, and many brave men lost
their lives in it, and his treasury was exhausted by it; so that he had
but a little time during the whole year to spend in pleasure, and even
then the fatigues he underwent were excessive. When his body was
at rest his mind was at work, for he had affairs in several places at
once, and would concern himself as much in those of his neighbours
as in his own, putting officers of his own over all the great families,
and endeavouring to divide their authority as much as possible. When
he was at war he laboured for a peace or a truce, and when he had

obtained it, he was impatient for war again. He troubled himself with many trifles in his government, which he had better have let alone: but it was his temper, and he could not help it; besides, he had a prodigious memory, and he forgot nothing, but knew everybody, as well in other countries as in his own.

And, in truth, he seemed better fitted to rule a world than to govern a single kingdom. I speak not of his minority, for then I was not with him; but when he was eleven years old, he was, by the advice of some of the nobility, and others of his kingdom, embroiled in a war with his father, Charles VII., which lasted not long, and was called the Praguerie. When he was arrived at man's estate, he was married, much against his inclination, to the King of Scotland's daughter;[1] and he regretted her existence during the whole course of her life. Afterwards, by reason of the broils and factions in his father's court, he retired into Dauphiny (which was his own), whither many persons of quality followed him, and indeed more than he could entertain. During his residence in Dauphiny he married the Duke of Savoy's daughter, and not long after he had great disputes with his father-in-law, and a terrible war was begun between them. His father, King Charles VII., seeing his son attended by so many good officers, and raising men at his pleasure, resolved to go in person against him, with a considerable body of forces, in order to disperse them. While he was upon his march he put out proclamations, requiring them all, as his subjects, under great penalties, to repair to him; and many obeyed, to the great displeasure of the Dauphin, who, finding his father incensed, though he was strong enough to resist, resolved to retire, and leave that country to him; and accordingly he removed, with but a slender retinue, into Burgundy, to Duke Philip's court, who received him honourably, furnished him nobly, and maintained him and his principal servants (as the Count de Comminges, the Lord de Montauban, and others), by way of pensions, and to the rest he gave presents, as he saw occasion, during the whole time of their residence there. However, the Dauphin entertained so many at his own expense, that his money often failed, to his great disgust and mortification; for he was forced to borrow, or his people would have forsaken him, which is certainly a great affliction to a prince who was utterly unaccustomed to those straits. So that during his residence at the court of Burgundy he had his anxieties, for he was constrained to cajole the duke and his ministers, lest they should think he was too burdensome, and had laid too long upon their hands, for he had been with them six years, and his father, King Charles, was constantly pressing and soliciting the Duke of Burgundy, by his ambassadors, either to deliver him up to him, or to banish him out of his dominions. And this, you may believe, gave the Dauphin some uneasy thoughts, and would not suffer him to be idle. In which season of his life, then, was it that he may be said to have enjoyed himself? I believe from his infancy and innocence to his death, his whole life was nothing but one continued scene of troubles and fatigues; and I am of opinion, that if all the days of his life were computed in which his joys and pleasures outweighed his pain and trouble, they would be found so few, that there would be twenty mournful ones to one pleasant. He lived about sixty-one years, yet he always fancied he should never outlive sixty, giving this for a reason, that for a long time no king of France had lived beyond that age. Some say, since the time of Charlemagne; but the king our master was far advanced in his sixty-first year.

What ease or what pleasure did Charles, Duke of Burgundy, enjoy more than our master King Louis? In his youth, indeed, he had less trouble, for he did not begin to enter upon any action till nearly the two-and-thirtieth year of his age; so that before that time he lived in great ease and quiet. His first quarrel was with his father's chief officers; and as his father took their part, he immediately withdrew from court, and retired into Holland, where being well received, he fell immediately into intelligence with the Gantois, and went and visited his father sometimes. He had no allowance from his father; but Holland, being a rich country, made him great presents, as did several other great towns, hoping thereby to insinuate themselves into his favour, and reap the advantage after Duke Philip's death. And it is the common custom of the world to worship the rising sun, and court him whose future authority will be great, rather than him who is already at the height of his fortune, and can never be higher. For this reason, when Duke Philip was informed that the Gantois had expressed great kindness for his son, and that he understood how to manage them, he answered, "They always love him who is to be their sovereign; but as soon as he is their lord they will hate him." And his saying was true, for from the time of Duke Philip's death and Charles's accession, their love began to decline, and they showed it openly, and he, on the other side, cared as little for them; yet they did more mischief to his posterity than they could possibly do to him.

But to continue these Memoirs. From the time Duke Charles undertook his war to recover the towns in Picardy (which our master had redeemed from Duke Philip), and joined himself with the lords of the kingdom in the war called the Public Good, what pleasure, what tranquillity had he? He had continual trouble and labour, without the least cessation or refreshment, either to his body or mind; for glory got entire possession of his heart, and constantly spurred him on to attempt new conquests. He was always in the field during summer, exposing his person to the greatest danger, taking the care and command of the whole army upon himself; and yet he thought his work too little. He was the first that rose, and the last that went to bed in the camp; and he slept in his clothes, like the poorest foot-soldier in the army. In winter, when the campaign was over, he was busily employed about raising money; six hours every morning he set apart for conferences, and for giving audience to ambassadors; and in this perpetual hurry of affairs he ended his days, and was killed by the Swiss in the battle of Nancy, as you have already heard; so that it cannot be said that he enjoyed one happy day from the time of his beginning to aggrandise himself to the hour of his death; and then what were the fruits of all his pains and labour? Or what necessity was there of his doing so? since he was a rich prince, and had towns and territories large enough already to have made him happy, if he could have been contented with them.

The next prince whom we shall have occasion to mention is Edward IV., King of England, a great and powerful monarch. In his minority he saw his father the Duke of York defeated and slain in battle, and with him the father of the Earl of Warwick, who governed the king in his youth, and managed all his affairs; and, to say the truth, it was the Earl of Warwick who made Edward king, and dethroned his old master, King Henry VI., who had reigned many years in England, and (in my judgment, and the judgment of the world), was the lawful king; but, in such cases, the disposal of kingdoms and great states is in the hands of God, who orders them as He pleases, for indeed all things proceed from Him. The reason of the Earl of Warwick's espousing the interest of the House of York against King Henry, who was of the Lancastrian family, was upon a difference that happened at court betwixt the Duke of Somerset and the Earl of Warwick. The king not having wisdom enough to compose it, it grew to that height that the queen (who was of the house of Anjou, and daughter to René, King of Sicily) interposed in it, and inclined to the duke's party against the Earl of Warwick; for all had acknowledged Henry, his father, and his grandfather, for their lawful kings. The queen would have acted much more prudently in endeavouring to have adjusted the dispute between them than in saying, "I am of this party, and will maintain it;" and it proved so by the event, for it occasioned many battles in England, and a war which continued nine-and-twenty years; and in the end nearly all the partisans of both sides were destroyed; so that factions and parties are very perilous and fatal, especially to the nobility, who are too prone to propagate and foment them. If it be alleged that by this means both parties are kept in awe, and the secret minds of his subjects are discovered to the prince, I agree that a young prince may encourage faction among his ladies, and it may be pleasant and diverting enough, and may give him opportunity of finding out some of their intrigues; but nothing is so dangerous to a nation as to nourish such factions and partialities among men of courage and magnanimity; it is no less than setting one's own house on fire; for immediately some or other cry out, "The king is against us," seize upon some fortified town, and correspond with his enemies. And certainly the factions of Orleans and Burgundy ought to make us wise on this point; for they began a war which lasted seventy-two years, in which the English were concerned, and thought by those unhappy divisions to have conquered the kingdom.

But to return from this digression. King Edward was a very young prince, and one of the handsomest men of his age, at the time he had overcome all his difficulties; so he gave himself up wholly to pleasures, and took no delight in anything but ladies, dancing, entertainments, and the chase; and in this voluptuous course of life, if I mistake not, he spent about sixteen years, till the quarrel happened between him and the Earl of Warwick. In which contest, though the king was driven out of the kingdom, yet his misfortune lasted not long; for he quickly returned, obtained a victory, and afterwards fell again to his pleasures, and indulged himself in them more recklessly than before. From this time he feared nobody; but he grew very fat, and his excess inclining him to diseases, in the very flower of his age, he died suddenly (as it was reported) of an apoplexy,[2] and his family perished after him (as you have heard), as regarded the succession in the male line.

In our time also, there reigned two wise and valiant princes, Matthias, King of Hungary,[3] and Mahomet Ottoman, Emperor of the Turks.[4] This King Matthias was the son of a very valiant gentleman,

called the White Knight of Wallachia,[5] a person of great honour
and prudence, who for a long time had governed the kingdom of
Hungary, and had gained several battles over the Turks, who are
neighbours to that country, by reason of the territories which they
have usurped in Sclavonia, Bosnia, and Greece. Not long after his
death, Lancelot[6] came to man's estate, who was heir to that kingdom,
and to the kingdoms of Bohemia and Poland besides. This Lancelot
was advised by some persons (as was reported) to seize upon the
two sons of the White Knight, on the pretence that, as their father
had obtained and exercised so much power and authority in that kingdom during his infancy, it was not improbable that his sons might do
the same. Upon which the said Lancelot resolved to have them both
apprehended, which was accordingly done. He put the eldest[7] to
death, and sent the other, which was Matthias, a prisoner to Buda, the
chief town in Hungary; but he did not remain long in confinement
(God Almighty being perhaps pleased with the services of his father), for, awhile after, King Lancelot was poisoned at Prague, in
Bohemia, by a lady of quality (whose brother I have seen), with
whom he had been in love, and she with him; but being incensed at
his intended marriage in France, with the daughter of King Charles
VII. (called now the Princess of Vienne), which was contrary to his
engagement to her, she poisoned him in a bath, by giving him an
apple to eat, and conveying poison into the haft of his knife. Upon
the death of Lancelot, the barons of Hungary assembled at Buda for
the election of a king, according to an ancient privilege which they
have, to elect their king when his predecessor has died without issue.
Whilst they were mightily divided, and in great controversy about
the election, the widow of the White Knight, and mother of Matthias, entered the town with a very splendid equipage; for she was
very rich, especially in ready money, which her husband had left her,
by means of which she was able to raise men immediately; and, besides, it is not improbable that she had partisans in the town, and
among the electors, upon account of the influence and authority her
husband had had in that kingdom. As soon as she came into the city,
she marched directly to the prison, and released her son; upon which
some of the barons and prelates who were assembled fled in terror
out of the town, and those that remained chose Matthias for their
king; and he reigned among them in great prosperity, with as much
applause and esteem as any of his predecessors, and in some things
with even more. He was a man of as much courage as any of that

age, and obtained many signal victories over the Turks, without any loss to his kingdom, which he much enlarged, as well towards Turkey as towards Bohemia (most of which was in his possession), and also in Wallachia (where he was born) and Sclavonia; and on the side towards Germany he took the greatest part of Austria from the Emperor Frederic, and kept it till his death, which happened in Vienna, the chief city of Austria, in the year 1491. He was a prince who managed his affairs discreetly, both in peace and in war. Towards the latter end of his days, finding he was become formidable, he began to affect a pompous and splendid way of living, and provided great store of rich hangings, jewels, and plate, for the adornment of his palace. All his business was dispatched by himself, or by his direction: he had also an inclination to make himself terrible to his own subjects, and became a very tyrant towards his latter end; after which he fell into a grievous and incurable distemper, as it were in his youth (for he was but eight-and-twenty[8] years of age), and died: his life having been one continued scene of labour and sorrow, without any great pleasure or ease.

The Turk, whom I mentioned before, was a wise and valiant prince, but he made more use of his cunning than of his courage. His father also was a valiant prince, who took Adrianople (that is to say, the city of Adrian), and left his son very great; and this son, at the age of twenty-three, took Constantinople, or the city of Constantine; I have seen his portrait painted at that age, which represented him vigorous and sprightly. It was a great disgrace to all Christendom to suffer that city to be lost; he took it by assault, and the Emperor of the East (whom we called Emperor of Constantinople) was slain in the breach. Many brave men were killed with him in this assault, many great ladies ravished, and no manner of cruelty was omitted. This was his first exploit, but he continued to perform great actions, and so many, that I heard a Venetian ambassador say once in the presence of Charles, Duke of Burgundy, that this Mahomet had conquered two empires, four kingdoms, and two hundred cities; he meant, indeed, the empires of Constantinople and Trebizond; the kingdoms of Bosnia, Syria, Armenia, and I think Morea was the fourth. He conquered likewise many fair islands in the Archipelago (where the Venetians have two settlements), among others, Negropont and Mitylene; besides which he subdued nearly all Albania and Sclavonia: and as his conquests were great over the Christians, so were they no less considerable over those of his own religion, among

whom he destroyed several great princes, as the Prince of Caramania,[9] and others.

The greatest part of his affairs were transacted by himself, according to the practice of our king and of the king of Hungary; and these
three were without all dispute the wisest princes that had reigned for
a hundred years. But the generosity of our master's conversation, and
his liberality to his servants, as well as to foreigners and others, distinguished him very much from the other two; and it is no wonder,
for he was styled the most Christian King. As to worldly pleasures
and enjoyments, this Turk had his share, and spent most of his time
in them; and, indeed, he would have done more mischief to Christendom, had he not been so employed. He indulged himself in all kinds
of sensuality, and was strangely given to gluttony, which brought
him numberless diseases, which continued upon him as long as he
lived. Every spring he had a swelling in his legs, that made them as
big as a man's waist (as I have heard from those who have seen it);
and the swelling never broke, but dispersed of its own accord, and no
surgeon could tell what to make of it, but all agreed his gluttony was
the occasion of it, though perhaps it was a judgment from heaven;
and one reason why he suffered himself to be seen so seldom, and
kept himself shut up in his seraglio, was, lest he should discover that
infirmity, and grow contemptible to his subjects. He died about the
fifty-second year of his age, and suddenly; yet he made a will, and I
have seen it, and, if it be true, he seemed to have some remorse for a
tax which he had lately laid upon his subjects. Let Christian princes
therefore consider what they do, since they have no reasonable power
to raise money, without the permission and consent of their people.

Thus have you seen the death of many illustrious persons in a
short time, who had borne so much sorrow, and endured so many
fatigues, only to extend their dominions, and advance their fame and
glory, as perhaps tended not only to the shortening of their lives, but
to the endangering the welfare of their immortal souls. I am not
speaking here of the Turk, for I question not but that he is gone to
his predecessors, but of our king and the rest, on whom I hope God
will have mercy. But to speak freely (as one that is no great scholar
or genius, but has had some experience in the world), would it not
have been better for them, and for all other great princes and subjects whatever, to choose a middle course in all their desires; that is,
not to be so solicitous and careful about temporal things, and have
such vast and unreasonable designs in view; but to be more cautious

of offending God, oppressing their subjects, and invading their neighbours, by so many cruel and unchristian ways, as I have mentioned before, and rather employ their time in tranquillity and innocent diversions? Their lives would be longer, their infirmities the later in coming, their deaths less desirable to other people, and less terrible to themselves. Can we desire any clearer examples to prove how poor and inconsiderable a creature man is, how short and miserable his life, and how little difference there is betwixt princes and private persons, since as soon as they are dead, whether rich or poor, their bodies become abominable, all people fly and shun them, and their souls are no sooner separated but they prepare to receive their doom, which is given by God at that very instant of time, according to every man's works, and bodily deserts.

TRANSLATOR'S NOTES

1. Margaret, daughter of James I., King of Scotland. She was married to the Dauphin on the 24th of June, 1436; and died on the 16th of August, 1444. Her lot in France was singularly wretched, as she was treated by her husband with marked contempt and dislike. The story of her adventure with Alain Chartier is well known. Finding the famous poet asleep in a saloon of the palace, she stooped down and kissed him, observing to her ladies, who were somewhat astonished at her proceeding, that she did not kiss the man, but the mouth which had uttered so many fine things.

2. This is the third explanation given by Commines of the cause of Edward's death. At Vol. 1. p. 394., he says he died of *melancholy,* and at p. 62. of this volume he ascribes his decease to a *catarrh.* Apoplexy is the most probable explanation of the event.

3. Matthias I., surnamed Corvinus, was the son of John Hunniades, and was proclaimed King of Hungary in 1458, at the age of sixteen years. He reigned for thirty-two years with considerable reputation, to which his patronage of learned men, who repaid his munificence with very profuse eulogies, did not a little contribute. He died in 1490.

4. Mahomet II., son of Amurath II., was proclaimed Sultan in 1451, and died in 1481. He is usually distinguished by European historians by the title of Mahomet the Great, first Emperor of the Turks. His reign was signalised by the capture of Constantinople, and the fall of the Byzantine empire.

5. John Hunniades, Voyvode of Transylvania, was Regent of Hungary during the minority of King Ladislaus. This hero stood in the breach for twelve years against the Turkish power, frequently defeated, but unconquered in defeat. "If the renown of Hunniades," says Mr. Hallam, "may

seem exaggerated by the partiality of writers who lived under the reign of his son, it is confirmed by more unequivocal evidence, by the dread and hatred of the Turks, whose children were taught obedience by threatening them with his name, and by the deference of a jealous aristocracy to a man of no distinguished birth." Hunniades was a Wallachian, of a small family. His last and most splendid service was the relief of Belgrade. That strong city was besieged by Mahomet II., three years after the fall of Constantinople; its capture would have laid open all Hungary. A tumultuary army, chiefly collected by the preaching of a friar, was entrusted to Hunniades. He penetrated into the city, and having repulsed the Turks in a fortunate sally, wherein Mahomet was wounded, had the honour of compelling him to raise the siege in confusion. The relief of Belgrade was more important in its effects than in its immediate circumstances: it revived the spirits of Europe, which had been appalled by the unceasing victories of the infidels. Mahomet himself seemed to acknowledge the importance of the blow, and seldom afterwards attacked the Hungarians. Hunniades died in 1456, soon after this achievement.

6. Ladislaus V., King of Hungary, was the posthumous son of Albert, Duke of Austria, who acquired the crown of Hungary for his progeny by marrying Elizabeth, daughter of the Emperor Sigismund. Ladislaus was born on the 22nd of February, 1440; became king on the 13th of February, 1453; and died on the 23rd of November, 1457.

7. Ladislaus, the eldest son of John Hunniades, was beheaded on the 8th of March, 1456, for having assassinated the Count of Cillei during the preceding year.

8. As might have been expected, from his having no personal knowledge of Hungarian affairs, Commines falls into many inaccuracies about Matthias Corvinus, who was forty-eight years old when he died, in the year 1490. His election to the kingdom is to be ascribed far less to any intrigues of his mother than to the aversion felt by the Hungarian nobles to the character and Austrian connections of the Emperor Frederic III., the other candidate for the crown.

9. Caramania, a province of Asiatic Turkey, on the south of Anatolia. Its emirs were formerly powerful princes; but Mahomet II greatly weakened them in 1440, and his son Bajazet incorporated their dominions with the Turkish empire in 1488.

8

The Renaissance Comes to Germany

CONRAD CELTIS was a poet, the first German to be crowned with the laurel. He was also an enthusiast of humanism, Latinizing his name, which was Conrad Pickel. Having caught the fever of classical studies from Italy, he strove to introduce them into Germany. In this Latin oration, which was his inaugural address to the faculty of the University of Ingolstadt in 1492, he mixed admiration for the Italians and criticism of the Germans with resentment of foreign domination and an appeal to German pride. Thus, from its inception humanism in Germany was linked with nationalism and patriotic mythology, fostering certain attitudes that have abided to the present.

Conrad Celtis (1459–1508), Public Oration Delivered in the University of Ingolstadt

I SHOULD HAVE DEEMED it in no way remarkable, distinguished fathers and excellent young men, that I, a German and a fellow-countryman of yours, should be able to address you in Latin, if those former geniuses of our native Germany were still flourishing and if that age had returned in which it is said that our ambassadors spoke Greek in preference to Latin. But since, through the iniquity of the ages and the change in the times, not only amongst you but even in Italy, the mother and ancient parent of literature, all the brilliance of letters has at length faded and died and all freeborn studies have been put to flight and overthrown by barbarous upheavals, I do not feel confident, in view of the sluggishness of my intellect and the paucity of my powers, that I can address you adequately in Latin. [The more so] since at least I cannot own that I have lacked what most of you lament [the lack of] from personal experience, namely

From Leonard Forster, ed., SELECTIONS FROM CONRAD CELTIS (Cambridge, 1948), pp. 37, 39, 41, 43, 45, 47, 53, 55, 57, 59, 61, 63, 65. Reprinted by permission of Cambridge University Press.

industry and expert teaching. Yet for fear I should be accused of coming in complete silence to this place honoured by your presence, I have preferred to risk offending your ears by hesitant delivery rather than pass over in silence my affection for you and for the commonwealth of letters. For I am confident that you will readily pardon me if you reflect that a mannikin born as some say in the midst of barbarians and drunkards cannot be expected to speak with that sobriety which is required by your most attentive ears and the place marked out for me in oratory and poetry at the public expense by George our illustrious prince and by your distinguished selves who are sharers in all his counsels.

Moreover I have decided that I cannot address you more worthily or more pleasantly, or choose any topic better suited to myself and you my audience than by encouraging your minds in virtue and the study of the liberal arts. For by these means how easily can true glory, immortal fame and happiness be secured in this short life of ours! Not one of you should be found so sluggish and cowardly as not to think it a fine, noble and glorious thing to strive for these great ends which can make a man truly blessed. I did not think it worth while to devote any special acuteness to treating of the favours of fortune or physical well-being or of those pleasures which are proper to vile slaves and tend to put out the light of the intellect. For all these things are fleeting and quickly fading and destined to perish with the body in its own brief span of life, or else soon to pass on to other masters. Hence no wise man is recorded to have striven for such things. On the contrary, if we examine the lives of those great men of old, we find that they had such great love of learning and wisdom (on which the human mind feeds as on nectar and ambrosia) that to attain them they left their native land, their dear wives and children, spent their ample patrimony and endured injuries, insults and infamy among the common herd, and exile too, with the greatest patience and tranquillity. Furthermore it is related of them that they voluntarily submitted to toils and heat and cold and difficult voyages because they wished to perceive and see with their own eyes what they had discovered with weary effort by close reflexion and much reading. Such was the power of their incredible zeal for the acquisition of wisdom and their love of astronomical and physical investigations. For these achievements they finally won divine renown and will continue to enjoy immortal fame; and being highly revered and wor-

shipped by all posterity they come to be called by the title of philosophers.

*   *   *

I shall be satisfied — and more than satisfied, O German men and
illustrious youths — if anything I may say to-day, however poor it be,
succeeds in adding and inculcating and, as it were, branding into your
minds some incentive to fame and virtue, so that you may have immortality above all things present before your eyes, that immortality
which can only be sought at the fountain-head of philosophy and eloquence. I cannot easily express with what great labour and sacrifice
of sleep you must brood and sweat over these two things, in other
words over the writings of the philosophers, poets and orators of
old. They alone have set out for us the way to live wisely and
happily and have set before us Nature, the parent of the human race
and course of all things, as it were for an example and mirror of
life for us to imitate. From them you will learn to praise good deeds
and hate wrong-doing, from them you will learn how to console
and to encourage, to persuade and to dissuade, and you will study
how to contemplate the ruler of all things and Nature herself, which
is the crown of human felicity. And though all these things can be
done by others, yet in some indefinable way it is in the hand of the
orator and the poet that the power to evoke compassion and to rouse
or check the spirit lies. Moreover those adornments of words and
sentiments which like stars embellish an oration are instruments
proper to the poet and the orator. These you must borrow and
employ them as occasion arises for your own purposes in your daily
discourse. For what in the world is the use of much knowledge and
a sense for the sublime and the beautiful if one is unable to enjoy
that unique element in human happiness, the power to transmit one's
thoughts to posterity? This is the truth, I dare be sworn: there is
nothing which so clearly shows a man to be learned and well educated as the way he speaks and writes, and this is conditioned by
eloquence.

But I now direct my speech to you, distinguished men and well-
born youths, to whom by virtue of the courage of your ancestors
and the unconquerable strength of Germany the Italian empire has
passed, who throng this university in preference to all others in this
Germany of ours, enrich it, and do it great honour and credit. I urge
you to direct your studies to those things first and foremost which

will ripen and improve the mind and call you away from the habits of the common herd to devote yourselves to higher pursuits. Keep before your eyes true nobility of spirit, considering that you bring not honour but dishonour to our empire if you neglect the study of literature only to rear horses and dogs and pursue ecclesiastical preferment. Consider how to add distinction to your dignified office by your virtue, and to increase your fame by learning, so that men may think you worthy of those dignities and may follow after you, instead of your following them, like fowlers after a flock of birds. Emulate, noble men, the ancient nobility of Rome, which, after taking over the empire of the Greeks, assimilated all their wisdom and eloquence, so much so that it is hard to decide whether it has equalled all the Greek discoveries and equipment of learning or surpassed them. In the same way you who have taken over the empire of the Italians should cast off repulsive barbarism and seek to acquire Roman culture. Do away with that old disrepute of the Germans in Greek, Latin and Hebrew writers, who ascribe to us drunkenness, cruelty, savagery and every other vice bordering on bestiality and excess. Consider it a great disgrace to be ignorant of the histories of the Greeks and Latins, and the height of shame to know nothing about the topography, the climate, the rivers, the mountains, the antiquities and the peoples of our region and our own country, in short all those facts which foreigners have so cleverly collected concerning us. I am greatly astonished to reflect on the painstaking exactitude and subtle learning with which the Greeks and Romans have surveyed our country, which is, to use their own words, the greatest part of Europe, and though it seems rough and wild, I imagine, in comparison with their own climate, they have expressed our customs, our emotional make-up and our spirits as graphically as a painter might delineate our bodies. Cast away, noble gentlemen, cast away and wipe out those acts of robbery which those authorities declare to have been held as proofs of courage amongst us! It is astonishing that that hereditary disease should have persisted still in certain parts of Germany for some fifteen hundred years, for even now when, after the draining of marshes and the cutting down of vast forests, our climate is more cheerful and our land populated with famous cities, we still fail to dislodge the leaders of that robber crew. So difficult is it to correct what has become a habit, what has lasted for centuries and is now a general practice. And so it has come about that the neighbouring countries vent their spleen upon us, and pursue our name with a kind of eternal hatred and calumny, maintaining that with the empire we have acquired many of the vices of foreign peoples. To them our characters are always suspect and dangerous. Let us be ashamed, noble gentlemen, that certain modern historians (who, publishing new Decads, boast that they have equalled the ancient Roman empire) should speak of our most famous leaders merely as 'the barbarians' and suppress their proper native title, in order to belabour and bitterly disparage the reputation of us Germans. Such has been the power of that long-standing and irreconcilable hatred between us and of that ancient strife between the protecting deities of our two nations, which would, in view of the hostile spirit on both sides, inevitably have led to mutual slaughter, had not prudent Nature separated us by the Alps and by rocks towering to the stars. Let us be ashamed, I pray, that although we have waged and won many memorable wars in Hungary, France and Italy and against that cruel tyrant of Asia who wallows in Christian blood, not one of you should be found to-day to hand down to posterity the deeds performed by German courage. Yet many foreigners will be found who in their historical works, contrary to all historical truth, will hiss like vipers against our courage with all the pretentious cajolery of their style and seek with falsifications and lying inventions (with which that sort of men is most prodigal for the purpose of singing their own praises) to belittle our glorious achievements. And I am quite at a loss to say whether it is due to our wisdom or our carelessness that lately of our own accord we have surrendered the insignia of authors and their companion, the imperial laurel, to Rome — an unhappy omen, as it were, for our empire, this abdication to others of the right to confer the laurel, foreshadowing that in the end not a single privilege of empire will remain in our possession.

Assume, O men of Germany, that ancient spirit of yours, with which you so often confounded and terrified the Romans, and turn your eyes to the frontiers of Germany; collect together her torn and broken territories. Let us be ashamed, ashamed, I say, to have placed upon our nation the yoke of slavery, and to be paying tributes and taxes to foreign and barbarian kings. O free and powerful people, O noble and valiant race, plainly worthy of the Roman empire, our famous harbour is held by the Pole and the gateway of our ocean by the Dane! In the east also powerful peoples live in slavery, the Bohemians, the Moravians, the Slovaks and the Silesians, who all live as it were separated from the body of our Germany. And I may add the

Transylvanian Saxons who also use our racial culture and speak our native language. In the west is France, which is so friendly and bountiful towards us by reason of the immortal virtue and incredible wisdom of Philip, Palatine of the Rhine, who rules both banks of the famous river and will ever rule them with fair-omened sway,

> While the pole wheels the stars, while winds smite the shores.

But from the south we are oppressed by a sort of distinguished slavery, and under the impulse of greed, that old and accursed aid to the acquirement of comfort and luxury, new commercial ventures are continually established, by which our country is drained of its wonderful natural wealth while we pay to others what we need for ourselves. So persistent is fortune or destiny in persecuting and wiping out the Germans, the last survivors of the Roman Empire. . . . To such an extent are we corrupted by Italian sensuality and by fierce cruelty in exacting filthy lucre, that it would have been far more holy and reverent for us to practise that rude and rustic life of old, living within the bounds of self-control, than to have imported the paraphernalia of sensuality and greed which are never sated, and to have adopted foreign customs. Hence it comes about that princes accept as their companions those who share their own interests, and exclude those who love learning and wisdom. Yet the founders of the Greek and Roman Empires honoured such men as these so highly as to decorate them with the offices of government and count them among their more intimate friends; even when they died they ordered them to be buried in their own tombs, because they considered that their own power and immortality were prolonged by the good services of such men and their use of literature on which alone immortality depends, so that they might be able to benefit humanity not only in life, but even after death. So their memory is alive to-day and always will be, as long as Greek and Latin letters are cultivated. And I will assign no other cause for the ever-flourishing condition of Italy than the fact that her people surpass us in no blessing other than the love of literature and its cultivation. By this they overawe other nations as if by force of arms, and win their admiration for their genius and industry. But among us there are frequent changes and the insatiable eagerness for revolution, as the learned poet says of us:

> Brothers eager to devise revolution, raging in hatred of peace with spirit and quick desire.

And so, for fear our horses should grow gouty or our weapons rusty, we run riot among ourselves with civil strife like Sulla and Marius or Caesar and Pompey. . . .

And so I now return to you, young men of Germany. Continue no longer in your childish ways, but learn to know the secrets of literature, which those writers allege to be beyond your grasp who sing to our shame:

> The waters of Castalia and the streams prophetic of destiny no barbarian shall ever drink with his polluted mouth.

Be ashamed that these words should be read and applied to you, the owners of the Roman Empire, and should survive down to the present day. Let no one try to bring up as contrary evidence the multitude of our universities, of which we have no less than fourteen, and maintain that because of them barbarism has been removed, that counsel has been taken and a way made clear for good character and honourable accomplishments. For, though the common herd flatters those of us who have the titles of magister or professor (much to their satisfaction), I confess to my sorrow that you will find few of such folk who either pursue or possess true knowledge of things, or combine research into natural science with purity of the Roman tongue. And the reason is that in our studies of such subjects (which I might almost call playing at study) all those who expound the Latin poets and authors are suppressed, and anyone who reveals the work of nature and the wisdom of its director by mathematical truth or whose perception goes a little deeper than that of the common herd is considered almost sacrilegious. To such an extent is philosophy trampled under foot and frittered away by men who have distorted the most beautiful majesty of nature into incorporeal concepts, monstrous abstractions and empty Chimaeras, as if they were poets. The latter [however] with their figures and apposite fables have transformed the natures of things with the aim of hiding the knowledge of lofty matters from the common herd, so that nature should be made known under honourable coverings and so to speak under a sacramental veil; for they know that she dislikes being displayed openly and nakedly. Moreover if the common herd understood certain secrets as the philosophers understand them, it would be difficult to restrain their impetuosity.

I will not now interpret in physical terms the fables of the Greek and Roman poets, who under a cloud of poetic invention have revealed the fountain-head of all divine discoveries to those who understand the truth. But we lay false accusations against such men as these and execrate them as if they were charlatans and worthless fellows. So much do we love our own worthlessness and our disgusting barbarism, to which in my view divine displeasure has led us, that we do not add to our possession of the Roman Empire that of the glory of Italian literature nor compete in this most beautiful style of writing with those whom we none the less admire. Though indeed, even among us, men are to be found who suffer from my personal failing and call themselves poets and orators. But they, neglecting all teaching in philosophy and rhetoric, strain every nerve of their intellect to achieve an empty loquacity and to nurture the minds of young men with indescribable fantasies. They are but artificers of smooth and sloppy diction, and shamelessly vomit forth whatever comes into their mouths, intoxicating chaste ears with certain filthy and disgusting discourses, as if vices ought to be laid bare to us in teaching, whereas in fact they always spring up unencouraged, ever more exuberantly, like worthless weeds. If anyone scrutinizes this learning of ours more closely he will find mortar without lime and a voice without blood, though we are ready enough to reprove others on mere points of vocabulary, like schoolboys. But we do not perceive our own rottenness, and indeed I think that the gods have been kind to us in giving us even this sort of plebeian and vulgar learning. Otherwise we should not allow others more learned than ourselves to utter a single syllable amid our nonsensical babble and verbal hogwash....

*   *   *

Turn then, Germans, turn to more cultured studies, which only philosophy and eloquence can teach you. Reflect that it was no accident that the founders of the Greek and Roman empires tended them so carefully and honoured the teachers of them wth the highest public offices [which they would never have done] if they had not realized that assemblies of men, cities, religions, the cult of the gods, the most virtuous habits in social life and the most powerful empires can all be preserved and governed by the power of the tongue. This fact was given eloquent expression by that divine poet, the glory and delight of Roman eloquence, in those celebrated verses:

And, like as mid a people great, full often will arise
Huge riot — and all the low-born herd to utter anger flies,
And sticks and stones are in the air, and fury arms doth find;
Then setting eyes perchance on one of weight for noble mind
And noble deeds, they hush them then and stand with pricked-up
    ears,
And he with words becomes their lord and smooth their anger
    wears.

It was assuredly a great and almost divine factor in the administration of their commonwealth that they sought to unite wisdom with eloquence and, for the purpose of attaining these, founded public performances in which by sublime persuasion and works of remarkable originality they exhorted the minds of the spectators to virtue, loyalty, self-restraint, courage and endurance of all hardships, warned young people against vices and inspired them to seek for glory, so that they might imbibe as it were in living images their duty to their country, their friends, their guests and their dear parents. That poetical allegory by which Orpheus is said to have soothed wild beasts and Amphion to have moved stones and led them where he pleased is thus not inappropriate, for it succeeds in showing metaphorically the power of eloquence and the function of the poet, who can move fierce, cruel and ungovernable minds to mildness, goodness and patriotism. It is therefore a wise practice on the part of the cities of ancient Greece and of modern Italy to instruct their children from the very beginning in the works of the poets. For in them they learn to recognize musical songs and sweet modulations of harmony (to which their age is peculiarly responsive), and their tender spirits, normally prone to laziness and indolence, are stimulated to industry, so that they are inspired to learn and to linger over their studies with joyful enthusiasm and eagerness. The dignity of words and sentiments imbibed by tender minds will thus last very likely to a more advanced age, and will continue to enjoy fresh vigour throughout a whole lifetime even till death. This is the type of teaching which Aristotle prescribes, when he advises that young people should be trained in music. For harmony rouses the native talent of boys so that they bend their energies towards oratory and musical composition. Moreover that training is most excellently suited to give the spirit relaxation, to console and uplift the mind, resounding in sacred hymns in praise of the gods and transporting it in divine meditation.

Wherefore Pythagoras and Plato, the greatest of the philosophers, have called poetry the first philosophy and theology, whch uses song for its demonstrations and proceeds in modulated speech. Another branch of composition however, namely oratory, wanders along in everyday, free and unshackled language. Poetry is more closely bound by rhythm and a little freer in the use of words, but similar and almost equal in many types of ornament. We should not neglect either of these, but from the beginning, men of Germany, the minds of boys should be trained and captivated by the lure of songs and poems. For, under the influence of the things worthy of sublime admiration, the things of beauty and the polish of language which such works contain, the minds of the young are moulded into shape; while at a more robust age, when young minds have been fortified by these beginnings and their powers of reflexion quickened, so that they are better equipped and prepared, they can betake themselves to the reading of the more weighty philosophers and orators. From these they can at length rise to original composition and the sublimity of the art of poetry with its imagery, finally to achieve the reputation of illustrious writers by composing histories and poems, and to win thereafter immortality for themselves and glory and renown for their native land. My speech is ended.

9

Columbus Lands on a New Continent

In October, 1498, Columbus wrote to Ferdinand and Isabella to report the achievements of his third voyage. He had sighted and landed upon a great continent hitherto unknown, discovered the mouth of a mighty river, met new peoples, and, best of all, found gold and pearls and spices. Columbus was probably the first European, since the Vikings at least, to land on the American continent. The mainland he had reached was the Paria Peninsula of present-day Venezuela and the river the Orinoco, but Columbus believed he was in the Indies, and to this belief he clung to his dying day. From this letter we can understand why. Schooled in the cosmography of the Bible and of the Ancients, anxious to prove to his royal patrons that he had not misled them, he could only interpret his findings as confirming evidence of what he was already convinced was true: that the world was made up of three great land masses, Europe, Africa, and Asia; that by sailing westward he had found the shortest and most direct route to the East; and that soon he would come upon the fabled sources of the riches which had first lured him out upon these uncharted seas.

Christopher Columbus (1451–1506), Third Voyage

Narrative of the voyage which Don Christopher Columbus made the third time that he came to the Indies, when he discovered terra firma, as he sent it to their majesties from the island of Hispaniola

MOST SERENE and most exalted and powerful Princes, the King and Queen, our Sovereigns: The Blessed Trinity moved your Highnesses to this enterprise of the Indies; and of His Infinite goodness has chosen me to proclaim it to you; wherefore as His ambassador I

From R. H. Major, ed., SELECT LETTERS OF CHRISTOPHER COLUMBUS (London, 2nd ed., 1870), pp. 108–112, 121–131, 135–139, 140–151.

approached your royal presence, moved by the consideration that I was appealing to the most exalted monarchs in Christendom, who exercised so great an influence over the Christian faith, and its advancement in the world. Those who heard of it looked upon it as impossible, for they fixed all their hopes on the favours of fortune, and pinned their faith solely upon chance. I gave to the subject six or seven years of great anxiety, explaining, to the best of my ability, how great service might be done to our Lord, by this undertaking, in promulgating His sacred name and our holy faith among so many nations; — an enterprise so exalted in itself, and so calculated to enhance the glory and immortalise the renown of great sovereigns. It was also requisite to refer to the temporal prosperity which was foretold in the writings of so many trustworthy and wise historians, who related that great riches were to be found in these parts. At the same time I thought it desirable to bring to bear upon the subject the sayings and opinions of those who have written upon the geography of the world, and finally, your Highnesses came to the determination that the undertaking should be entered upon. In this your Highnesses exhibited the noble spirit which has been always manifested by you on every great subject; for all others who had thought of the matter or heard it spoken of, unanimously treated it with contempt, with the exception of two friars, who always remained constant in their belief of its practicability. I, myself, in spite of fatiguing opposition, felt sure that the enterprise would nevertheless prosper, and continue equally confident of it to this day, because it is a truth, that though everything will pass away, the Word of God will not, and everything that he has said will be fulfilled; who so clearly spoke of these lands, by the mouth of the prophet Isaiah, in so many places in Scripture, that from Spain the holy name of God was to be spread abroad. Thus I departed in the name of the Holy Trinity, and returned very soon, bringing with me an account of the practical fulfilment of everything I had said. Your Highnesses again sent me out, and in a short space of time, by God's mercy, not by [ms. incomplete here].

I discovered three hundred and thirty-three leagues of terra firma on the eastern side, and seven hundred islands, besides those which I discovered on the first voyage; I also succeeded in circumnavigating the island of Española, which is larger in circumference than all Spain, the inhabitants of which are countless, and all of whom may be laid under tribute. It was then that complaints arose, disparaging the enterprise that I had undertaken, because, forsooth, I had not immediately sent the ships home laden with gold, — no allowance being made for the shortness of the time, and all the other impediments of which I have already spoken. On this account (either as a punishment for my sins, or, as I trust, for my salvation), I was held in detestation, and had obstacles placed in the way of every thing I said, or for which I petitioned. I therefore resolved to apply to your Highnesses, to inform you of all the wonderful events that I had experienced, and to explain the reason of every proposition that I made, making reference to the nations that I had seen, among whom, and by whose instrumentality, many souls may be saved. I related how the natives of Española had been laid under tribute to your Highnesses, and regarded you as their sovereigns. And I laid before your Highnesses abundant samples of gold and copper, — proving the existence of extensive mines of those metals. I also laid before your Highnesses many sorts of spices, too numerous to detail; and I spoke of the great quantity of brazil-wood, and numberless other articles found in those lands. All this was of no avail with some persons, who began, with determined hatred, to speak ill of the enterprise, not taking into account the service done to our Lord in the salvation of so many souls, nor the enhancement of your Highnesses' greatness to a higher pitch than any earthly prince has yet enjoyed; nor considering, that from the exercise of your Highnesses' goodness, and the expense incurred, both spiritual and temporal advantage was to be expected, and that Spain must in the process of time derive from thence, beyond all doubt, an unspeakable increase of wealth. This might be manifestly seen by the proofs given in the written descriptions of the voyages already made, showing that the fulfillment of every other hope may be reasonably expected. Nor were they affected by the consideration of what great princes throughout the world have done to increase their fame: as, for example, Solomon, who sent from Jerusalem, to the uttermost parts of the east, to see Mount Sopora [Σωφίρ, Ophir], in which expedition his ships were detained three years; and which mountain your Highnesses now possess in the island of Española. Nor, as in the case of Alexander, who sent to observe the mode of government in the island of Taprobana, in India; and Caesar Nero, to explore the sources of the Nile, and to learn the causes of its increase in the summer, when water is needed; and many other mighty deeds that princes have done, and which it is allotted to princes to achieve. Nor was it of any avail that no prince of Spain, as far as I have read, has ever hitherto gained possession of land out of Spain; and that the world of which I speak is different from that of which the Romans, and Alexander, and the Greeks made mighty efforts with great armies to gain possession. Nor have they been affected by the recent noble example of the kings of Portugal, who have had the courage to explore as far as Guinea, and to make the discovery of it, expending so much gold and so many lives in the undertaking, that a calculation of the population of the kingdom would show that one half of them have died in Guinea: and though it is now a long time since they commenced these great exertions, the return for their labour and expense has hitherto been but trifling; this people has also dared to make conquests in Africa, and to carry on their exploits to Ceuta, Tangier, Argilla, and Alcazar, repeatedly giving battle to the Moors; and all this at great expense; simply because it was an exploit worthy of a prince, undertaken for the service of God, and to advance the enlargement of His kingdom. The more I said on the subject, the more two-fold was reproach cast upon it, even to the expression of abhorrence, no consideration being given to the honour and fame that accrued to your Highnesses throughout all Christendom from your Highnesses having undertaken this enterprise; so that there was neither great nor small who did not desire to hear tidings of it. Your Highnesses replied to me encouragingly, and desired that I should pay no regard to those who spoke ill of the undertaking, inasmuch as they had received no authority or countenance whatever from your Highnesses.

*   *   *

. . . When I reached the point of Arenal, I found that the island of Trinidad formed with the land of Gracia a strait of two leagues' width from west to east, and as we had to pass through it to go to the north, we found some strong currents which crossed the strait, and which made a great roaring, so that I concluded there must be a reef of sand or rocks, which would preclude our entrance; and behind this current there was another and another, all making a roaring noise like the sound of breakers against the rocks. I anchored there, under the said point of Arenal, outside of the strait, and found the water rush from east to west with as much impetuosity as that of the Guadalquivir at its conflux with the sea; and this continued constantly day and night, so that it appeared to be impossible to move backwards for the current or forwards for the shoals. In the dead of night, while I was on deck, I heard an awful roaring that came from the south towards the ship; I stopped to observe what it might be, and I saw the sea rolling from west to east like a mountain as high as the ship, and approaching by little and little; on the top of this rolling sea came a mighty wave roaring with a frightful noise and the same terrific uproar as the other currents, producing, as I have already said, a sound as of breakers upon the rocks. To this day I have a vivid recollection of the dread I then felt, lest the ship might founder under the force of that tremendous sea; but it passed by, and reached the mouth of the beforementioned passage, where the uproar lasted for a considerable time. On the following day I sent out boats to take soundings, and found that in the strait, at the deepest part of the embouchure, there were six or seven fathoms of water, and that there were constant contrary currents, one running inwards, and the other outwards. It pleased the Lord, however, to give us a favourable wind, and I passed inwards through that strait and soon came to still water. In fact some water which was drawn up from the sea, proved to be fresh. I then sailed northwards till I came to a very high mountain, at about twenty-six leagues from the Punta del Arenal; here two lofty headlands appeared, one towards the east, and forming part of the island of Trinidad, and the other, on the west, being part of the land which I have already called Gracia; we found here a channel still narrower than that of Arenal, with similar currents, and a tremendous roaring of water; the water here also was fresh. Hitherto I had held no communication with any of the people of this country, although I very earnestly desired it; I therefore sailed along the coast westwards, and the further I advanced, the fresher and more wholesome I found the water; and when I had proceeded a considerable distance, I reached a spot where the land appeared to be cultivated. There I anchored, and sent the boats ashore, and the men who went in them found the natives had recently left the place; they also observed that the mountain was covered with monkeys. They came back, and as the coast at that part presented nothing but a chain of mountains, I concluded that further west we should find the land flatter, and consequently in all probability inhabited. Actuated by this thought I weighed anchor, and ran along the coast until we came to the end of the cordillera; I then anchored at the mouth of a river, and we were soon visited by a great number of the inhabitants, who informed us, that the country was called Paria, and that further westward it was more fully peopled. I took four of these natives, and proceeded on my westward voyage; and when I had gone eight leagues further, I found on the other side of a point which I called Punta de la Aguja (Needle Point) one of the most lovely countries in the world, and very thickly peopled: it was three o'clock in the morning when I reached it, and seeing its verdure and beauty, I resolved to anchor there and communicate with the inhabitants. Some of the natives soon came out to the ship, in canoes, to beg me, in the name of their king, to go on shore; and when they saw that I paid no attention to them, they came to the ship in their canoes in countless numbers, many of them wearing pieces of gold on their breasts, and some with bracelets of pearls on their arms; on seeing which I was much delighted, and made many inquiries with the view of learning where they found them. They informed me, that they were to be procured in their own neighbourhood, and also northward of that country. I would have remained here, but the provisions of corn, and wine, and meats, which I had brought out with so much care for the people whom I had left behind, were nearly wasted, so that all my anxiety was to get them into a place of safety, and not to stop for any thing. I wished, however, to get some of the pearls that I had seen, and with that view sent the boats on shore. The natives are very numerous, and all handsome in person, and of the same colour as the Indians we had already seen; they are, moreover, very affable, and received our men who went on shore most courteously, seeming very well disposed towards us. These men relate, that when the boats reached the shore, two of the chiefs, whom they took to be father and son, came forward in advance of the mass of the people, and conducted them to a very large house with façades, and not round and tent-shaped as the other houses were; in this house were many seats, on which they made our men sit down, they themselves sitting with them. They then caused bread to be brought, with many kinds of fruits, and various sorts of wine, both white and red, not made of grapes, but apparently produced from different fruits. The most reasonable inference is, that they use maize, which is a plant that bears an ear like that of wheat, some of which I took with me to Spain, where it now grows abundantly; the best of this they seemed to regard as most excellent, and set a great value upon it. The men remained together at one end of the house, and the women at the other. Great vexation was felt by both parties that they could not understand each other, for they were mutually anxious to make in-

quiries respecting each other's country. After our men had been entertained at the house of the elder Indian, the younger took them
to his house, and gave them an equally cordial reception; after which
they returned to their boats and came on board. I weighed anchor
forthwith, for I was hastened by my anxiety to save the provisions
which were becoming spoiled, and which I had procured and preserved with so much care and trouble, as well as to attend to my own
health, which had been affected by long watching; and although
on my former voyage, when I went out to discover terra firma, I
passed thirty-three days without natural rest, and was all that time
without seeing it, yet never were my eyes so much affected with
bleeding or so painful as at this period. These people, as I have
already said, are very graceful in form, — tall, and lithe in their movements, and wear their hair very long and smooth. They also bind their
heads with handsome worked handkerchiefs, which from a distance
look like silk or gauze; others use the same material in a longer form,
wound round them so as to cover them like trousers, and this is
done by both the men and the women. These people are of a whiter
skin than any I have seen in the Indies. It is the fashion among all
classes to wear something at the breast, and on the arms, and many
wear pieces of gold hanging low on the bosom. Their canoes are
larger, lighter, and of better build than those of the islands which I
have hitherto seen, and in the middle of each they have a cabin or
room, which I found was occupied by the chiefs and their wives. I
called this place "Jardines," that is "the Gardens," for it corre-
sponded to that appellation. I made many inquiries as to where they
found the gold, in reply to which, all of them directed me to an
elevated tract of land at no great distance, on the confines of their
country, lying to the westward; but they all advised me not to go
there, for fear of being eaten, and at the time, I imagined that by
their description they wished to imply, that they were cannibals who
dwelt there, but I have since thought it possible, that they meant
merely to express, that the country was filled with beasts of prey.
I also inquired of them where they obtained the pearls, and in reply
to this question likewise, they directed me to the westward, and
also to the north, behind the country they occupied. I did not put
this information to the test, on account of the provisions, and the
weakness of my eyes, and because the large ship that I had with me
was not calculated for such an undertaking. The short time that I
spent with them was all passed in putting questions; and at the hour

of vespers [six P.M.], as I have already said, we returned to the ships, upon which I weighed anchor and sailed to the westward. I proceeded onwards on the following day, until I found that we were only in three fathoms of water; at this time I was still under the idea that it was but an island, and that I should be able to make my exit by the north. With this view I sent a light caravel in advance of us, to see whether there was any exit, or whether the passage was closed. The caravel proceeded a great distance, until it reached a very large gulf, in which there appeared to be four smaller gulfs, from one of which debouched a large river. They invariably found ground at five fathoms, and a great quantity of very fresh water, indeed, I never tasted any equal to it. I was very disappointed when I found that I could make no exit, either by the north, south, or west, but that I was enclosed on all three sides by land. I therefore weighed anchor, and sailed in a backward direction, with the hope of finding a passage to the north by the strait, which I have already described; but I could not return along the inhabited part where I had already been, on account of the currents, which drove me entirely out of my course. But constantly, at every headland, I found the water sweet and clear, and we were carried eastwards very powerfully towards the two straits already mentioned. I then conjectured, that the currents and the overwhelming mountains of water which rushed into these straits with such an awful roaring, arose from the contest between the fresh water and the sea. The fresh water struggled with the salt to oppose its entrance, and the salt contended against the fresh in its efforts to gain a passage outwards. I also formed the conjecture, that at one time there was a continuous neck of land from the island of Trinidad to the land of Gracia, where the two straits now are, as your Highnesses will see, by the drawing which accompanies this letter. I passed out by this northern strait, and found the fresh water come even there; and when, by the force of the wind, I was enabled to effect a passage, I remarked, while on one of the watery billows which I have described, that the water on the inner side of the current was fresh, and on the outside salt.

* * *

. . . Ptolemy and the other philosophers, who have written upon the globe, thought that it was spherical, believing that this hemisphere was round as well as that in which they themselves dwelt, the centre of which was in the island of Arin which is under the equinoctial line between the Arabian Gulf and the Gulf of Persia; and the circle passes over Cape St. Vincent, in Portugal, westward, and eastward, by Cangara and the Seras, in which hemisphere I make no difficulty as to its being a perfect sphere as they describe; but this western half of the world, I maintain, is like the half of a very round pear, having a raised projection for the stalk, as I have already described, or like a woman's nipple on a round ball. Ptolemy and the others who have written upon the globe, had no information respecting this part of the world, which was then unexplored; they only established their arguments with respect to their own hemisphere, which, as I have already said, is half of a perfect sphere. And now that your Highnesses have commissioned me to make this voyage of discovery, the truths which I have stated are evidently proved, because in this voyage, when I was off the island of Hargin, and its vicinity, which is twenty degrees to the north of the equinoctial line, I found the people are black, and the land very much burnt; and when after that I went to the Cape Verde islands, I found the people there much darker still, and the more southward we went, the more they approach the extreme of blackness; so that when I reached the parallel of Sierra Leone, where, as night came on, the north star rose five degrees, the people there were excessively black; and as I sailed westward, the heat became extreme. But after I had passed the meridian, or line which I have already described, I found the climate become gradually more temperate; so that when I reached the island of Trinidad, where the north star rose five degrees as night came on, there, and in the land of Gracia, I found the temperature exceedingly mild; the fields and the foliage likewise were remarkably fresh and green, and as beautiful as the gardens of Valencia in April. The people there are very graceful in form, less dark than those whom I had before seen in the Indies, and wear their hair long and smooth; they are also more shrewd, intelligent, and courageous. The sun was then in the sign of Virgo, over our heads and theirs; therefore, all this must proceed from the extreme blandness of the temperature, which arises, as I have said, from this country being the most elevated in the world, and the nearest to the sky. On these grounds, therefore, I affirm, that the globe is not spherical, but that there is the difference in its form which I have described; the which is to be found in this hemisphere, at the point where the Indies meet the ocean, the extremity of the hemisphere being below the equinoctial line. And a great confirmation of this is, that when our Lord made the sun, the first light appeared in the first point of the east, where the most elevated point of the globe is; and although it was the opinion of Aristotle, that the antarctic pole, or the land under it, was the highest part of the world, and the nearest to the heavens, other philosophers oppose him, and say, that the highest part was below the arctic pole, by which reasoning it appears, that they understood, that one part of the world must be loftier, and nearer the sky, than the other; but it never struck them that it might be under the equinoctial, in the way that I have said, which is not to be wondered at, because they had no certain knowledge respecting this hemisphere, but merely vague suppositions, for no one has ever gone or been sent to investigate the matter, until now that your Highnesses have sent me to explore both the sea and the land.

*　　*　　*

I do not find, nor have ever found, any account by the Romans or Greeks, which fixes in a positive manner the site of the terrestrial paradise, neither have I seen it given in any mappe-monde, laid down from authentic sources. Some placed it in Ethiopia, at the sources of the Nile, but others, traversing all these countries, found neither the temperature nor the altitude of the sun correspond with their ideas respecting it; nor did it appear that the overwhelming waters of the deluge had been there. Some pagans pretended to adduce arguments to establish that it was in the Fortunate Islands, now called the Canaries, etc.

St. Isidore, Bede, Strabo, and the Master of scholastic history, with St. Ambrose, and Scotus, and all the learned theologians, agree that the earthly paradise is in the east, etc.

I have already described my ideas concerning this hemisphere and its form, and I have no doubt, that if I could pass below the equinoctial line, after reaching the highest point of which I have spoken, I should find a much milder temperature, and a variation in the stars and in the water; not that I suppose that elevated point to be navigable, nor even that there is water there; indeed, I believe it is impossible to ascend thither, because I am convinced that it is the spot of the earthly paradise, whither no one can go but by God's permission; but this land which your Highnesses have now sent me to explore, is very extensive, and I think there are many other countries in the south, of which the world has never had any knowledge.

I do not suppose that the earthly paradise is in the form of a rugged mountain, as the descriptions of it have made it appear, but that it is on the summit of the spot, which I have described as being in the form of the stalk of a pear; the approach to it from a distance must be by a constant and gradual ascent; but I believe that, as I have already said, no one could ever reach the top; I think also, that the water I have described may proceed from it, though it be far off, and that stopping at the place which I have just left, it forms this lake. There are great indications of this being the terrestrial paradise, for its site coincides with the opinion of the holy and wise theologians whom I have mentioned; and moreover, the other evidences agree with the supposition, for I have never either read or heard of fresh water coming in so large a quantity, in close conjunction with the water of the sea; the idea is also corroborated by the blandness of the temperature; and if the water of which I speak, does not proceed from the earthly paradise, it seems to be a still greater wonder, for I do not believe that there is any river in the world so large or so deep.

When I left the Dragon's Mouth, which is the northernmost of the two straits which I have described, and which I so named on the day of our Lady of August, I found that the sea ran so strongly to the westward, that between the hour of mass, when I weighed anchor, and the hour of complines, I made sixty-five leagues of four miles each; and not only was the wind not violent, but on the contrary very gentle, which confirmed me in the conclusion, that in sailing southward, there is a continuous ascent, while there is a corresponding descent towards the north.

I hold it for certain, that the waters of the sea move from east to west with the sky, and that in passing this track, they hold a more rapid course, and have thus eaten away large tracts of land, and hence has resulted this great number of islands; indeed, these islands themselves afford an additional proof of it, for on the one hand all those which lie west and east, or a little more obliquely north-west and south-east, are broad; while those which lie north and south, or north-east and south-west, that is, in a directly contrary direction to the said winds, are narrow; furthermore, that these islands should possess the most costly productions, is to be accounted for by the mild temperature, which comes to them from heaven, since these are the most elevated parts of the world. It is true, that in some parts, the waters do not appear to take this course, but this only occurs in certain spots, where they are obstructed by land, and hence they appear to take different directions.

Pliny writes that the sea and land together form a sphere, but that the ocean forms the greatest mass, and lies uppermost, while the earth is below and supports the ocean, and that the two afford a mutual support to each other, as the kernel of a nut is confined by its shell. The Master of scholastic history, in commenting upon Genesis, says, that the waters are not very extensive; and that although when they were first created they covered the earth, they were yet vaporous like a cloud, and that afterwards they became condensed, and occupied but small space, and in this notion Nicolas de Lira agrees. Aristotle says that the world is small, and the water very limited in extent, and that it is easy to pass from Spain to the Indies; and this is confirmed by Avenruyz, and by the Cardinal Pedro de Aliaco, who, in supporting this opinion, shows that it agrees with that of Seneca, and says that Aristotle had been enabled to gain information respecting the world by means of Alexander the Great, and Seneca by means of the Emperor Nero, and Pliny through the Romans; all of them having expended large sums of money, and employed a vast number of people, in diligent inquiry concerning the secrets of the world, and in spreading abroad the knowledge thus obtained. The said cardinal allows to these writers greater authority than to Ptolemy, and other Greeks and Arabs; and in confirmation of their opinion concerning the small quantity of water on the surface of the globe, and the limited amount of land covered by that water, in comparison of what had been related on the authority of Ptolemy and his disciples, he finds a passage in the third book of Esdras, where that sacred writer says, that of seven parts of the world six are discovered, and the other is covered with water. The authority of the third and fourth books of Esdras is also confirmed by holy persons, such as St. Augustin, and St. Ambrose in his *Exameron,* where he says, — "Here my son Jesus shall first come, and here my son Christ shall die!" These holy men say that Esdras was a prophet as well as Zacharias, the father of St. John, and *El Braso* Simon; authorities which are also quoted by Francis de Mairones. With respect to the dryness of the land, experience has shown that it is greater than is commonly believed; and this is no wonder, for the further one goes the more one learns.

I now return to my subject of the land of Gracia, and of the river and lake found there, which latter might more properly be called a sea; for a lake is but a small expanse of water, which, when it becomes great, deserves the name of a sea, just as we speak of the Sea af Galilee and the Dead Sea; and I think that if the river mentioned does not proceed from the terrestrial paradise, it comes from an immense tract of land situated in the south, of which no knowledge has been hitherto obtained. But the more I reason on the subject, the more satisfied I become that the terrestrial paradise is situated in the spot I have described; and I ground my opinion upon the arguments and authorities already quoted. May it please the Lord to grant your Highnesses a long life, and health and peace to follow out so noble an investigation; in which I think our Lord will receive great service, Spain considerable increase of its greatness, and all Christians much consolation and pleasure, because by this means the name of our Lord will be published abroad.

In all the countries visited by your Highnesses' ships, I have caused a high cross to be fixed upon every headland, and have proclaimed, to every nation that I have discovered, the lofty estate of your Highnesses, and of your court in Spain. I also tell them all I can respecting our holy faith and of the belief in the holy mother Church, which has its members in all the world; and I speak to them also of the courtesy and nobleness of all Christians, and of the faith they have in the Holy Trinity. May it please the Lord to forgive those who have calumniated and still calumniate this excellent enterprise, and oppose and have opposed its advancement, without considering how much glory and greatness will accrue from it to your Highnesses throughout all the world. They cannot state anything in disparagement of it, except its expense, and that I have not immediately sent back the ships loaded with gold. They speak this without considering the shortness of the time, and how many difficulties there are to contend with; and that every year there are individuals who singly earn by their deserts out of your Majesties' own household, more revenue than would cover the whole of this expense. Nor do they take into consideration that the princes of Spain have never gained possession of any land out of their own country, until now that your Highnesses have become the masters of another world, where our holy faith may become so much increased, and whence such stores of wealth may be derived; for although we have not sent home ships laden with gold, we have, nevertheless, sent satisfactory samples, both of gold and of other valuable commodities, by which it may be judged that in a short time large profit may be derived. Neither do they take into consideration the noble spirit of the princes of Portugal, who so long ago carried into execution the exploration of Guinea, and still follow it up along the coast of Africa, in which one-half of the population of the country has been employed, and yet the King is more determined on the enterprise than ever. The Lord grant all that I have said, and lead them to think deeply upon what I have written; which is not the thousandth part of what might be written of the deeds of princes who have set their minds upon gaining knowledge, and upon obtaining territory and keeping it.

I say all this, not because I doubt the inclination of your Highnesses to pursue the enterprise while you live, — for I rely confidently on the answers your Highnesses once gave me by word of mouth, — nor because I have seen any change in your Highnesses, but from the fear of what I have heard from those of whom I have been speaking; for I know that water dropping on a stone will at length make a hole. Your Highnesses responded to me with that nobleness of feeling which all the world knows you to possess, and told me to pay no attention to these calumniations; for that your intention was to follow up and support the undertaking, even if nothing were gained by it but stones and sand. Your Highnesses also desired me to be in no way anxious about the expense, for that much greater cost had been incurred on much more trifling matters, and that you considered all the past and future expense as well laid out; for that your Highnesses believed that our holy faith would be increased, and your royal dignity enhanced, and that they were no friends of the royal estate who spoke ill of the enterprise.

And now, during the despatch of the information respecting these lands which I have recently discovered, and where I believe in my soul that the earthly paradise is situated, the "Adelantado" will proceed with three ships, well stocked with provisions, on a further investigation, and will make all the discoveries he can about these parts. Meanwhile, I shall send your Highnesses this letter, accompanied by a map of the country, and your Majesties will determine on what is to be done, and give your orders as to how it is your pleasure that I should proceed: the which, by the aid of the Holy Trinity, shall be carried into execution with all possible diligence, in the faithful service and to the entire satisfaction of your Majesties. Thanks be to God.

10

Erasmus on the Follies of His Age

LIKE ITS TITLE, Moriae Encomium, which means "Praise of (Thomas) More" as well as "Praise of Folly," this little book of 1511 must be understood in more than one sense. It is not only a lampoon of human foibles; it is also a sympathetic statement of the human condition, to be compared to those of Petrarch, Vives, and Montaigne, and it is a work of social criticism. In this selection Erasmus reminds the humanists, the Stoics, and the scientists of the irrationalities which make life possible; but in a later part of the book he bitterly criticizes the follies of churchmen and others and he ends with a eulogy of the unworldly "foolishness" of Christian teaching.

Desiderius Erasmus (1469–1536), The Praise of Folly

An oration, of feigned matter, spoken by Folly in her own person

AT WHAT RATE SOEVER the world talks of me (for I am not ignorant what an ill report Folly has got, even among the most foolish), yet that I am that she, that only she, whose deity recreates both gods and men, even this is a sufficient argument, that I no sooner stepped up to speak to this full assembly than all your faces put on a kind of new and unwonted pleasantness. So suddenly have you cleared your brows, and with so frolic and hearty a laughter given me your applause, that in troth as many of you as I behold on every side of me, seem to me no less than Homer's gods drunk with nectar and nepenthe; whereas before, you sat as lumpish and pensive as if you had come from consulting an oracle. And as it usually happens when the sun begins to show his beams, or when after a sharp winter the spring breathes afresh on the earth, all things immediately get a new face, new colour, and recover as it were a

From John Wilson, trans., THE PRAISE OF FOLLY (London, 1668), pp. 7–8, 11–12, 15–16, 26, 46–49, 51–60.

certain kind of youth again, in like manner, by but beholding me you have in an instant gotten another kind of countenance; and so what the otherwise great rhetoricians with their tedious and long-studied orations can hardly effect, to wit, to remove the trouble of the mind, I have done it at once with my single look.

But if you ask me why I appear before you in this strange dress, be pleased to lend me your ears, and I'll tell you; not those ears, I mean, you carry to church, but abroad with you, such as you are wont to prick up to jugglers, fools, and buffoons, and such as our friend Midas once gave to Pan. For I am disposed awhile to play the sophister with you; not of their sort who nowadays boozle young men's heads with certain empty notions and curious trifles, yet teach them nothing but a more than womanish obstinacy of scolding; but I'll imitate those ancients who, that they might the better avoid that infamous appellation of *sophi,* or *wise,* chose rather to be called sophisters. Their business was to celebrate the praises of the gods and valiant men. And the like encomium shall you hear from me, but neither of Hercules nor Solon, but my own dear self, that is to say, Folly. . . .

*   *   *

Nor will it be amiss also to imitate the rhetoricians of our times, who think themselves in a manner gods if like horse leeches they can but appear to be double-tongued, and believe they have done a mighty act if in their Latin orations they can but shuffle in some ends of Greek like mosaic work, though altogether by head and shoulders and less to the purpose. And if they want hard words they run over some worm-eaten manuscript and pick out half a dozen of the most old and obsolete to confound their reader, believing, no doubt, that they that understand their meaning will like it the better, and they that do not will admire it the more by how much the less they understand it. Nor is this way of ours of admiring what seems most foreign without its particular grace; for if there happen to be any more ambitious than others, they may give their applause with a smile, and, like the ass, shake their ears that they may be thought to understand more than the rest of their neighbours.

*   *   *

And now, lest I may seem to have taken upon me the name of goddess without cause, you shall in the next place understand how far my deity extends and what advantage by it I have brought both to gods and men. For, if it was not unwisely said by somebody, that this only is to be a god, to help men; and if they are deservedly enrolled among the gods that first brought in corn and wine and such other things as are for the common good of mankind, why am not I of right the *alpha,* or first, of all the gods? who being but one, yet bestow all things on all men. For first, what is more sweet or more precious than life? And yet from whom can it more properly be said to come than from me? For neither the crab-favoured Pallas' spear nor the cloud-gathering Jupiter's shield either beget or propagate mankind; but even he himself, the father of gods and king of men at whose very beck the heavens shake, must lay by his forked thunder and those looks wherewith he conquered the giants and with which at pleasure he frightens the rest of the gods, and like a common stage player put on a disguise as often as he goes about that, which now and then he does, that is to say the getting of children. And the Stoics too, that conceive themselves next to the gods, yet show me one of them, nay the veriest bigot of the sect, and if he do not put off his beard, the badge of wisdom, though yet it be no more than what is common with him and goats; yet at least he must lay by his supercilious gravity, smooth his forehead, shake off his rigid principles, and for some time commit an act of folly and dotage. In fine, that wise man whoever he be, if he intends to have children, must have recourse to me. . . .

*   *   *

. . . So provident has that great parent of mankind, Nature, been that there should not be anything without its mixture and, as it were, seasoning of Folly. For since according to the definition of the Stoics, wisdom is nothing else than to be governed by reason, and on the contrary Folly, to be given up to the will of our passions, that the life of man might not be altogether disconsolate and hard to away with, of how much more passion than reason has Jupiter composed us? putting in, as one would say, "scarce half an ounce to a pound." Besides, he has confined reason to a narrow corner of the brain and left all the rest of the body to our passions; has also set up against this one, two as it were, masterless tyrants — anger, that possesses the region of the heart, and consequently the very fountain of life, the heart itself, and lust, that stretches its empire everywhere. Against which double force how powerful reason is let common experience declare, inasmuch as she, which yet is all she can do, may call out to us till she be hoarse again and tell us the rules of honesty and virtue; while they give up the reins to their governor and make a hideous clamor, till at last being wearied, he suffer himself to be carried whither they please to hurry him.

*   *   *

. . . Be present then awhile, and assist me, you daughters of Jupiter, while I make it out that there is no way to that so much famed wisdom nor access to that fortress as they call it of happiness, but under the banner of Folly. And first 'tis agreed of all hands that our passions belong to Folly, inasmuch as we judge a wise man from a fool by this, that the one is ordered by them, the other by reason; and therefore the Stoics remove from a wise man all disturbances of mind as so many diseases. But these passions do not only the office of a tutor to such as are making towards the port of wisdom, but are in every exercise of virtue as it were spurs and incentives, nay and encouragers to well doing: which though that great Stoic Seneca most strongly denies, and takes from a wise man all affections whatever, yet in doing that he leaves him not so much as a man but rather a new kind of god that was never yet nor ever like to be. Nay, to speak plainer, he sets up a stony semblance of a man, void of all sense and common feeling of humanity. And much good to them with this wise man of theirs; let them enjoy him to themselves, love him without competitors, and live with him in Plato's Commonwealth, the country of ideas, or Tantalus' orchards. For who would not shun and startle at such a man as at some unnatural accident or spirit? A man dead to all sense of nature and common affections, and no more moved with love or pity than if he were a flint or rock; whose censure nothing escapes; that commits no errors himself, but has a lynx's eyes upon others; measures everything by an exact line, and forgives nothing; pleases himself with himself only; the only rich, the only wise, the only free man, and only king; in brief, the only man that is everything, but in his own single judgment only; that cares not for the friendship of any man, being himself a friend to no man; makes no doubt to make the gods stoop to him, and condemns and laughs at the whole actions of our life? And yet such a beast is this their perfect wise man. But tell me pray, if the thing were to be carried by most voices, what city would choose him for its governor, or what army desire him for their general? What woman would have such a husband, what good fellow such a guest, or what servant would either wish or endure such a master? Nay, who had not rather have one of the middle sort of fools, who, being a fool himself, may the better know how to command or obey fools, and who though he please his like, 'tis yet the greater number; one that is kind to his wife, merry among his friends, a boon companion, and easy to be lived with; and lastly one that thinks nothing of humanity should be a stranger to him? But I am weary of this wise man, and therefore I'll proceed to some other advantages.

Go to then. Suppose a man in some lofty high tower, and that he could look round him, as the poets say Jupiter was now and then wont. To how many misfortunes would he find the life of man subject? How miserable, to say no worse, our birth, how difficult our education; to how many wrongs our childhood exposed, to what pains our youth; how unsupportable our old age, and grievous our unavoidable death? As also what troops of diseases beset us, how many casualties hang over our heads, how many troubles invade us, and how little there is that is not steeped in gall? To say nothing of those evils one man brings upon another, as poverty, imprisonment, infamy, dishonesty, racks, snares, treachery, reproaches, actions, deceits — but I'm got into as endless a work as numbering the sands — for what offenses mankind have deserved these things, or what angry god compelled them to be born into such miseries is not my present business. Yet he that shall diligently examine it with himself, would he not, think you, approve the example of the Milesian virgins and kill himself? But who are they that for no other reason but that they were weary of life have hastened their own fate? Were they not the next neighbors to wisdom? amongst whom, to say nothing of Diogenes, Xenocrates, Cato, Cassius, Brutus, that wise man Chiron, being offered immortality, chose rather to die than be troubled with the same thing always.

And now I think you see what would become of the world if all men should be wise; to wit it were necessary we got another kind of clay and some better potter. But I, partly through ignorance, partly unadvisedly, and sometimes through forgetfulness of evil, do now and then so sprinkle pleasure with the hopes of good, and sweeten men up in their greatest misfortunes, that they are not willing to leave this life, even then when according to the account of the destinies this life has left them; and by how much the less reason they have to live by so much the more they desire it; so far are they from being sensible of the least wearisomeness of life. . . .

But methinks I hear the philosophers opposing it and saying 'tis a miserable thing for a man to be foolish, to err, mistake and know nothing truly. Nay, rather this is to be a man. And why they should call it miserable, I see no reason; forasmuch as we are so born, so bred, so instructed, nay such is the common condition of us all. And nothing can be called miserable that suits with its kind, unless perhaps you'll think a man such because he can neither fly with birds nor walk on all four with beasts and is not armed with horns as a bull. For by the same reason he would call the warlike horse unfortunate, because he understood not grammar, nor ate cheesecakes; and the bull miserable, because he'd make so ill a wrestler. And therefore, as a horse that has no skill in grammar is not miserable, no more is man in this respect, for that they agree with his nature. But again, the *virtuosi* may say that there was particularly added to man the knowledge of sciences, by whose help he might recompense himself in understanding for what nature cut him short in other things. As if this had the least face of truth, that Nature that was so solicitously watchful in the production of gnats, herbs, and flowers should have so slept when she made man, that he should have need to be helped by sciences, which that old devil Theuth, the evil genius of mankind, first invented for his destruction, and are so little conducive to happiness that they rather obstruct it; to which purpose they are properly said to be first found out, as that wise king in Plato argues touching the invention of letters.

Sciences therefore crept into the world with the other pests of mankind, from the same head from whence all other mischiefs spring; we'll suppose it devils, for so the name imports when you call them demons, that is to say, 'knowing.' For that simple people of the Golden Age, being wholly ignorant of everything called learning, lived only by the guidance and dictates of nature; for what use of grammar, where every man spoke the same language and had no further design than to understand one another? What use of logic, where there was no bickering about the double-meaning words? What need of rhetoric, where there were no lawsuits? Or to what purpose laws, where there were no ill manners? from which without doubt good laws first came. Besides, they were more religious than with an impious curiosity to dive into the secrets of nature, the dimension of stars, the motions, effects, and hidden causes of things, as believing it a crime for any man to attempt to be wise beyond his condition. And as to the inquiry of what was beyond heaven, that madness never came into their heads. But the purity of the Golden Age declining by degrees, first, as I said before, arts were invented by the evil genii; and yet but few, and those too received by fewer. After that the Chaldean superstition and Greek new-fangledness, that had little to do, added I know not how many more mere torments of wit, and that so great that even grammar alone is work enough for any man for his whole life.

Though yet among these sciences those only are in esteem that come nearest to common sense, that is to say, folly. Divines are half starved, naturalists out of heart, astrologers laughed at, and logicians slighted; only the physician is worth all the rest. And among them too, the more unlearned, impudent, or unadvised he is, the more he is esteemed, even among princes. For physic, especially as it is now professed by most men, is nothing but a branch of flattery, no less than rhetoric. Next them, the second place is given to our law-drivers, if not the first, whose profession, though I say it myself, most men laugh at as the ass of philosophy; yet there's scarce any business, either so great or so small, but is managed by these asses. These purchase their great lordships, while in the meantime the divine, having run through the whole body of divinity, sits gnawing a radish and is in continual warfare with lice and fleas. As therefore those arts are best that have the nearest affinity with folly, so are they most happy of all others that have least commerce with sciences and follow the guidance of Nature, who is in no wise imperfect, unless perhaps we endeavor to leap over those bounds she has appointed to us. Nature hates all false coloring and is ever best where she is least adulterated with art.

Go to then, don't you find among the several kinds of living creatures that they thrive best that understand no more than what Nature taught them? What is more prosperous or wonderful than the bee? And though they have not the same judgment of sense as other bodies have, yet wherein has architecture gone beyond their building of houses? What philosopher ever founded the like republic? Whereas the horse, that comes so near man in understanding and is therefore so familiar with him, is also partaker of his misery. For while he thinks it a shame to lose the race, it often happens that he cracks his wind; and in the battle, while he contends for victory, he's cut down himself, and, together with his rider "lies biting the earth"; not to mention those strong bits, sharp spurs, close stables, arms, blows, rider, and briefly, all that slavery he willingly submits to, while, imitating those men of valour, he so eagerly strives to be revenged of the enemy. Than which how much more were the life of flies or birds to be wished for, who living by the instinct of nature, look no further than the present, if yet man would but let them alone in it. And if at anytime they chance to be taken, and being shut up in cages endeavor to imitate our speaking, 'tis strange how they degenerate from their native gaiety. So much better in every respect are the works of nature than the adulteries of art.

In like manner I can never sufficiently praise that Pythagoras in a dunghill cock, who being but one had been yet everything, a philosopher, a man, a woman, a king, a private man, a fish, a horse, a frog, and, I believe too, a sponge, and at last concluded that no creature was more miserable than man, for that all other creatures are content with those bounds that nature set them, only man endeavors to exceed them. And again, among men he gives the precedency not to the learned or the great, but the fool. Nor had that Gryllus less with than Ulysses with his many counsels, who chose rather to lie grunting in a hog sty than be exposed with the other to so many hazards. Nor does Homer, that father of trifles, dissent from me; who not only called all men "wretched and full of calamity," but often his great pattern of wisdom, Ulysses, "miserable"; Paris, Ajax, and Achilles nowhere. And why, I pray but that, like a cunning fellow and one that was his craft's master, he did nothing without the advice of Pallas? In a word he was too wise, and by that means ran wide of nature. As therefore among men they are least happy that study wisdom, as being in this twice fools, that when they are born men, they should yet so far forget their condition as to affect the life of gods; and after the example of the giants, with their philosophical gimcracks make a war upon nature: so they on the other side seem as little miserable as is possible who come nearest to beasts and never attempt anything beyond man. Go to then, let's try how demonstrable this is; not by enthymemes or the imperfect syllogisms of the Stoics, but by plain, downright, and ordinary examples.

And now, by the immortal gods! I think nothing more happy than that generation of men we commonly call fools, idiots, lackwits, and dolts; splendid titles too, as I conceive them. I'll tell you a thing, which at first perhaps may seem foolish and absurd, yet nothing more true. And first they are not afraid of death — no small evil, by Jupiter! They are not tormented with the conscience of evil acts, not terrified with the fables of ghosts, nor frightened with spirits and goblins. They are not distracted with the fear of evils to come nor the hopes of future good. In short, they are not disturbed with those thousand of cares to which this life is subject. They are neither modest, nor fearful, nor ambitious, nor envious, nor love they any man. And lastly, if they should come nearer even to the very ignorance of brutes, they could not sin, for so hold the divines. And now tell me, you wise fool, with how many troublesome cares your mind is continually perplexed; heap together all the discommodities of your life, and then you'll be sensible from how many evils I have delivered my fools. Add to this that they are not only merry, play, sing, and laugh themselves, but make mirth wherever they come, a special privilege it seems the gods have given them to refresh the pensiveness of life. Whence it is that whereas the world is so differently affected one towards another, that all men indifferently admit them as their companions, desire, feed, cherish, embrace them, take their parts upon all occasions, and permit them without offense to do or say what they like. And so little does everything desire to hurt them, that even the very beasts, by a kind of natural instinct of their innocence no doubt, pass by their injuries. For of them it may be truly said that they are consecrate to the gods, and therefore and not without cause do men have them in such esteem. Whence is it else that they are in so great request with princes that they can neither eat nor drink, go anywhere, or be an hour without them? Nay, and in some degree they prefer these fools before their crabbish wise men, whom yet they keep about them for state sake. Nor do I conceive the reason so difficult, or that it should seem strange why they are preferred before the others, for that these wise men speak to princes about nothing but grave, serious matters, and trusting to their own parts and learning do not fear sometimes "to grate their tender ears with smart truths"; but fools fit them with that they most delight in, as jests, laughter, abuses of other men, wanton pastimes, and the like.

Again, take notice of this no contemptible blessing which Nature has given fools, that they are the only plain, honest men and such as speak truth. And what is more commendable than truth? For though that proverb of Alcibiades in Plato attributes truth to drunkards and children, yet the praise of it is particularly mine, even from the testimony of Euripides, among whose other things there is extant that his honorable saying concerning us, "A fool speaks foolish things." For whatever a fool has in his heart, he both shows it in his looks and expresses it in his discourse; while the wise men's are those two tongues which the same Euripides mentions, whereof the one speaks truth, the other what they judge most seasonable for the occasion. These are they "that turn black into white," blow hot and cold with the same breath, and carry a far different meaning in their breast from what they feign with their tongue. Yet in the midst of all their prosperity, princes in this respect seem to me most unfortunate, because, having no one to tell them truth, they are forced to receive flatterers for friends.

But, someone may say, the ears of princes are strangers to truth, and for this reason they avoid those wise men, because they fear lest someone more frank than the rest should dare to speak to them things rather true than pleasant; for so the matter is, that they don't much care for truth. And yet this is found by experience among my fools, that not only truths but even open reproaches are heard with pleasure; so that the same thing which, if it came from a wise man's mouth might prove a capital crime, spoken by a fool is received with delight. For truth carries with it a certain peculiar power of pleasing, if no accident fall in to give occasion of offense; which faculty the gods have given only to fools. And for the same reasons is it that women are so earnestly delighted with this kind of men, as being more propense by nature to pleasure and toys. And whatsoever they may happen to do with them, although sometimes it be of the most serious, yet they turn it to jest and laughter, as that sex was ever quickwitted, especially to color their own faults.

But to return to the happiness of fools, who when they have passed over this life with a great deal of pleasantness and without so much as the least fear or sense of death, they go straight forth into the Elysian field, to recreate their pious and careless souls with such sports as they used here. Let's proceed then, and compare the condition of any of your wise men with that of this fool. Fancy to me now some example of wisdom you'd set up against him; one that had spent his childhood and youth in learning the sciences and lost the sweetest part of his life in watchings, cares, studies, and for the remaining part of it never so much as tasted the least of pleasure;

ever sparing, poor, sad, sour, unjust, and rigorous to himself, and troublesome and hateful to others; broken with paleness, leanness, crassness, sore eyes, and an old age and death contracted before their time (though yet, what matter is it, when he die that never lived?); and such is the picture of this great wise man.

11

The Dignity of Man

JUAN VIVES, A SPANIARD, wrote this fable shortly after meeting Erasmus in 1518. It is a charming rendition of the theme, widespread in the Renaissance, of man's godlike ability to shape himself to whatever form he chooses. The most famous version of the theme is Pico della Mirandola's Oration on the Dignity of Man of 1486, from which Vives obviously drew; but Vives' fable contains some ideas not in Pico's oration, such as the representation of human life as a theater. Its simplicity is deceptive, for it masks certain important theological positions: predestination, man's distinctive nature — or rather his lack of one — and man's power to ascend to heaven by human efforts alone. As a statement of the human condition, Vives' fable represents a point of view considerably different from Erasmus' Praise of Folly and Montaigne's Essays.

Juan Luis Vives (1492–1540), A Fable about Man

I SHOULD like to begin this essay of mine on man by some fables and plays, since man is himself a fable and a play. Once upon a time, after a certain lavish and sumptuous feast given by Juno on her birthday for all the gods, they, feeling carefree and elated by the nectar, asked whether she had prepared some plays which they might watch after the banquet. Thus nothing would be lacking to complete their happiness on this august occasion.

To gratify this wish of the immortal gods, Juno earnestly asked her brother and husband Jupiter, since he was all-powerful, to improvise an amphitheater and to bring forth new characters, after the manner of regular plays, lest in this respect a day which she wanted most distinguished seem deficient to the gods. Thereupon, all of a sudden, at a command of almighty Jupiter, by whom alone

From E. Cassirer, P. O. Kristeller, and J. H. Randall, Jr., eds., THE RENAISSANCE PHILOSOPHY OF MAN (Chicago, 1948), pp. 387–393. Translation by Nancy Lenkeith. Reprinted by permission of University of Chicago Press.

all things are done, this whole world appeared, so large, so elaborate, so diversified, and beautiful in places, just as you see it. This was the amphitheater: uppermost, to wit in the skies, were the stalls and seats of the divine spectators; nethermost — some say in the middle — the earth was placed as a stage for the appearance of the actors, along with all the animals and everything else.

When everything was ready and the banquet tables carried away, Mercurius Braubeta announced that the players were already on the stage. Joyfully the spectators went forth and were seated, each according to his rank. The great Jupiter was director of the plays, and when he saw that all were there, he gave the signal. Since he was the maker, he ordered everything and explained it to all that they might understand. Lest something be done differently from what he himself liked, he prescribed to the company of actors the entire arrangement and sequence of the plays, from which not even by the breadth of a finger, as they say, should they depart.

Indeed, as soon as the voice and signal of the great Jupiter reached the actors, each in their turn they came onto the stage, and there with such skill and poise, and so much in the manner of Roscius, did they perform tragedies, comedies, satires, mimes, farces, and other things of the sort that the gods swore that a more beautiful spectacle they had never beheld. Overjoyed at the delight and satisfaction of the gods, and quite elated herself, Juno kept asking them, one by one, how they liked the games. All agreed wholeheartedly that there had never been a more admirable spectacle, nothing worthier of Juno herself and of the birthday which they were celebrating.

This greatest spouse of the greatest god could not contain her excitement; briskly she would skip among the stalls of the immortal gods and, besides other things, repeatedly asked everyone which of the actors they considered the greatest. The wisest of the gods answered that none was more praiseworthy than man, and the father of the gods himself nodded his assent. Indeed, the more intently they watched the gestures, the words, and all the actions of this character, the greater was the astonishment that struck them. It pleased Jupiter to see so much admiration and praise given to man, his own offspring, by all the gods.

Those who sat at Jupiter's side, seeing how much pleasure he took in this human archmime, easily understood that he himself had made this personage; nay, looking more carefully, they recognized in man himself a great resemblance to Jupiter, so that even the dullest of gods might have known that man was born of Jupiter. Verily, man, peering oft through the mask which hides him, almost ready to burst forth and revealing himself distinctly in many things, is divine and Jupiter-like, participating in the immortality of Jupiter himself, in his wisdom, prudence, memory, sharing so many of his talents that it was easy to know that these great gifts had been bestowed upon him by Jupiter from out of his treasury and even from his own person.

Then, as he of gods the greatest, embracing all things in his might, is all things, they saw man, Jupiter's mime, be all things also. He would change himself so as to appear under the mask of a plant, acting a simple life without any power of sensation. Soon after, he withdrew and returned on the stage as a moral satirist, brought into the shapes of a thousand wild beasts: namely, the angry and raging lion, the rapacious and devouring wolf, the fierce and wild boar, the cunning little fox, the lustful and filthy sow, the timid hare, the envious dog, the stupid donkey. After doing this, he was out of sight for a short time; then the curtain was drawn back and he returned a man, prudent, just, faithful, human, kindly, and friendly, who went about the cities with the others, held the authority and obeyed in turn, cared for the public interest and welfare, and was finally in every way a political and social being.

The gods were not expecting to see him in more shapes when, behold, he was remade into one of their own race, surpassing the nature of man and relying entirely upon a very wise mind. O great Jupiter, what a spectacle for them! At first they were astonished that they, too, should be brought to the stage and impersonated by such a convincing mime, whom they said to be that multiform Proteus, the son of the Ocean. Thereupon there was an unbelievable outburst of applause, and they prevented that great player from acting any longer. They begged Juno to let him into the stalls of the gods, unmasked, and to make of him a spectator rather than an actor. She was already eagerly going about obtaining this of her husband, when at that very moment, man came out upholding the great Jupiter, the worthiest of gods, and with marvelous and indescribable gestures impersonating his father. He had transcended the characters of the lower gods and was piercing into that inaccessible light surrounded by darkness where Jupiter dwells, of kings and gods the king.

When the gods first saw him, they were roused and upset at the thought that their master and father had stooped to the stage. Soon, however, with composed minds, they glanced repeatedly at Jupiter's stall wondering whether he himself was sitting there or whether he had appeared masked to play a part. Seeing him there, they gazed back again at man and then at Jupiter. With such skill and propriety did he play Jupiter's part that, up and down, from Jupiter's stall to the stage, they kept glancing, lest they be misled by a likeness or the accurate mimic of an actor. Among the other players there were some who swore that this was not man but Jupiter himself, and they underwent severe punishment for their error.

Yet the gods, out of respect for this image of the father of all gods, and by their own suffrage, unanimously decreed that divine honors be granted to man. They prevailed upon Jupiter, through Juno's intercession, that man, who had so rightly played the parts of Jupiter and the gods, put off his mask and be seated among the gods. Jupiter complied with the gods, granting them what he himself, long before, had decided to bestow gratuitously upon man. Thus man was recalled from the stage, seated by Mercury among the gods, and proclaimed victor. There were no cheers to greet him but a silence of wonder. The whole man lay bare, showing the immortal gods his nature akin to theirs, this nature which, covered with mask and body, had made of him an animal so diverse, so desultory, so changing like a polypus and a chameleon, as they had seen him on the stage. Jupiter was then declared and proclaimed the father not only of the gods but also of men. With a gentle and mild countenance, he took delight in both, and was hailed and adored as a parent by both. With pleasure he received this august double name; and now, using also this favored title, we proclaim him of gods and men the father.

Now, when Mercury first came into the stalls of the gods, carrying in his arms the stage costumes, the gods looked at them with great interest; having examined them attentively, a long while, they praised Jupiter's wisdom and skill and adored him, for the costumes which he had made were no less appropriate than useful for all the acts. There was the lofty head, stronghold and court of the divine mind; in it the five senses arranged and placed ornately and usefully. The ears, accordingly, did not droop with soft skin, nor were they firmly fixed with a hard bone, but both were rounded by a sinuous cartilage. Thus they could receive sounds from all directions, and the dust, straw, fluff, gnats which might be flying around would not penetrate into the head but be caught in the folds. The eyes in equal number, two indeed, were high up so that they could observe all things and protected by a fine wall of lashes and eyelids against the same bits of straw and fluff, dust and tiny insects. They were the gauge of the soul and the noblest part of the human face. Then came the very attire of the mask or the mask itself, so handsomely shaped, divided into arms and legs which were long and ending with fingers, so good-looking and useful for all purposes. As there is no time to go through all that which others have related at great length, I shall add this conclusion. All is so well fitted and interrelated that if one were to withdraw or change or add something, all that harmony and beauty and the whole efficacy would be immediately lost. By no ingenuity could a more appropriate mask be conceived for a man, unless someone perhaps wish for the impossible.

When the gods saw man and embraced their brother, they deemed it unworthy of him to appear on a stage and practice the disreputable art of the theater, and they could not find enough praise for their own likeness and that of their father. They investigated one by one and examined the many hidden secrets of man and derived more pleasure from this than from the spectacle of all the plays, "Nor having seen him once are they content; they wish to linger on." There indeed was a mind full of wisdom, prudence, knowledge, reason, so fertile that by itself it brought forth extraordinary things. Its inventions are: towns and houses, the use of herbs, stones and metals, the designations and names of all things, which foremost among his other inventions have especially caused wise men to wonder. Next and no less important, with a few letters he was able to comprise the immense variety of the sounds of the human voice. With these letters so many doctrines were fixed in writing and transmitted, including religion itself and the knowledge and cult of Jupiter the father and of the other brother-gods. This one thing, which is found in no other animal but man, shows his relationship to the gods. Of little good would all these inventions have been if there had not been added, as the treasury of all things and for the safe-keeping of these divine riches, a memory, the storehouse of all that we have enumerated. From religion and memory, foreknowledge is almost obtained, with the prophecy of the future, evidently a spark of that divine and immense science which perceives all future events as if they were present.

The gods were gazing at these and other things, as yet sateless; just as those who contemplate their beautiful reflection in a mirror take delight in these things and willingly tarry on, so the gods, seeing themselves and Jupiter their father so well portrayed in man, wished to look more and more at what they had already beheld, inquiring about one thing after another. How did he act plants, herbs, even wild animals, man, gods, the god king Jupiter, by what craft and gesture?

While man explained all this calmly and clearly, Jupiter ordered that ambrosia and nectar from the remains of the feast be placed before him. Cheerfully neglecting the plays, many of the gods had their afternoon refreshment with him. They were charmed by their brotherly guest or fellow-citizen, who, refreshed by heavenly victuals after the toil of the plays, wrapped like the other gods in the purple *praetexta* and bearing the crown, went forth to watch the spectacle. Many of the gods stood up for him, many gave up their seats. In different directions they pulled his cloak and retarded his progress that he might stay next to them, until the great Jupiter nodded to Mercury, who led him, that he was to be received in the orchestra among the gods of the first rank, who considered this a great honor. Far was it from those gods of the highest order to despise man, who had been an actor a short time before. He was received by them with respect and invited to the front seats. He sat in their company and watched the games which proceeded without interruption, until Apollo himself reduced the light at Juno's request (for the masters of the feast and other servants, warned by the cooks, announced that supper was more than ready), and night fell upon them. Chandeliers, torches, wax tapers, candlesticks, and oil lamps brought by the stars were lighted, and they were entertained at supper with the same pomp as they had been at dinner. Juno also invited man, and Jupiter the father "assented and with a nod made all Olympus tremble."

Man, just as he had watched the plays with the highest gods, now reclined with them at the banquet. He put on his mask, which he had meanwhile laid aside, for this stage costume was so greatly honored. Since it had so well met the needs of man, it was deemed worthy of the most sumptuous feast and of the table of the gods. Thus it was given the power of perception and enjoyed the eternal bliss of the banquet.

12

Machiavelli on Republics

To MOST PEOPLE Machiavelli was the cynical author of an amoral book, The Prince, in which he discussed how to gain and how to keep power. But Machiavelli was a many-sided man. He also wrote history, bawdy plays, and religious poetry. Moreover, his real labor of love was The Discourses, a treatise on republics which he worked on during the years of his involuntary retirement from service in the Florentine government after the Medici returned to power in 1512. In The Discourses Machiavelli shows his love of liberty as well as his pessimism, his faith in a government of laws as well as his unsentimental attitude towards the use of naked power. Whether he reconciled these dichotomies, and with what constructive results, has always been a matter for argument.

Niccolò Machiavelli (1469–1527), Discourses, First Book

Introduction

ALTHOUGH the envious nature of men, so prompt to blame and so slow to praise, makes the discovery and introduction of any new principles and systems as dangerous almost as the exploration of unknown seas and continents, yet, animated by that desire which impels me to do what may prove for the common benefit of all, I have resolved to open a new route, which has not yet been followed by any one, and may prove difficult and troublesome, but may also bring me some reward in the approbation of those who will kindly appreciate my efforts.

And if my poor talents, my little experience of the present and insufficient study of the past, should make the result of my labors defective and of little utility, I shall at least have shown the way to others, who will carry out my views with greater ability, eloquence,

From Niccolò Machiavelli, THE PRINCE AND THE DISCOURSES (New York, 1940), pp. 103–105, 110–117, 121–124, 138–141. Translation by Christian E. Detmold. Reprinted by permission of The Modern Library.

and judgment, so that if I do not merit praise, I ought at least not to incur censure.

When we consider the general respect for antiquity, and how often — to say nothing of other examples — a great price is paid for some fragments of an antique statue, which we are anxious to possess to ornament our houses with, or to give to artists who strive to imitate them in their own works; and when we see, on the other hand, the wonderful examples which the history of ancient kingdoms and republics presents to us, the prodigies of virtue and of wisdom displayed by the kings, captains, citizens, and legislators who have sacrificed themselves for their country, — when we see these, I say, more admired than imitated, or so much neglected that not the least trace of this ancient virtue remains, we cannot but be at the same time as much surprised as afflicted. The more so as in the differences which arise between citizens, or in the maladies to which they are subjected, we see these same people have recourse to the judgments and the remedies prescribed by the ancients. The civil laws are in fact nothing but decisions given by their jurisconsults, and which, reduced to a system, direct our modern jurists in their decisions. And what is the science of medicine, but the experience of ancient physicians, which their successors have taken for their guide? And yet to found a republic, maintain states, to govern a kingdom, organize an army, conduct a war, dispense justice, and extend empires, you will find neither prince, nor republic, nor captain, nor citizen, who has recourse to the examples of antiquity! This neglect, I am persuaded, is due less to the weakness to which the vices of our education have reduced the world, than to the evils caused by the proud indolence which prevails in most of the Christian states, and to the lack of real knowledge of history, the true sense of which is not known, or the spirit of which they do not comprehend. Thus the majority of those who read it take pleasure only in the variety of the events which history relates, without ever thinking of imitating the noble actions, deeming that not only difficult, but impossible; as though heaven, the sun, the elements, and men had changed the order of their motions and power, and were different from what they were in ancient times.

Wishing, therefore, so far as in me lies, to draw mankind from this error, I have thought it proper to write upon those books of Titus Livius that have come to us entire despite the malice of time; touching upon all those matters which, after a comparison between the ancient and modern events, may seem to me necessary to facilitate their proper understanding. In this way those who read my remarks may derive those advantages which should be the aim of all study of history; and although the undertaking is difficult, yet, aided by those who have encouraged me in this attempt, I hope to carry it sufficiently far, so that but little may remain for others to carry it to its destined end.

*   *   *

Chapter ii, of the different kinds of republics, and of what kind the Roman republic was

I WILL leave aside what might be said of cities which from their very birth have been subject to a foreign power, and will speak only of those whose origin has been independent, and which from the first governed themselves by their own laws, whether as republics or as principalities, and whose constitution and laws have differed as their origin. Some have had at the very beginning, or soon after, a legislator, who, like Lycurgus with the Lacedæmonians, gave them by a single act all the laws they needed. Others have owed theirs to chance and to events, and have received their laws at different times, as Rome did. It is a great good fortune for a republic to have a legislator sufficiently wise to give her laws so regulated that, without the necessity of correcting them, they afford security to those who live under them. Sparta observed her laws for more than eight hundred years without altering them and without experiencing a single dangerous disturbance. Unhappy, on the contrary, is that republic which, not having at the beginning fallen into the hands of a sagacious and skilful legislator, is herself obliged to reform her laws. More unhappy still is that republic which from the first has diverged from a good constitution. And that republic is furthest from it whose vicious institutions impede her progress, and make her leave the right path that leads to a good end; for those who are in that condition can hardly ever be brought into the right road. Those republics, on the other hand, that started without having even a perfect constitution, but made a fair beginning, and are capable of improvement, — such republics, I say, may perfect themselves by the aid of events. It is very true, however, that such reforms are never effected without danger, for the majority of men never willingly adopt any new law tending to change the constitution of the state, unless the necessity of the change is clearly demonstrated; and as such a necessity cannot make itself felt without being accompanied with danger, the republic may easily be destroyed before having perfected its constitution. That of Florence is a complete proof of this: reorganized after the revolt of Arezzo, in 1502, it was overthrown after the taking of Prato, in 1512.

Having proposed to myself to treat of the kind of government established at Rome, and of the events that led to its perfection, I must at the beginning observe that some of the writers on politics distinguished three kinds of government, viz. the monarchical, the aristocratic, and the democratic; and maintain that the legislators of a people must choose from these three the one that seems to them most suitable. Other authors, wiser according to the opinion of many, count six kinds of governments, three of which are very bad, and three good in themselves, but so liable to be corrupted that they become absolutely bad. The three good ones are those which we have just named; the three bad ones result from the degradation of the other three, and each of them resembles its corresponding original, so that the transition from the one to the other is very easy. Thus monarchy becomes tyranny; aristocracy degenerates into oligarchy; and the popular government lapses readily into licentiousness. So that a legislator who gives to a state which he founds, either of these three forms of government, constitutes it but for a brief time; for no precautions can prevent either one of the three that are reputed good, from degenerating into its opposite kind; so great are in these the attractions and resemblances between the good and the evil.

Chance has given birth to these different kinds of governments amongst men; for at the beginning of the world the inhabitants were few in number, and lived for a time dispersed, like beasts. As the human race increased, the necessity for uniting themselves for defence made itself felt; the better to attain this object, they chose the strongest and most courageous from amongst themselves and placed him at their head, promising to obey him. Thence they began to know the good and the honest, and to distinguish them from the bad and vicious; for seeing a man injure his benefactor aroused at once two sentiments in every heart, hatred against the ingrate and love for the benefactor. They blamed the first, and on the contrary honored those the more who showed themselves grateful, for each felt that he in turn might be subject to a like wrong; and to prevent similar evils, they set to work to make laws, and to institute punishments for those who contravened them. Such was the origin of justice. This caused them, when they had afterwards to choose a prince, neither to look to the strongest nor bravest, but to the wisest and most just. But when they began to make sovereignty hereditary and non-elective, the children quickly degenerated from their fathers; and, so far from trying to equal their virtues, they considered that a prince had nothing else to do than to excel all the rest in luxury, indulgence, and every other variety of pleasure. The prince consequently soon drew upon himself the general hatred. An object of hatred, he naturally felt fear; fear in turn dictated to him precautions and wrongs, and thus tyranny quickly developed itself. Such were the beginning and causes of disorders, conspiracies, and plots against the sovereigns, set on foot, not by the feeble and timid, but by those citizens who, surpassing the others in grandeur of soul, in wealth, and in courage, could not submit to the outrages and excesses of their princes.

Under such powerful leaders the masses armed themselves against the tyrant, and, after having rid themselves of him, submitted to these chiefs as their liberators. These, abhorring the very name of prince, constituted themselves a new government; and at first, bearing in mind the past tyranny, they governed in strict accordance with the laws which they had established themselves; preferring public interests to their own, and to administer and protect with greatest care both public and private affairs. The children succeeded their fathers, and ignorant of the changes of fortune, having never experienced its reverses, and indisposed to remain content with this civil equality, they in turn gave themselves up to cupidity, ambition, libertinage, and violence, and soon caused the aristocratic government to degenerate into an oligarchic tyranny, regardless of all civil rights. They soon, however, experienced the same fate as the first tyrant; the people, disgusted with their government, placed themselves at the command of whoever was willing to attack them, and this disposition soon produced an avenger, who was sufficiently well seconded to destroy them. The memory of the prince and the wrongs committed by him being still fresh in their minds, and having overthrown the oligarchy, the people were not willing to return to the government of a prince. A popular government was therefore resolved upon, and it was so organized that the authority should not again fall into the hands of a prince or a small number of nobles.

And as all governments are at first looked up to with some degree of reverence, the popular state also maintained itself for a time, but which was never of long duration, and lasted generally only about as long as the generation that had established it; for it soon ran into that kind of license which inflicts injury upon public as well as private interests. Each individual only consulted his own passions, and a thousand acts of injustice were daily committed, so that, constrained by necessity, or directed by the counsels of some good man, or for the purpose of escaping from this anarchy, they returned anew to the government of a prince, and from this they generally lapsed again into anarchy, step by step, in the same manner and from the same causes as we have indicated.

Such is the circle which all republics are destined to run through. Seldom, however, do they come back to the original form of government, which results from the fact that their duration is not sufficiently long to be able to undergo these repeated changes and preserve their existence. But it may well happen that a republic lacking strength and good counsel in its difficulties becomes subject after a while to some neighboring state, that is better organized than itself; and if such is not the case, than they will be apt to revolve indefinitely in the circle of revolutions. I say, then, that all kinds of government are defective; those three which we have qualified as good because they are too short-lived, and the three bad ones because of their inherent viciousness. Thus sagacious legislators, knowing the vices of each of these systems of government by themselves, have chosen one that should partake of all of them, judging that to be the most stable and solid. In fact, when there is combined under the same constitution a prince, a nobility, and the power of the people, then these three powers will watch and keep each other reciprocally in check.

Amongst those justly celebrated for having established such a constitution, Lycurgus beyond doubt merits the highest praise. He organized the government of Sparta in such manner that, in giving to the king, the nobles, and the people each their portion of authority and duties, he created a government which maintained itself for over eight hundred years in the most perfect tranquillity, and reflected infinite glory upon this legislator. On the other hand, the constitution given by Solon to the Athenians, by which he established only a popular government, was of such short duration that before his death he saw the tyranny of Pisistratus arise. And although forty years afterwards the heirs of the tyrant were expelled, so that Athens recovered her liberties and restored the popular government according to the laws of Solon, yet it did not last over a hundred years; although a number of laws that had been overlooked by Solon were adopted, to maintain the government against the insolence of the nobles and the license of the populace. The fault he had committed in not tempering the power of the people and that of the prince and his nobles, made the duration of the government of Athens very short, as compared with that of Sparta.

But let us come to Rome. Although she had no legislator like Lycurgus, who constituted her government, at her very origin, in a manner to secure her liberty for a length of time, yet the disunion which existed between the Senate and the people produced such extraordinary events, that chance did for her what the laws had failed to do. Thus, if Rome did not attain the first degree of happiness, she at least had the second. Her first institutions were doubtless defective, but they were not in conflict with the principles that might bring her to perfection. For Romulus and all the other kings gave her many and good laws, well suited even to a free people; but as the object of these princes was to found a monarchy, and not a republic, Rome, upon becoming free, found herself lacking all those institutions that are most essential to liberty, and which her kings had not established. And although these kings lost their empire, for the reasons and in the manner which we have explained, yet those who expelled them appointed immediately two consuls in place of the king; and thus it was found that they had banished the title of king from Rome, but not the regal power. The government, composed of Consuls and a Senate, had but two of the three elements of which we have spoken, the monarchical and the aristocratic; the popular power was wanting. In the course of time, however, the insolence of the nobles, produced by the causes which we shall see further on, induced the people to rise against the others. The nobility, to save a portion of their power, were forced to yield a share of it to the people; but the Senate and the Consuls retained sufficient to maintain their rank in the state. It was then that the Tribunes of the people were created, which strengthened and confirmed the republic, being now composed of the three elements of which we have spoken above. Fortune favored her, so that, although the authority passed successively from the kings and nobles to the people, by the same degrees and for the same reasons that we have spoken of, yet the royal authority was never entirely abolished to bestow it upon the nobles; and these were never entirely deprived of their authority to give it to the people; but a combination was formed of the three powers, which rendered the constitution perfect, and this perfection was attained by the disunion of the Senate and the people, as we shall more fully show in the following two chapters.

* * *

Chapter v, to whom can the guardianship of liberty more safely be confided, to the nobles or to the people? and which of the two have most cause for creating disturbances, those who wish to acquire, or those who desire to conserve?

All the legislators that have given wise constitutions to republics have deemed it an essential precaution to establish a guard and protection to liberty; and according as this was more or less wisely placed, liberty endured a greater or less length of time. As every republic was composed of nobles and people, the question arose as to whose hands it was best to confide the protection of liberty. The Lacedæmonians, and in our day the Venetians, gave it into the hands of the nobility; but the Romans intrusted it to the people. We must examine, therefore, which of these republics made the best choice. There are strong reasons in favor of each, but, to judge by the results, we must incline in favor of the nobles, for the liberties of Sparta and Venice endured a longer space of time than those of Rome. But to come to the reasons, taking the part of Rome first, I will say, that one should always confide any deposit to those who have least desire of violating it; and doubtless, if we consider the objects of the nobles and of the people, we must see that the first have a great desire to dominate, whilst the latter have only the wish not to be dominated, and consequently a greater desire to live in the enjoyment of liberty; so that when the people are intrusted with the care of any privilege or liberty, being less disposed to encroach upon it, they will of necessity take better care of it; and being unable to take it away themselves, will prevent others from doing so.

On the contrary, it is said, in favor of the course adopted by Sparta and Venice, that the preference given to the nobility, as guardians of public liberty, has two advantages: the first, to yield something to the ambition of those who, being more engaged in the management of public affairs, find, so to say, in the weapon which the office places in their hands, a means of power that satisfies them; the other, to deprive the restless spirit of the masses of an authority calculated from its very nature to produce trouble and dissensions, and apt to drive the nobles to some act of desperation, which in time may cause the greatest misfortunes. Rome is even adduced as an example of this; for having confided, it is said, this authority to the tribunes of the people, these were seen not to be content with having only one Consul taken from this class, but wanted both to be plebeians. They afterwards claimed the Censure, the Prætoriate, and all the other dignities of the republic. And not satisfied with these advantages, and urged on by the same violence, they came in the end to idolize all those whom they saw disposed to attack the nobles, which gave rise to the power of Marius and to the ruin of Rome.

And, truly, whoever weighs all these reasons accurately may well remain in doubt which of the two classes he would choose as the guardians of liberty, not knowing which would be least dangerous, — those who seek to acquire an authority which they have not, or those who desire to preserve that which they already possess. After the nicest examination, this is what I think may be concluded from it. The question refers either to a republic that desires to extend its empire, as Rome, or to a state that confines itself merely to its own preservation. In the first case Rome should be imitated, and in the second the example of Sparta and Venice should be followed; and in the next chapter we shall see the reasons why and the means by which this is to be done.

To come back now to the question as to which men are most dangerous in a republic, those who wish to acquire power or those who fear to lose that which they possess, I will remark that Menenius and M. Fulvius, both plebeians, were named, the one Dictator and the other Commander of the Cavalry, to make investigations on the occasion of a conspiracy formed at Capua against Rome. They were also commissioned to find out all those who from ambition and by extraordinary means sought to obtain the Consulate and the other important offices of the republic. The nobility, believing that such an authority given to the Dictator was aimed against them, spread the report throughout the city that it was not they who sought thus to arrive at these honors from ambition or by illicit proceedings, but rather the plebeians, who, trusting neither to their birth nor their personal merits, thus employed extraordinary means to obtain these honors, and they particularly charged it upon the Dictator himself. This accusation was so actively followed up that Menenius felt himself obliged to convoke an assembly of the people; where, after having complained of the calumnies spread against him by the nobles, he deposed the Dictatorship and submitted himself to the judgment of the people. The cause having been pleaded, Menenius was absolved. On that occasion there was much discussion as to which was the most ambitious, he who wished to preserve power or he who wished to acquire it; as both the one and the other of these motives may be the cause of great troubles. It seems, however, that they are most frequently occasioned by those who possess; for the fear to lose stirs the same passions in men as the desire to gain, as men do not believe themselves sure of what they already possess except by acquiring still more; and, moreover, these new acquisitions are so many means of strength and power for abuses; and what is still worse is that the haughty manners and insolence of the nobles and the rich excite in the breasts of those who have neither birth nor wealth, not only the desire to possess them, but also the wish to revenge themselves by depriving the former of those riches and honors which they see them employ so badly.

*   *   *

Chapter ix, to found a new republic, or to reform entirely the old institutions of an existing one, must be the work of one man only

It may perhaps appear to some that I have gone too far into the details of Roman history before having made any mention of the founders of that republic, or of her institutions, her religion, and her military establishment. Not wishing, therefore, to keep any longer in suspense the desires of those who wish to understand these matters, I say that many will perhaps consider it an evil example that the founder of a civil society, as Romulus was, should first have killed his brother, and then have consented to the death of Titus Tatius, who had been elected to share the royal authority with him; from which it might be concluded that the citizens, according to the example of their prince, might, from ambition and the desire to rule, destroy those who attempt to oppose their authority. This opinion would be correct, if we do not take into consideration the object which Romulus had in view in committing that homicide. But we must assume, as a general rule, that it never or rarely happens that a republic or monarchy is well constituted, or its old institutions entirely reformed, unless it is done by only one individual; it is even necessary that he whose mind has conceived such a constitution should be alone in carrying it into effect. A sagacious legislator of a republic, therefore, whose object is to promote the public good, and not his private interests, and who prefers his country to his own successors, should concentrate all authority in himself; and a wise mind will never censure any one for having employed any extraordinary means for the purpose of establishing a kingdom or constituting a republic. It is well that, when the act accuses him, the result should excuse him; and when the result is good, as in the case of Romulus, it will always absolve him from blame. For he is to be reprehended who commits violence for the purpose of destroying, and not he who employs it for beneficent purposes. The lawgiver should, however, be sufficiently wise and virtuous not to leave this authority which he has assumed either to his heirs or to any one else; for mankind, being more prone to evil than to good, his successor might employ for evil purposes the power which he had used only for good ends. Besides, although one man alone should organize a government, yet it will not endure long if the administration of it remains on the shoulders of a single individual; it is well, then, to confide this to the charge of many, for thus it will be sustained by the many. Therefore, as the organization of anything cannot be made by many, because the divergence of their opinions hinders them from agreeing as to what is best, yet, when once they do understand it, they will not readily agree to abandon it. That Romulus deserves to be excused for the death of his brother and that of his associate, and that what he had done was for the general good, and not for the gratification of his own ambition, is proved by the fact that he immediately instituted a Senate with which to consult, and according to the opinions of which he might form his resolutions. And on carefully considering the authority which Romulus reserved for himself, we see that all he kept was the command of the army in case of war, and the power of convoking the Senate. This was seen when Rome became free, after the expulsion of the Tarquins, when there was no other innovation made upon the existing order of things than the substitution of two Consuls, appointed annually, in place of an hereditary king; which proves clearly that all the original institutions of that city were more in conformity with the requirements of a free and civil society than with an absolute and tyrannical government.

The above views might be corroborated by any number of examples, such as those of Moses, Lycurgus, Solon, and other founders of monarchies and republics, who were enabled to establish laws suitable for the general good only by keeping for themselves an exclusive authority; but all these are so well known that I will not further refer to them. I will adduce only one instance, not so celebrated, but which merits the consideration of those who aim to become legislators: it is this. Agis, king of Sparta, desired to bring back the Spartans to the strict observance of the laws of Lycurgus, being convinced that, by deviating from them, their city had lost much of her ancient virtue, and consequently her power and dominion; but the Spartan Ephores had him promptly killed, as one who attempted to make himself a tyrant. His successor, Cleomenes, had conceived the same desire, from studying the records and writings of Agis, which he had found, and which explained his aims and intentions. Cleomenes was convinced that he would be unable to render this service to his country unless he possessed sole authority; for he judged that, owing to the ambitious nature of men, he could not promote the interests of the many against the will of the few; and therefore he availed of a convenient opportunity to have all the Ephores slain, as well as all such others as might oppose his project, after which he restored the laws of Lycurgus entirely. This course was calculated to resuscitate the greatness of Sparta, and to give Cleomenes a reputation equal to that of Lycurgus, had it not been for the power of the Macedonians and the weakness of the other Greek republics. For being soon after attacked by the Macedonians, and Sparta by herself being inferior in strength, and there being no one whom he could call to his aid, he was defeated; and thus his project, so just and laudable, was never put into execution. Considering, then, all these things, I conclude that, to found a republic, one must be alone; and that Romulus deserves to be absolved from, and not blamed for, the death of Remus and of Tatius.

13

Luther Defines Christian Liberty

1520 WAS THE GREEN YEAR of Luther's development as a Reformer, In The Freedom of a Christian, the Address to the Nobility of the German Nation, and The Babylonian Captivity of the Church, often called "the Reformation treatises," he spelled out the implications of his idea of justification through faith alone. Although Luther intended, in his Freedom of a Christian, to conciliate the Pope, the treatise etched more sharply than anything he had previously written the lines of difference between his views and accepted Catholic doctrine, setting forth a new ideal of Christian piety. It also gave inspiration to more ardent rebels against the existing social order and more radical opponents of "Popery" who misunderstood his position on both social and spiritual equality.

Martin Luther (1483–1546), The Freedom of a Christian

MAN has a twofold nature, a spiritual and a bodily one. According to the spiritual nature, which men refer to as the soul, he is called a spiritual, inner, or new man. According to the bodily nature, which men refer to as flesh, he is called a carnal, outward, or old man, of whom the Apostle writes in II Cor. 4 [:16], "Though our outer nature is wasting away, our inner nature is being renewed every day." Because of this diversity of nature the Scriptures assert contradictory things concerning the same man, since these two men in the same man contradict each other, "for the desires of the flesh are against the Spirit, and the desires of the Spirit are against the flesh," according to Gal. 5 [:17].

First, let us consider the inner man to see how a righteous, free, and pious Christian, that is, a spiritual, new, and inner man, becomes

From Harold J. Grimm, ed., LUTHER'S WORKS, vol. 31, CAREER OF THE REFORMER: 1 (Philadelphia, 1957). Translation by W. A. Lambert, revised by Harold J. Grimm. Reprinted by permission of The Muhlenberg Press.

what he is. It is evident that no external thing has any influence in producing Christian righteousness or freedom, or in producing unrighteousness or servitude. A simple argument will furnish the proof of this statement. What can it profit the soul if the body is well, free, and active, and eats, drinks, and does as it pleases? For in these respects even the most godless slaves of vice may prosper. On the other hand, how will poor health or imprisonment or hunger or thirst or any other external misfortune harm the soul? Even the most godly men, and those who are free because of clear consciences, are afflicted with these things. None of these things touch either the freedom or the servitude of the soul. It does not help the soul if the body is adorned with the sacred robes of priests or dwells in sacred places or is occupied with sacred duties or prays, fasts, abstains from certain kinds of food, or does any work that can be done by the body and in the body. The righteousness and the freedom of the soul require something far different since the things which have been mentioned coud be done by any wicked person. Such works produce nothing but hypocrites. On the other hand, it will not harm the soul if the body is clothed in secular dress, dwells in unconsecrated places, eats and drinks as others do, does not pray aloud, and neglects to do all the above-mentioned things which hypocrites can do.

Furthermore, to put aside all kinds of works, even contemplation, meditation, and all that the soul can do, does not help. One thing, and only one thing, is necessary for Christian life, righteousness, and freedom. That one thing is the most holy Word of God, the gospel of Christ, as Christ says, John 11 [:25], "I am the resurrection and the life; he who believes in me, though he die, yet shall he live"; and John 8 [:36], "So if the Son makes you free, you will be free indeed"; and Matt. 4 [:4], "Man shall not live by bread alone, but by every word that proceeds from the mouth of God." Let us then consider it certain and firmly established that the soul can do without anything except the Word of God and that where the Word of God is missing there is no help at all for the soul. If it has the Word of God it is rich and lacks nothing since it is the Word of life, truth, light, peace, righteousness, salvation, joy, liberty, wisdom, power, grace, glory, and of every incalculable blessing. This is why the prophet in the entire Psalm [119] and in many other places yearns and sighs for the Word of God and uses so many names to describe it.

On the other hand, there is no more terrible disaster with which the wrath of God can afflict men than a famine of the hearing of his Word, as he says in Amos [8:11]. Likewise there is no greater mercy than when he sends forth his Word, as we read in Psalm 107 [:20]: "He sent forth his word, and healed them, and delivered them from destruction." Nor was Christ sent into the world for any other ministry except that of the Word. Moreover, the entire spiritual estate — all the apostles, bishops, and priests — has been called and instituted only for the ministry of the Word.

You may ask, "What then is the Word of God, and how shall it be used, since there are so many words of God?" I answer: The Apostle explains this in Romans 1. The Word is the gospel of God concerning his Son, who was made flesh, suffered, rose from the dead, and was glorified through the Spirit who sanctifies. To preach Christ means to feed the soul, make it righteous, set it free, and save it, provided it believes the preaching. Faith alone is the saving and efficacious use of the Word of God, according to Rom. 10 [:9]: "If you confess with your lips that Jesus is Lord and believe in your heart that God raised him from the dead, you will be saved." Furthermore, "Christ is the end of the law, that every one who has faith may be justified" [Rom. 10:4]. Again, in Rom. 1 [:17], "He who through faith is righteous shall live." The Word of God cannot be received and cherished by any works whatever but only by faith. Therefore it is clear that, as the soul needs only the Word of God for its life and righteousness, so it is justified by faith alone and not any works; for if it could be justified by anything else, it would not need the Word, and consequently it would not need faith.

This faith cannot exist in connection with works — that is to say, if you at the same time claim to be justified by works, whatever their character — for that would be the same as "limping with two different opinions" [I Kings 18:21], as worshiping Baal and kissing one's own hand [Job 31:27–28], which, as Job says, is a very great iniquity. Therefore the moment you begin to have faith you learn that all things in you are altogether blameworthy, sinful, and damnable, as the Apostle says in Rom. 3 [:23], "Since all have sinned and fall short of the glory of God," and, "None is righteous, no, not one; . . . all have turned aside, together they have gone wrong," Rom. 3 [:10–12]. When you have learned this you will know that you need Christ, who suffered and rose again for you so that, if you believe in him, you may through this faith become a new man in so far as your sins are forgiven and you are justified by the merits of another, namely, of Christ alone.

Since, therefore, this faith can rule only in the inner man, as Rom. 10 [:10] says, "For man believes with his heart and so is justified," and since faith alone justifies, it is clear that the inner man cannot be justified, freed, or saved by any outer work or action at all, and that these works, whatever their character, having nothing to do with this inner man. On the other hand, only ungodliness and unbelief of heart, and no outer work, make him guilty and a damnable servant of sin. Wherefore it ought to be the first concern of every Christian to lay aside all confidence in works and increasingly to strengthen faith alone and through faith to grow in the knowledge, not of works, but of Christ Jesus, who suffered and rose for him, as Peter teaches in the last chapter of his first Epistle, I Pet. [5:10]. No other work makes a Christian. . . .

*　　*　　*

. . . Here we must point out that the entire Scripture of God is divided into two parts: commandments and promises. Although the commandments teach things that are good, the things taught are not done as soon as they are taught, for the commandments show us what we ought to do but do not give us the power to do it. They are intended to teach man to know himself, that through them he may recognize his inability to do good and may despair of his own ability. That is why they are called the Old Testament and constitute the Old Testament. For example, the commandment, "You shall not covet" [Exod. 20:17], is a command which proves us all to be sinners, for no one can avoid coveting no matter how much he may struggle against it. Therefore, in order not to covet and to fulfil the commandment, a man is compelled to despair of himself, to seek the help which he does not find in himself elsewhere and from someone else, as stated in Hosea [13:9]: "Destruction is your own, O Israel: your help is only in me." As we fare with respect to one commandment, so we fare with all, for it is equally impossible for us to keep any one of them.

Now when a man has learned through the commandments to recognize his helplessness and is distressed about how he might satisfy the law — since the law must be fulfilled so that not a jot or tittle shall be lost, otherwise man will be condemned without hope — then, being truly humbled and reduced to nothing in his own eyes, he finds in himself nothing whereby he may be justified and saved. Here the second part of Scripture comes to our aid, namely, the promises of God which declare the glory of God, saying, "If you wish to fulfil the law and not covet, as the law demands, come, believe in Christ in whom grace, righteousness, peace, liberty, and all things are promised you. If you believe, you shall have all things; if you do not believe, you shall lack all things." That which is impossible for you to accomplish by trying to fulfil all the works of the law — many and useless as they all are — you will accomplish quickly and easily through faith. God our Father has made all things depend on faith so that whoever has faith will have everything, and whoever does not have faith will have nothing. "For God has consigned all men to disobedience, that he may have mercy upon all," as it is stated in Rom. 11 [:32]. Thus the promises of God give what the commandments of God demand and fulfil what the law prescribes so that all things may be God's alone, both the commandments and the fulfilling of the commandments. He alone commands, he alone fulfils. Therefore the promises of God belong to the New Testament. Indeed, they are the New Testament.

Since these promises of God are holy, true, righteous, free, and peaceful words, full of goodness, the soul which clings to them with a firm faith will be so closely united with them and altogether absorbed by them that it not only will share in all their power but will be saturated and intoxicated by them. If a touch of Christ healed, how much more will this most tender spiritual touch, this absorbing of the Word, communicate to the soul all things that belong to the Word. This, then, is how through faith alone without works the soul is justified by the Word of God, sanctified, made true, peaceful, and free, filled with every blessing and truly made a child of God, as John 1 [:12] says: "But to all who . . . believed in his name, he gave power to become children of God."

*   *   *

From this you once more see that much is ascribed to faith, namely, that it alone can fulfil the law and justify without works. You see that the First Commandment, which says, "You shall worship one God," is fulfilled by faith alone. Though you were nothing but good works from the soles of your feet to the crown of your head, you would still not be righteous or worship God or fulfil the First Commandment, since God cannot be worshiped unless you ascribe to him the glory of truthfulness and all goodness which is due him. This cannot be done by works but only by the faith of the heart. Not by the doing of works but by believing do we glorify God and acknowledge that he is truthful. Therefore faith alone is the righteousness of a Christian and the fulfilling of all the command-ments, for he who fulfils the First Commandment has no difficulty in fulfilling all the rest.

But works, being inanimate things, cannot glorify God, although they can, if faith is present, be done to the glory of God. Here, how-ever, we are not inquiring what works and what kind of works are done, but who it is that does them, who glorifies God and brings forth the works. This is done by faith which dwells in the heart and is the source and substance of all our righteousness. Therefore it is a blind and dangerous doctrine which teaches that the command-ments must be fulfilled by works. The commandments must be fulfilled before any works can be done, and the works proceed from the fulfilment of the commandments [Rom. 13:10], as we shall hear.

That we may examine more profoundly that grace which our inner man has in Christ, we must realize that in the Old Testament God consecrated to himself all the first-born males. The birthright was highly prized for it involved a twofold honor, that of priest-hood and that of kingship. The first-born brother was priest and lord over all the others and a type of Christ, the true and only first-born of God the Father and the Virgin Mary and true king and priest, but not after the fashion of the flesh and the world, for his kingdom is not of this world [John 18:36]. He reigns in heavenly and spiritual things and consecrates them — things such as righteous-ness, truth, wisdom, peace, salvation, etc. This does not mean that all things on earth and in hell are not also subject to him — other-wise how could he protect and save us from them? — but that his kingdom consists neither in them nor of them. Nor does his priest-hood consist in the outer splendor of robes and postures like those of the human priesthood of Aaron and our present-day church; but it consists of spiritual things through which he by an invisible serv-ice intercedes for us in heaven before God, there offers himself as a sacrifice, and does all things a priest should do, as Paul describes him under the type of Melchizedek in the Epistle to the Hebrews [Heb. 6–7]. Nor does he only pray and intercede for us but he teaches us inwardly through the living instruction of his Spirit, thus performing the two real functions of a priest, of which the prayers and the preaching of human priests are visible types.

Now just as Christ by his birthright obtained these two prerogatives, so he imparts them to and shares them with everyone who believes in him according to the law of the above-mentioned marriage, according to which the wife owns whatever belongs to the husband. Hence all of us who believe in Christ are priests and kings in Christ, as 1 Pet. 2 [:9] says: "You are a chosen race, God's own people, a royal priesthood, a priestly kingdom, that you may declare the wonderful deeds of him who called you out of darkness into his marvelous light."

The nature of this priesthood and kingship is something like this: First, with respect to the kingship, every Christian is by faith so exalted above all things that, by virtue of a spiritual power, he is lord of all things without exception, so that nothing can do him any harm. As a matter of fact, all things are made subject to him and are compelled to serve him in obtaining salvation. Accordingly Paul says in Rom. 8 [:28], "All things work together for good for the elect," and in 1 Cor. 3 [:21–23], "All things are yours whether . . . life or death or the present or the future, all are yours; and you are Christ's. . . ." This is not to say that every Christian is placed over all things to have and control them by physical power — a madness with which some churchmen are afflicted — for such power belongs to kings, princes, and other men on earth. Our ordinary experience in life shows us that we are subjected to all, suffer many things, and even die. As a matter of fact, the more Christian a man is, the more evils, sufferings, and deaths he must endure, as we see in Christ the first-born prince himself, and in all his brethren, the saints. The power of which we speak is spiritual. It rules in the midst of enemies and is powerful in the midst of oppression. This means nothing else than that "power is made perfect in weakness" [II Cor. 12:9] and that in all things I can find profit toward salvation [Rom. 8:28], so that the cross and death itself are compelled to serve me and to work together with me for my salvation. This is a splendid privilege and hard to attain, a truly omnipotent power, a spiritual dominion in which there is nothing so good and nothing so evil but that it shall work together for good to me, if only I believe. Yes, since faith alone suffices for salvation, I need nothing except faith exercising the power and dominion of its own liberty. Lo, this is the inestimable power and liberty of Christians.

Not only are we the freest of kings, we are also priests forever, which is far more excellent than being kings, for as priests we are worthy to appear before God to pray for others and to teach one another divine things. These are the functions of priests, and they cannot be granted to any unbeliever. Thus Christ has made it possible for us, provided we believe in him, to be not only his brethren, co-heirs, and fellow-kings, but also his fellow-priests. Therefore we may boldly come into the presence of God in the spirit of faith [Heb. 10:19, 22] and cry "Abba, Father!" pray for one another, and do all things which we see done and foreshadowed in the outer and visible works of priests.

* * *

From this anyone can clearly see how a Christian is free from all things and over all things so that he needs no works to make him righteous and save him, since faith alone abundantly confers all these things. Should he grow so foolish, however, as to presume to become righteous, free, saved, and a Christian by means of some good work, he would instantly lose faith and all its benefits, a foolishness aptly illustrated in the fable of the dog who runs along a stream with a piece of meat in his mouth and, deceived by the reflection of the meat in the water, opens his mouth to snap at it and so loses both the meat and the reflection.

You will ask, "If all who are in the church are priests, how do these whom we now call priests differ from laymen?" I answer: Injustice is done those words "priest," "cleric," "spiritual," "ecclesiastic," when they are transferred from all Christians to those few who are now by a mischievous usage called "ecclesiastics." Holy Scripture makes no distinction between them, although it gives the name "ministers," "servants," "stewards" to those who are now proudly called popes, bishops, and lords and who should according to the ministry of the Word serve others and teach them the faith of Christ and the freedom of believers. Although we are all equally priests, we cannot all publicly minister and teach. We ought not do so even if we could. Paul writes accordingly in 1 Cor. 4 [:1], "This is how one should regard us, as servants of Christ and stewards of the mysteries of God."

* * *

To return to our purpose, I believe that it has now become clear that it is not enough or in any sense Christian to preach the works, life, and words of Christ as historical facts, as if the knowledge of these would suffice for the conduct of life; yet this is the fashion among those who must today be regarded as our best preachers. Far less is it sufficient or Christian to say nothing at all about Christ and to teach instead the laws of men and the decrees of the fathers. Now there are not a few who preach Christ and read about him that they may move men's affections to sympathy with Christ, to anger against the Jews, and such childish and effeminate nonsense. Rather ought Christ to be preached to the end that faith in him may be established that he may not only be Christ, but be Christ for you and me, and that what is said of him and is denoted in his name may be effectual in us. Such faith is produced and preserved in us by preaching why Christ came, what he brought and bestowed, what benefit it is to us to accept him. This is done when that Christian liberty which he bestows is rightly taught and we are told in what way we Christians are all kings and priests and therefore lords of all and may firmly believe that whatever we have done is pleasing and acceptable in the sight of God, as I have already said.

What man is there whose heart, upon hearing these things, will not rejoice to its depth, and when receiving such comfort will not grow tender so that he will love Christ as he never could by means of any laws or works? Who would have the power to harm or frighten such a heart? If the knowledge of sin or the fear of death should break in upon it, it is ready to hope in the Lord. It does not grow afraid when it hears tidings of evil. It is not disturbed when it sees its enemies. This is so because it believes that the righteousness of Christ is its own and that its sin is not its own, but Christ's, and that all sin is swallowed up by the righteousness of Christ. This, as has been said above, is a necessary consequence on account of faith in Christ. So the heart learns to scoff at death and sin and to say with the Apostle, "O death, where is thy victory? O death, where is thy sting? The sting of death is sin, and the power of sin is the law. But thanks be to God, who gives us the victory through our Lord Jesus Christ" [1 Cor. 15:55–57]. Death is swallowed up not only in the victory of Christ but also by our victory, because through faith his victory has become ours and in that faith we also are conquerors.

Let this suffice concerning the inner man, his liberty, and the source of his liberty, the righteousness of faith. He needs neither laws nor good works but, on the contrary, is injured by them if he believes that he is justified by them.

Now let us turn to the second part, the outer man. Here we shall answer all those who, offended by the word "faith" and by all that has been said, now ask, "If faith does all things and is alone sufficient unto righteousness, why then are good works commanded? We will take our ease and do no works and be content with faith." I answer: not so, you wicked men, not so. That would indeed be proper if we were wholly inner and perfectly spiritual men. But such we shall be only at the last day, the day of the resurrection of the dead. As long as we live in the flesh we only begin to make some progress in that which shall be perfected in the future life. For this reason the Apostle in Rom. 8 [:23] calls all that we attain in this life "the first fruits of the Spirit" because we shall indeed receive the greater portion, even the fulness of the Spirit, in the future. This is the place to assert that which was said above, namely, that a Christian is the servant of all and made subject to all. Insofar as he is free he does no works, but insofar as he is a servant he does all kinds of works. How this is possible we shall see.

Although, as I have said, a man is abundantly and sufficiently justified by faith inwardly, in his spirit, and so has all that he needs, except insofar as this faith and these riches must grow from day to day even to the future life; yet he remains in this mortal life on earth. In this life he must control his own body and have dealings with men. Here the works begin; here a man cannot enjoy leisure; here he must indeed take care to discipline his body by fastings, watchings, labors, and other reasonable discipline and to subject it to the Spirit so that it will obey and conform to the inner man and faith and not revolt against faith and hinder the inner man, as it is the nature of the body to do if it is not held in check. The inner man, who by faith is created in the image of God, is both joyful and happy because of Christ in whom so many benefits are conferred upon him; and therefore it is his one occupation to serve God joyfully and without thought of gain, in love that is not constrained.

* * *

In doing these works, however, we must not think that a man is justified before God by them, for faith, which alone is righteousness before God, cannot endure that erroneous opinion. We must, however, realize that these works reduce the body to subjection and purify it of its evil lusts, and our whole purpose is to be directed only toward the driving out of lusts. Since by faith the soul is cleansed and made to love God, it desires that all things, and especially its own body, shall be purified so that all things may join with it in loving and praising God. Hence a man cannot be idle, for the need of his body drives him and he is compelled to do many good works to reduce it to subjection. Nevertheless the works themselves do not justify him before God, but he does the works out of spontaneous love in obedience to God and considers nothing except the approval of God, whom he would most scrupulously obey in all things.

*   *   *

From this it is easy to know how far good works are to be rejected or not, and by what standard all the teachings of men concerning works are to be interpreted. If works are sought after as a means to righteousness, are burdened with this perverse leviathan, and are done under the false impression that through them one is justified, they are made necessary and freedom and faith are destroyed; and this addition to them makes them no longer good but truly damnable works. They are not free, and they blaspheme the grace of God since to justify and to save by faith belongs to the grace of God alone. What the works have no power to do they nevertheless — by a godless presumption through this folly of ours — pretend to do and thus violently force themselves into the office and glory of grace. We do not, therefore, reject good works; on the contrary, we cherish and teach them as much as possible. We do not condemn them for their own sake but on account of this godless addition to them and the perverse idea that righteousness is to be sought through them; for that makes them appear good outwardly, when in truth they are not good. They deceive men and lead them to deceive one another like ravening wolves in sheep's clothing [Matt. 7:15].

*   *   *

Our faith in Christ does not free us from works but from false opinions concerning works, that is, from the foolish presumption that justification is acquired by works. Faith redeems, corrects, and preserves our consciences so that we know that righteousness does not consist in works, although works neither can nor ought to be wanting; just as we cannot be without food and drink and all the works of this mortal body, yet our righteousness is not in them, but in faith; and yet those works of the body are not to be despised or neglected on that account. In this world we are bound by the needs of our bodily life, but we are not righteous because of them. "My kingship is not of this world" [John 18:36], says Christ. He does not, however, say, "My kingship is not here, that is, in this world." And Paul says, "Though we live in the world we are not carrying on a worldly war" [II Cor. 10:3], and in Gal. 2 [:20], "The life I now live in the flesh I live by faith in the Son of God." Thus what we do, live, and are in works and ceremonies, we do because of the necessities of this life and of the effort to rule our body. Nevertheless we are righteous, not in these, but in the faith of the Son of God. . . .

14

Anabaptist Piety

MUNTZER AND GREBEL were both referred to as Anabaptists, but they had reached their radical and somewhat different positions on evangelical religion independently of each other. Here Grebel and his friends are trying to make common cause with Müntzer without ignoring the real differences between their views. The letters show why the Anabaptists rejected both Luther's and Zwingli's more conservative evangelicalism as well as Catholicism. They also show that once the Reformers used the principle of "Scripture alone" to repudiate the old authorities they could not find a common standard. In this connection Grebel's attack on "false forbearance" and "anti-Christian caution" is significant. For their part the more conservative Reformers could argue that Grebel's criticism of "superficial faith, without fruits of faith" led away from Luther's doctrine of justification by faith alone and back to a doctrine of works.

Conrad Grebel (?–1526) and Friends, Letters to Thomas Müntzer, Zurich, September 5, 1524

The text]

TO THE SINCERE *and true proclaimer of the gospel, Thomas Müntzer at Allstedt in the Hartz, our true and beloved brother with us in Christ: May peace, grace, and mercy from God, our Father, and Jesus Christ, our Lord, be with us all. Amen*

Dear Brother Thomas:

For God's sake do not marvel that we address thee without title, and request thee like a brother to communicate with us by writing, and that we have ventured, unasked and unknown to thee,

From George H. Williams, ed., SPIRITUAL AND ANABAPTIST WRITERS (Philadelphia, 1957), pp. 73–85. Translation by Walter Rauschenbusch. Reprinted by permission of the Westminster Press and Student Christian Movement Press Ltd.

to open communications between us. God's Son, Jesus Christ, who offers himself as the one master and head of all who would be saved, and bids us be brethren by the one common word given to all brethren and believers, has moved us and compelled us to make friendship and brotherhood and to bring the following points to thy attention. Thy writing of two tracts on fictitious faith has further prompted us. Therefore we ask that thou wilt take it kindly for the sake of Christ our Saviour. If God wills, it shall serve and work to our good. Amen.

Just as our forebears fell away from the true God and from the one true, common, divine Word, from the divine institutions, from Christian love and life, and lived without God's law and gospel in human, useless, unchristian customs and ceremonies, and expected to attain salvation therein, yet fell far short of it, as the evangelical preachers have declared, and to some extent are still declaring, so today too every man wants to be saved by superficial faith, without fruits of faith, without baptism of trial and probation, without love and hope, without right Christian practices, and wants to persist in all the old manner of personal vices, and in the common ritualistic and anti-Christian customs of baptism and of the Lord's Supper, in disrespect for the divine Word and in respect for the word of the pope and of the antipapal preachers, which yet is not equal to the divine Word nor in harmony with it. In respecting persons and in manifold seduction there is grosser and more pernicious error now than ever has been since the beginning of the world. In the same error we too lingered as long as we heard and read only the evangelical preachers who are to blame for all this, in punishment for our sins. But after we took Scripture in hand too, and consulted it on many points, we have been instructed somewhat and have discovered the great and harmful error of the shepherds, of ours too, namely, that we do not daily beseech God earnestly with constant groaning to be brought out of this destruction of all godly life and out of human abominations, to attain to the true faith and divine practice. The cause of all this is false forbearance, the hiding of the divine Word, and the mixing of it with the human. Aye, we say it harms all and frustrates all things divine. There is no need of specifying and reciting.

While we were marking and deploring these facts, thy book against false faith and baptism was brought to us, and we were more fully informed and confirmed, and it rejoiced us wonderfully that we found one who was of the same Christian mind with us and dared to show the evangelical preachers their lack, how that in all the chief points they falsely forbear and act and set their own opinions, and even those of Antichrist, above God and against God, as befits not the ambassadors of God to act and preach. Therefore we beg and admonish thee as a brother by the name, the power, the word, the spirit, and the salvation, which has come to all Christians through Jesus Christ our Master and Saviour (*seligmacher*), that thou wilt take earnest heed to preach only the divine Word without fear, to set up and guard only divine institutions, to esteem as good and right only what may be found in pure and clear Scripture, to reject, hate, and curse all devices, words, customs, and opinions of men, including thy own.

1] We understand and have seen that thou hast translated the Mass into German and hast introduced new German hymns. That cannot be for the good, since we find nothing taught in the New Testament about singing, no example of it. Paul scolds the learned among the Corinthians more than he praises them, because they mumbled in meeting as if they sang, just as the Jews and the Italians chant their words song-fashion.   2] Since singing in Latin grew up without divine instruction and apostolic example and custom, without producing good or edifying, it will still less edify in German and will create a faith of outward appearance only.   3] Paul very clearly forbids singing in Eph. 5:19 and Col. 3:16 since he says and teaches that they are to speak to one another and teach one another with psalms and spiritual songs, and if anyone would sing, he should sing and give thanks in his heart.   4] Whatever we are not taught by clear passages or examples must be regarded as forbidden, just as if it were written: "This do not; sing not."   5] Christ in the Old and especially in the New Testament bids his messengers (*botten*) simply proclaim the word. Paul too says that the word of Christ profits us, not the song. Whoever sings poorly gets vexation by it; whoever can sing well gets conceit.   6] We must not follow our notions; we must add nothing to the word and take nothing from it.   7] If thou wilt abolish the Mass, it cannot be accomplished with German chants, which is thy suggestion perhaps, or comes from Luther.   8] It must be rooted up by the word and command of Christ.   9] For it is not planted by God.   10] The Supper of fellowship Christ did institute and plant.   11] The words found in Matt., ch. 26, Mark, ch. 14, Luke, ch. 22, and 1 Cor., ch. 11, alone are to be used, no more, no less. 12] The server from out of the congregation should pronounce them from one of the Evangelists or from Paul. 13] They are the words of the instituted meal of fellowship, not words of consecration. 14] Ordinary bread ought to be used, without idols and additions. 15] For [the latter] creates an external reverence and veneration of the bread, and a turning away from the inward. An ordinary drinking vessel too ought to be used. 16] This would do away with the adoration and bring true understanding and appreciation of the Supper, since the bread is nought but bread. In faith, it is the body of Christ and the incorporation with Christ and the brethren. But one must eat and drink in the Spirit and love, as John shows in ch. 6 and the other passages, Paul in I Cor., chs. 10 and 11, and as is clearly learned in Acts, ch. 2. 17] Although it is simply bread, yet if faith and brotherly love precede it, it is to be received with joy, since, when it is used in the church, it is to show us that we are truly one bread and one body, and that we are and wish to be true brethren with one another, etc. 18] But if one is found who will not live the brotherly life, he eats unto condemnation, since he eats it without discerning, like any other meal, and dishonors love, which is the inner bond, and the bread, which is the outer bond. 19] For also it does not call to his mind Christ's body and blood, the covenant of the cross, nor that he should be willing to live and suffer for the sake of Christ and the brethren, of the head and the members. 20] Also it ought not to be administered by thee. That was the beginning of the Mass that only a few would partake, for the Supper is an expression of fellowship, not a Mass and sacrament. Therefore none is to receive it alone, neither on his deathbed nor otherwise. Neither is the bread to be locked away, etc., for the use of a single person, since no one should take for himself alone the bread of those in unity, unless he is not one with himself — which no one is, etc. 21] Neither is it to be used in "temples" according to all Scripture and example, since that creates a false reverence. 22] It should be used much and often. 23] It should not be used without the rule of Christ in Matt. 18:15–18, otherwise it is not the Lord's Supper, for without that rule every man will run after the externals. The inner matter, love, is passed by, if brethren and false brethren approach or eat it [together]. 24] If ever thou desirest to serve it, we should wish that it would be done without priestly garment and vestment of the Mass, without singing, without addition. 25] As for the time, we know that Christ gave it to the apostles at supper and that the Corinthians had the same usage. We fix no definite time with us, etc.

Let this suffice, since thou art much better instructed about the Lord's Supper, and we only state things as we understand them. If we are not in the right, teach us better. And do thou drop singing and the Mass, and act in all things only according to the Word, and bring forth and establish by the Word the usages of the apostles. If that cannot be done, it would be better to leave all things in Latin and unaltered and mediated [by a priest]. If the right cannot be established, do not then administer according to thy *own* or the priestly usage of Antichrist. And at least teach how it ought to be, as Christ does in John, ch. 6, and teaches how we must eat and drink his flesh and blood, and takes no heed of backsliding and anti-Christian caution, of which the most learned and foremost evangelical preachers have made a veritable idol and propagated it in all the world. It is much better that a few be rightly taught through the Word of God, believing and walking aright in virtues and practices, than that many believe falsely and deceitfully through adulterated doctrine. Though we admonish and beseech thee, we hope that thou wilt do it of thy own accord; and we admonish the more willingly, because thou hast so kindly listened to our brother and confessed that thou too hast yielded too much, and because thou and Carlstadt are esteemed by us the purest proclaimers and preachers of the purest Word of God. And if ye two rebuke, and justly, those who mingle the words and customs of men with those of God, ye must by rights cut yourselves loose and be completely purged of popery, benefices, and all new and ancient customs, and of your own and ancient notions. If your benefices, as with us, are supported by interest and tithes, which are both true usury, and it is not the whole congregation which supports you, we beg that ye free yourselves of your benefices. Ye know well how a shepherd should be sustained.

We have good hopes of Jacob Strauss and a few others, who are little esteemed by the slothful scholars and doctors at Wittenberg. We too are thus rejected by our learned shepherds. All men follow them, because they preach a sinful sweet Christ, and they lack clear discernment, as thou hast set forth in thy tracts, which have taught and strengthened beyond measure us who are poor in spirit. And so we are in harmony in all points, except that we have learned with sorrow that thou hast set up tablets, for which we find no text or example in the New Testament. In the Old it [the law] was to be written outwardly, but now in the New it is to be written on the fleshly tablets of the heart, as the comparison of both Testaments proves, as we are taught by Paul, II Cor. 3:3; Jer. 31:33; Heb. 8:10; Ezek. 36:26. Unless we are mistaken, which we do not think and believe, do thou abolish the tablets again. The matter has grown out of thy own notions, a futile expense, which will increase and become quite idolatrous, and spread into all the world, just as happened with the idolatrous images. It would also create the idea that something external always had to stand and be set up in place of the idols, whereby the unlearned might learn — even if it be only the external word which is so used, as is declared to us, according to all example and commandment of Scripture, especially I Cor. 14:16 and Col. 3:16. This kind of learning from this word only might in time become insidious, and even if it would never do any harm, yet I would never want to invent and set up anything new and to follow and imitate the slothful and misleading scholars with their false forbearance, and from my own opinion invent, teach, and establish a single thing.

Go forward with the Word and establish a Christian church with the help of Christ and his rule, as we find it instituted in Matt. 18:15–18 and applied in the Epistles. Use determination and common prayer and decision according to faith and love, without command or compulsion. Then God will help thee and thy little sheep to all sincerity, and the singing and the tablets will cease. There is more than enough of wisdom and counsel in the Scripture, how all classes and all men may be taught, governed, instructed, and turned to piety. Whoever will not amend and believe, but resists the Word and action of God and thus persists, such a man, after Christ and his Word and rule have been declared to him and he has been admonished in the presence of the three witnesses and the church, such a man, we say, taught by God's Word, shall not be killed, but regarded as a heathen and publican and let alone.

Moreover, the gospel and its adherents are not to be protected by the sword, nor are they thus to protect themselves, which, as we learn from our brother, is thy opinion and practice. True Christian believers are sheep among wolves, sheep for the slaughter; they must be baptized in anguish and affliction, tribulation, persecution, suffering, and death; they must be tried with fire, and must reach the fatherland of eternal rest, not by killing their bodily, but by mortifying their spiritual, enemies. Neither do they use worldly sword or war, since all killing has ceased with them — unless, indeed, we would still be of the old law. And even there [in the Old Testament], so far as we recall, war was a misfortune after they had once conquered the Promised Land. No more of this.

On the matter of baptism thy book pleases us well, and we desire to be further instructed by thee. We understand that even an adult is not to be baptized without Christ's rule of binding and loosing. The Scripture describes baptism for us thus, that it signifies that, by faith and the blood of Christ, sins have been washed away for him who is baptized, changes his mind, and believes before and after; that it signifies that a man is dead and ought to be dead to sin and walks in newness of life and spirit, and that he shall certainly be saved if, according to this meaning, by inner baptism he lives his faith; so that the water does not confirm or increase faith, as the scholars at Wittenberg say, and [does not] give very great comfort [nor] is it the final refuge on the deathbed. Also baptism does not save, as Augustine, Tertullian, Theophylact, and Cyprian have taught, dishonoring faith and the suffering of Christ in the case of the old and adult, and dishonoring the suffering of Christ in the case of the unbaptized infants. We hold (according to the following passages: Gen. 8:21; Deut. 1:39; 30:6; 31:13; and 1 Cor. 14:20; Wisdom of Solomon 12:19; 1 Peter 2:2; Rom., chs. 1; 2; 7; 10 [allusions uncertain]; Matt. 18:1–6; 19:13–15; Mark 9:33–47; 10:13–16; Luke 18:15–17; etc.) that all children who have not yet come to the discernment of the knowledge of good and evil, and have not yet eaten of the tree of knowledge, that they are surely saved by the suffering of Christ, the new Adam, who has restored their vitiated life, because they would have been subject to death and condemnation only if Christ had not suffered; but they're not yet grown up to the infirmity of our broken nature — unless, indeed, it can be proved that Christ did not suffer for children. But as to the objection that faith is demanded of all who are to be saved, we exclude children from this and hold that they are saved without faith, and we do not believe from the above passages [that children must be baptized], and we conclude from the description of baptism and from the accounts of it (according to which no child was baptized), also from the above passages (which alone apply to the question of children, and all other scriptures do not refer to children), that infant baptism is a senseless, blasphemous abomination, contrary to all Scripture, contrary even to the papacy; since we find, from Cyprian and Augustine, that for many years after apostolic times believers and unbelievers were baptized together for six hundred years, etc. Since thou knowest this ten times better and hast published thy protests against infant baptism, we hope that thou art not acting against the eternal word, wisdom, and commandment of God, according to which only believers are to be baptized, and art not baptizing children. If thou or Carlstadt will not write sufficiently against infant baptism with all that applies, as to how and why we should baptize, etc., I (Conrad Grebel) will try my hand, and I have already begun to reply to all who have hitherto (excepting thyself) misleadingly, and knowingly, written on baptism and have deceived concerning the senseless, blasphemous form of baptism, as for instance Luther, Leo, Osiander, and the men at Strassburg, and some have done even more shamefully. Unless God avert it, I and we all are and shall be surer of persecution on the part of the scholars, etc., than of other people. We pray thee not to use nor to receive the old customs of the Antichrists, such as sacrament, Mass, signs, etc., but to hold to and rule by the word alone, as becomes all ambassadors (*gesanten*), and especially thee and Carlstadt, and ye do more than all the preachers of all nations.

Regard us as thy brethren and take this letter as an expression of great joy and hope toward you through God, and admonish, comfort, and strengthen us as thou art well able. Pray to God the Lord for us that he may come to the aid of our faith, since we desire to believe. And if God will grant us also to pray, we too will pray for thee and all, that we all may walk according to our calling and estate. May God grant it through Jesus Christ our Saviour. Amen. Greet all brethren, the shepherds and the sheep, who receive the word of faith and salvation with desire and hunger, etc.

One point more. We desire an answer, and if thou dost publish anything, that thou wilt send it to us by this messenger and others. We also desire to be informed if thou and Carlstadt are of one mind. We hope and believe it. We commend this messenger to thee, who has also carried letters from us to our brother Carlstadt. And if thou couldst visit Carlstadt, so that ye could reply jointly, it would be a sincere joy to us. The messenger is to return to us; what is lacking in his pay shall be made up when he returns.

God be with us.

Whatever we have not understood correctly, inform and instruct us.
Given at Zurich on the fifth day of September in the year 1524.

Conrad Grebel, Andrew Castelberg, Felix Mantz, John Ockenfuss, Bartholomew Pur, Henry Aberli, and other brethren of thine in Christ, if God will, who have written this to thee, wish for thee and us all and all thy flock till further message and true word of God, true faith, love, and hope with all peace and grace from God through Jesus Christ. Amen.

I, C. Grebel, meant to write to Luther in the name of all of us, and to exhort him to cease from his [policy of] caution, which he uses without [authority of] Scripture and which he established in the world, and others after him. But my affliction and time would not permit. Do it according to your duty; etc.

Postscript or second letter

Dearly beloved Brother Thomas:

When I had subscribed all our names in a hurry and had thought this messenger would not wait until we wrote to Luther too, he had to bide and wait on account of rain. So I wrote to Luther too, on behalf of my brethren and thine, and have exhorted him to cease from the false sparing of the weak, who are [really] themselves. Andrew Castelberg has written to Carlstadt. Meanwhile there has come here to Hans Hujuff of Halle, our fellow citizen and brother, who recently visited thee, a letter and shameful tract by Luther, which no man ought to write who wants to be first fruits like the apostles. Paul teaches differently: *porro servum Domini*, etc. I see that he wants to have thee outlawed and deliver thee to the prince to whom he has tied his gospel, even as Aaron had to hold Moses as a god. As for thy tracts and protestations I find thee without guilt, unless thou dost reject baptism entirely, which I do not gather from them, but that thou dost condemn infant baptism and the mis-understanding of baptism. What "water" means in John 3:5 we shall examine carefully in thy book and the Scripture. The brother of Hujuff writes that thou hast preached against the princes, that they are to be attacked with the fist. Is it true? If thou are willing to defend war, the tablets, singing, or other things which thou dost not find in express words of Scripture, as thou dost not find the points mentioned, then I admonish thee by the common salvation of us all that thou wilt cease therefrom and from all notions of thy own now and hereafter. Then wilt thou be completely pure, who in other points pleasest us better than anyone in this German and other countries. If thou fallest into the hands of Luther or the Duke, drop the points mentioned, and stand by the others like a hero and champion of God. Be strong. Thou hast the Bible (of which Luther has made bible, blare, babble) for defense against the idolatrous caution of Luther, which he and the learned shepherds in our parts have propagated in all the world; against the deceitful, weak-kneed faith, against their preaching in which they do not teach Christ as they should, although they have just opened the gospel for all the world so people might or should read for themselves. But not many do it, for everybody follows their authority. With us there are not twenty who believe the word of God; they trust persons: Zwingli, Leo [Judae], and others, who elsewhere are esteemed learned. And if thou must suffer for it, thou knowest well that it cannot be otherwise. Christ must suffer still more in his members. But he will strengthen and keep them steadfast to the end. May God give grace to thee and us. For our shepherds also are so wroth and furious against us, rail at us as knaves from the pulpit in public, and call us *Satanas in angelos lucis conversos.* We too shall in time see persecution come upon us through them. Therefore pray to God for us. Once more we admonish thee, and we do so because we love and honor thee so heartily for the clearness of thy word and hence dare write thee trustfully. Do not act, teach, or establish anything according to human opinion, your own or that of others, and abolish again what has been so established; but establish and teach only the clear word and practices of God, with the rule of Christ, unadulterated baptism and unadulterated Supper, as we have touched upon in the first letter, and upon which thou art better informed than a hundred of us. If thou and Carlstadt, Jacob Strauss and Michael Stiefel do not give sincere diligence to it (as I and my brethren hope that you will do), it will be a sorry gospel that has come into the world. But ye are far purer than our men here and those at Wittenberg, who flounder from one perversion of Scripture into the next, and daily from one blindness into another and greater. I think and believe that they propose to become true papists and popes. Now no more.

God, our Captain, with his Son Jesus Christ, our Saviour, and with his spirit and word be with thee and us all.

Conrad Grebel, Andrew Castelberg, Felix Mantz, Henry Aberli, Johannes Pannicellus, John Ockenfuss, John Hujuff, thy country-man of Halle, thy brethren, and seven new young Müntzers against Luther. . . .

15

Calvin Appeals to His King in the Name of the Gospel

IN 1536 CALVIN, an exile from his native France, published the first edition of his theological treatise The Institutes of the Christian Religion. Calvin dedicated the work to his king, Francis I, in the hope that he could persuade him to stop the persecution of Protestants in France. Later Calvin settled in Geneva, Switzerland, where he began building the New Jerusalem; but he never gave up his dream of converting his native France to the evangelical cause, and in later years he bent his efforts to this end again. This dedication to King Francis is a convenient summary in layman's language of some of Calvin's key positions. Calvin answers Catholic charges, levels some of his own, and does not hesitate to lecture his king on the religious duties of rulers.

John Calvin (1509–1564), The Institutes of the Christian Religion

Dedication]

TO HIS MOST *Christian Majesty, Francis, King of the French and his Sovereign, John Calvin wisheth peace and salvation in Christ*]

When I began this work, Sire, nothing was farther from my thoughts than writing a book which would afterwards be presented to your Majesty. My intention was only to lay down some elementary principles, by which inquirers on the subject of religion might be instructed in the nature of true piety. And this labour I undertook chiefly for my countrymen, the French, of whom I apprehended multitudes to be hungering and thirsting after Christ, but saw very few possessing any real knowledge of him. That this was

From John Calvin, THE INSTITUTES OF THE CHRISTIAN RELIGION (Philadelphia, 1816), pp. 7–13, 15–20, 22–23, 25–26. Translation by John Allen.

my design, the book itself proves by its simple method and un-adorned composition. But when I perceived that the fury of certain wicked men in your kingdom had grown to such a height, as to leave no room in the land for sound doctrine, I thought I should be usefully employed, if in the same work I delivered my instructions to them, and exhibited my confession to you, that you may know the nature of that doctrine, which is the object of such unbounded rage to those madmen, who are now disturbing your kingdom with fire and sword. For I shall not be afraid to acknowledge, that this treatise contains a summary of that very doctrine, which, according to their clamours, deserves to be punished with imprisonment, banishment, proscription, and flames, and to be exterminated from the face of the earth. . . . But it shall be yours, Sire, not to turn away your ears or thoughts from so just a defence, especially in a cause of such importance as the maintenance of God's glory un-impaired in the world, the preservation of the honour of divine truth, and the continuance of the kingdom of Christ uninjured among us. This is a cause worthy of your attention, worthy of your cog-nizance, worthy of your throne. This consideration constitutes true royalty, to acknowledge yourself in the government of your king-dom to be the minister of God. For where the glory of God is not made the end of the government, it is not a legitimate sovereignty, but an usurpation. And he is deceived, who expects lasting pros-perity in that kingdom which is not ruled by the sceptre of God, that is, his holy word; for that heavenly oracle cannot fail, which declares that "where there is no vision the people perish." [Prov. xxix 18] Nor should you be seduced from this pursuit by a con-tempt of our meanness. We are fully conscious to ourselves how very mean and abject we are, being miserable sinners before God, and accounted most despicable by men; being (if you please) the refuse of the world, deserving of the vilest appellations that can be found; so that nothing remains for us to glory in before God, but his mercy alone, by which, without any merit of ours, we have been admitted to the hope of eternal salvation, and before men nothing but our weakness, the slightest confession of which is esteemed by them as the greatest disgrace. But our doctrine must stand, exalted above all the glory, and invincible by all the power of the world; because it is not ours, but the doctrine of the living God, and of his Christ, whom the Father hath constituted King, that he may have dominion from sea to sea, and from the river even to the ends of the earth, and that he may rule in such a manner, that the whole earth, with its strength of iron and brass, with its splendour of gold and silver, smitten by the rod of his mouth, may be broken to pieces like a potter's vessel: [Dan. ii. 34. Isaiah xi. 4. Psalm ii. 9] for thus do the prophets foretell the magnificence of his kingdom.

Our adversaries reply, that our pleading the word of God is a false pretence, and that we are nefarious corruptors of it. But that this is not only a malicious calumny, but egregious impudence, by reading our confession, you will, in your wisdom, be able to judge. Yet something farther is necessary to be said, to excite your attention, or at least to prepare your mind for this perusal. Paul's direction, that every prophecy be framed "according to the analogy of faith," [Rom. xii. 6] has fixed an invariable standard by which all interpretation of Scripture ought to be tried. If our principles be examined by this rule of faith, the victory is ours. For what is more consistent with faith, than to acknowledge ourselves naked of all virtue, that we may be clothed by God; empty of all good, that we may be filled by him; slaves to sin, that we may be liberated by him; blind, that we may be enlightened by him; lame, that we may be guided by him; weak, that we may be supported by him; to divest ourselves of all ground of glorying, that he alone may be eminently glorious, and that we may glory in him? When we advance these and similar sentiments, they interrupt us with complaints that this is the way to overturn, I know not what blind light of nature, pretended preparations, free will, and works meritorious of eternal salvation, together with all their supererogations; because they cannot bear that the praise and glory of all goodness, strength, righteousness, and wisdom, should remain entirely with God. But we read of none being reproved for having drawn too freely from the fountain of living waters; on the contrary, they are severely upbraided who "have hewed them out cisterns, broken cisterns that can hold no water." [Jer. ii. 13] Again, what is more consistent with faith, than to assure ourselves of God being a propitious Father, where Christ is acknowledged as a brother and Mediator? than securely to expect all prosperity and happiness from him, whose unspeakable love towards us went so far, that "he spared not his own Son, but delivered him up for us?" [Rom. viii. 32] than to rest in the certain expectation of salvation and eternal life, when we reflect upon the Father's gift of Christ, in whom such treasures are hidden? Here they oppose us, and complain that this certainty of confidence is chargeable with arrogance and presumption. But as we ought to presume nothing of ourselves, so we should presume every thing of God; nor are we divested of vain glory for any other reason than that we may learn to glory in the Lord. . . . Now look at our adversaries, (I speak of the order of priests, at whose will and direction others carry on these hostilities against us,) and consider a little, with me, by what principle they are actuated. The true religion, which is taught in the Scriptures, and ought to be universally maintained, they readily permit both themselves and others to be ignorant of, and to treat with neglect and contempt. They think it very unimportant what any one holds or denies concerning God and Christ, provided he submits his mind with an implicit faith (as they call it) to the judgment of the Church. Nor are they much affected, if the glory of God happen to be violated with open blasphemies, provided no one lift a finger against the primacy of the Apostolic See, and the authority of their holy Mother Church. Why, therefore, do they contend with such extreme bitterness and cruelty for the mass, purgatory, pilgrimages, and similar trifles, and deny that any piety can be maintained without a most explicit faith, so to speak, in these things; whereas they prove none of them from the Word of God? . . .

* * *

Nor do their attacks on our doctrine cease here; they urge every topic of accusation and abuse to render it an object of hatred or suspicion. They call it novel, and of recent origin, — they cavil at it as doubtful and uncertain, — they inquire by what miracles it is confirmed, — they ask whether it is right for it to be received contrary to the consent of so many holy fathers, and the custom of the highest antiquity? — they urge us to confess that it is schismatical in stirring up opposition against the Church, or that the Church was wholly extinct for many ages, during which no such thing was known. — Lastly, they say, all arguments are unnecessary, for that its nature may be determined by its fruits, since it has produced such a multitude of sects, so many factious tumults, and such great licentiousness of vices. It is indeed very easy for them to insult a deserted cause with the credulous and ignorant multitude, but if we had also the liberty of speaking in our turn, this acrimony, which they now discover in violently foaming against us with equal licentiousness and impunity, would presently cool.

In the first place, their calling it novel is highly injurious to God, whose holy word deserves not to be accused of novelty. I have no doubt of its being new to them, to whom Jesus Christ and the Gospel are equally new. But those who know the antiquity of this preaching of Paul, "that Jesus Christ died for our sins, and rose again for our justification," [Rom. iv. 25. Cor. xv. 3, 17.] will find no novelty among us. That it has long been concealed, buried, and unknown, is the crime of human impiety. Now that the goodness of God has restored it to us, it ought at least to be allowed its just claim of antiquity.

From the same source of ignorance springs the notion of its being doubtful and uncertain. This is the very thing which the Lord complains of by his prophets; that "the ox knoweth his owner, and the ass his master's crib," [Isaiah i. 3.] but that his people know not him. But however they may laugh at its uncertainty; if they were called to seal their own doctrine with their blood and lives, it would appear how much they value it. Very different is our confidence, which dreads neither the terrors of death, nor even the tribunal of God. . . .

*   *   *

Another calumny is their charging us with opposition to the fathers, I mean the writers of the earlier and purer ages, as if those writers were abetters of their impiety; whereas if the contest were to be terminated by this authority, the victory in most parts of the controversy, to speak in the most modest terms, would be on our side. But though the writings of those fathers contain many wise and excellent things, yet in some respects they have suffered the common fate of mankind; these very dutiful children reverence only their errors and mistakes, but their excellencies they either overlook, or conceal, or corrupt; so that it may be truly said to be their only study to collect dross from the midst of gold. . . . But if they insist on preserving the landmarks of those whom they understand to be intended, why do they at pleasure so freely transgress them themselves? There were two fathers, of whom one said, that our God neither eats nor drinks, and therefore needs neither cups nor dishes; the other, that sacred things require no gold, and that gold is no recommendation of that which is not purchased with gold. This landmark therefore is transgressed by those who in sacred things are so much delighted with gold, silver, ivory, jewels, muslins, and silks, and suppose that God is not rightly worshipped, unless all these things abound in exquisite splendour, or rather extravagant profusion. There was a father who said he freely partook of flesh on a day when others abstained from it, because he was a Christian. They trangress the landmarks therefore when they curse the soul that tastes flesh in Lent. There were two fathers, of whom one said, that a monk who labours not with his hands is on a level with a cheat or a robber; and the other, that it is unlawful for monks to live on what is not their own, notwithstanding their assiduity in contemplations, studies, and prayers: and they have transgressed this landmark by placing the idle and distended carcases of monks in cells and brothels, to be pampered on the substance of others. There was a father who said, that to see a painted image of Christ, or of any saint, in the temples of Christians, is a dreadful abomination. Nor was this merely the sentence of an individual; it was also decreed by an ecclesiastical council, that the object of worship should not be painted on the walls. They are far from confining themselves within these landmarks, for every corner is filled with images. Another father has advised that after having discharged the office of humanity towards the dead by the rites of sepulture, we should leave them to their repose. They break through these landmarks by inculcating a constant solicitude for the dead. There was one of the fathers who asserted that the substance of bread and wine in the eucharist ceases not, but remains, just as the substance of the human nature remains in the Lord Christ united with the divine. They transgress this landmark therefore by pretending, that on the words of the Lord being recited, the substance of bread and wine ceases, and is transubstantiated into his body and blood. There were fathers who, while they exhibited to the universal Church only one eucharist, and forbade all scandalous and immoral persons to approach it, at the same time severely censured all who when present did not partake of it. How far have they removed these landmarks, when they fill not only the churches, but even private houses with their masses, admit all who choose to be spectators of them, and every one the more readily in proportion to the magnitude of his contribution, however chargeable with impurity and wickedness; they invite none to faith in Christ and a faithful participation of the sacraments; but rather for purposes of gain bring forward their own work instead of the grace and merit of Christ. There were two fathers, of whom one contended that the use of Christ's sacred supper should be wholly forbidden to those who, content with partaking of one kind, abstained from the other; the other strenuously maintained that Christian people ought not to be refused the blood of their Lord, for the confession of whom they are required to shed their own. These landmarks also they have removed, in appointing, by an inviolable law, that very thing which the former punished with excommunication, and the latter gave a powerful reason for disapproving. There was a father who asserted the temerity of deciding on either side of an obscure subject, without clear and evident testimonies of Scripture. This landmark they forgot when they made so many constitutions, canons, and judicial determinations, without any authority from the word of God. There was a father who upbraided Montanus with having, among other heresies, been the first imposer of laws for the observance of fasts. They have gone far beyond this landmark also, in establishing fasts by the strictest laws. There was a father who denied that marriage ought to be forbidden to the ministers of the Church, and pronounced cohabitation with a wife to be real chastity; and there were fathers who assented to his judgment. They have transgressed these landmarks by enjoining on their priests the strictest celibacy. There was a father who thought that attention should be paid to Christ only, of whom it is said, "Hear ye him," and that no regard should be had to what others before us have either said or done, only to what has been commanded by Christ who is pre-eminent over all. This landmark they neither prescribe to themselves, nor permit to be observed by others, when they set up over themselves and others any masters rather than Christ. There was a father who contended that the Church ought not to take the precedence of Christ, because his judgment is always according to truth, but ecclesiastical judges, like other men, may generally be deceived. Breaking down this landmark also, they scruple not to assert, that all the authority of the Scripture depends on the decision of the Church. All the fathers with one heart and voice have declared it execrable and detestable for the holy word of God to be contaminated with the subtleties of sophists, and perplexed by the wrangles of logicians. Do they confine themselves within these landmarks, when the whole business of their lives is to involve the simplicity of the Scripture in endless controversies, and worse than sophistical wrangles? So that if the fathers were now restored to life, and heard this act of wrangling, which they call speculative divinity, they would not suspect the dispute to have the least reference to God. . . .

*   *   *

Nor are we so embarrassed by their dilemmas as to be obliged to confess, either that the Church was for some time extinct, or that we have now a controversy with the Church. The Church of Christ has lived, and will continue to live, as long as Christ shall reign at the right hand of the Father, by whose hand she is sustained, by whose protection she is defended, by whose power she is preserved in safety. For he will undoubtedly perform what he once promised, to be with his people "even to the end of the world." [Matt. xxviii. 20.] We have no quarrel against the Church, for with one consent we unite with all the company of the faithful in worshipping and adoring the one God and Christ the Lord, as he has been adored by all the pious in all ages. But our opponents deviate widely from the truth when they acknowledge no Church but what is visible to the corporeal eye, and endeavour to circumscribe it by those limits within which it is far from being included. Our controversy turns on the two following points: — first, they contend that the form of the Church is always apparent and visible; secondly, they place that form in the see of the Roman Church and her order of prelates. We assert, on the contrary, first, that the Church may exist without any visible form; secondly, that its form is not contained in that external splendour which they foolishly admire, but is distinguished by a very different criterion, *viz.* the pure preaching of God's word, and the legitimate administration of the sacraments. They are not satisfied unless the Church can always be pointed out with the finger. But how often among the Jewish people was it so disorganized, as to have no visible form left? What splendid form do we suppose could be seen, when Elias deplored his being left alone? How long, after the coming of Christ, did it remain without any external form? How often, since that time, have wars, seditions, and heresies, oppressed and totally obscured it? If they had lived at that period, would they have believed that any Church existed? Yet Elias was informed that there were "left seven thousand" who had "not bowed the knee to Baal." Nor should we entertain any doubt of Christ's having always reigned on earth ever since his ascension to heaven. But if the pious at such periods had sought for any form evident to their senses, must not their hearts have been quite discouraged? Indeed it was already considered by Hilary in his day as a grievous error, that people were absorbed in foolish admiration of the episcopal dignity, and did not perceive the dreadful mischiefs concealed under that disguise. For this is his language: "One thing I advise you, beware of Antichrist, for you have an improper attachment to walls; your veneration for the Church of God is misplaced on houses and buildings; you wrongly introduce under them the name of peace. Is there any doubt that they will be seats of Antichrist? I think mountains, woods, and lakes, prisons and whirlpools, less dangerous, for these were the scenes of retirement or banishment in which the prophets prophesied." But what excites the veneration of the multitude in the present day for their horned bishops, but the supposition that those are the holy prelates of religion whom they see presiding over great cities? Away then with such stupid admiration. Let us rather leave this to the Lord, since he alone "knoweth them that are his," and sometimes removes from human observation all external knowledge of his Church. . . .

* * *

. . . But if they speak their real sentiments, let them answer me sincerely, what nation or place they consider as the seat of the Church, from the time when, by a decree of the council of Basil, Eugenius was deposed and degraded from the pontificate, and Amadeus substituted in his place. They cannot deny that the council, as far as relates to external forms, was a lawful one, and summoned not only by one pope, but by two. There Eugenius was pronounced guilty of schism, rebellion, and obstinacy, together with all the host of cardinals and bishops, who had joined him in attempting a dissolution of the council. Yet afterwards, assisted by the favour of princes, he regained the quiet possession of his former dignity. That election of Amadeus, though formally made by the authority of a general and holy synod, vanished into smoke, and he was appeased with a cardinal's hat, like a barking dog with a morsel. From the bosom of those heretics and rebels have proceeded all the popes, cardinals, bishops, abbots, and priests, ever since. Here they must stop. For to which party will they give the title of the Church? Will they deny that this was a general council, which wanted nothing to complete its external majesty, being solemnly convened by two papal bulls, consecrated by a presiding legate of the Roman see, and well regulated in every point of order, and invariably preserving the same dignity to the last? Will they acknowledge Eugenius to be a schismatic, with all his adherents, by whom they have all been consecrated? Either therefore let them give a different definition of the form of the Church, or, whatever be their number, we shall account them all schismatics, as having been knowingly and voluntarily ordained by heretics. But if it had never been ascertained before, that the Church is not confined to external pomps, they would themselves afford us abundant proof of it, who have so long superciliously exhibited themselves to the world under the title of the Church, though they were at the same time the deadly plagues of it. I speak not of their morals, and those tragical exploits with which all their lives abound, since they profess themselves to be Pharisees, who are to be heard and not imitated. I refer to the very doctrine itself, on which they found their claim to be considered as the Church. If you devote a portion of your leisure, Sire, to the perusal of our writings, you will clearly discover that doctrine to be a fatal pestilence of souls, the firebrand, ruin, and destruction of the Church.

16

A Jesuit's Confession of Faith

ROBERT PERSONS WAS AN Englishman educated at Balliol College, Oxford. Suspected of disloyalty to the established church, he left his fellowship in the University and went to the continent where he first entered the Catholic Church, then the Society of Jesus. In 1580 Persons and Edmund Campion, the future martyr, returned in secret to England to serve their Church and their fellow English Catholics. This was a dangerous mission, and Persons prepared the following confession of faith in case he was caught. In making some telling points against Protestantism, he also reveals the struggle between contending faiths and irreconcilable loyalties that went on in many consciences during the Reformation. He also gives us some sense of the spirit of self-dedication that made the Jesuits such effective agents of their Church.

Robert Persons, S.J. (1546–1610), Confession of Faith for the London Magistrates, July 19, 1580

MOST NOBLE LORDS,

From the very day on which I was appointed to England by my superiors for this purpose which I am presently about to declare with the utmost candour, I did not fail to weigh in my mind all the things that were in store for one who undertakes an affair of this sort: as for instance, that you may arrest me or that I may happen to fall into your hands: again, that God may permit you to take every harsh and extreme action against me, and that I may have to undergo what in various parts of the world my comrades are suffering every day, or expecting to suffer, in this same cause from the enemies of Christ and of the aforesaid faith; moreover, the fact that, before I came here, I was informed (though to be sure the fact is not hidden,

From L. Hicks, S. J., ed., LETTERS AND MEMORIALS OF FATHER ROBERT PERSONS. S. J. (London, 1942), pp. 35–41. Reprinted by permission of Catholic Record Society.

and now we are about to learn from actual experience whether it is true) that men who are Catholics have been arrested and brought before Your Worships, and that magistrates of lower rank and sprung from the people are still less inclined than you to tolerate any man producing in his defence any thing containing a vindication of his faith or an account of his conferences; nay, that, on the very threshold as it were, they are overwhelmed with questions that are clearly irrelevant and of their own home invention and usually by recourse to the statutes so that they may be brought within the scope of these and thereby the people be made to believe that these men are punished, not for their religion and for conscience' sake, as is plainly the case (two things which, so far as words go, the Protestants proclaim should be free) but on the count of high treason and on the pretext of violation of the general laws of the realm; and for this they are quietly shut up in prison, either to be consumed and waste away there, as being implicated in these matters, or, if they should so decide, to be condemned to death under cover of some decree or other and done away with; lastly the fact that it was made known to me that *once a man was arrested as a Catholic and shut up* (especially if he bore some reputation for learning) there was no hope left of his being allowed to speak, however humble and abject the prayers with which he strove for permission; nay, that *anyone thus imprisoned was not only refused permission to speak again, but that even the words and arguments he had previously used* were all suppressed or were reproduced in an entirely changed form, sayings of his being slyly quoted in a distorted sense, or certain monstrous crimes being falsely attributed to him, such as conspiracy, rebellion, or the crime of high treason or such like! this with the sole object that he may be involved in the meshes of this deceit and so be less in favour with the people. And because I myself have the greatest horror of these unchristian and cruel deeds, and partly because I was afraid in my heart that they might be employed one day against me, and this perhaps with greater injury to others than inconvenience to myself, I therefore considered it reasonable that I should approach the task of my defence and of giving account of my actions (if ever I should be delivered into your hands) not entirely without preparation. And so what I then planned in my mind, I have now set down briefly in writing, to be a reminder to myself and to enlighten other people, and I here very humbly bring it to Your Worships' notice. And I beg you by Him, who one day will have to judge you as well as me and to pronounce that sentence from which there is no future appeal, to read and ponder over it and, in so far as these declarations I have made seem to Your Worships, to be honourable and my requests to be just, to deal with me in this same spirit, remembering always (and I hope Your Worships will never forget it) that, however I may differ from you in my actual view of what is the true religion and be unable at will to make my conscience agree with yours, nevertheless I am a Christian and also an Englishman, to whom apart from all other considerations such a measure of humanity should be granted as equity itself dictates; and this especially by you, men of that race whose rare nobility, even prior to receiving the Christian faith, is extolled as having always won praise for a certain humanity such as nature herself demands, and as having shrunk from all the barbarous cruelty of tyrants as from some kind of disease. I shall reduce this my defence to certain principal headings in due order to the best of my power.

To begin with, then, I confess that I am a Catholic, and not only that but a priest as well, little credit though I do to such a high calling; and further that I am a professed religious and an insignificant member of the Society of Jesus. All this I acknowledge as the greatest blessing from God and in the same way I proclaim it now solely for His glory, as I hope; and I frankly confess the depth of my own unworthiness. Now in regard to this name of 'Jesuit' although in this place, and in these times especially, and in the eyes of the judges here, I know that it is a source not of favour but of hatred, not of safety but of danger, yet I ought not from fear of this tribunal either to disown it or to dissemble. For this most blessed Society has so loaded me with benefits from God that by no confession of mine, even though it were sealed by my very blood, can I adequately show my gratitude to Him who gave me my vocation to it. For it is my opinion that of the means to my salvation, other of course than the most holy sacraments of Confession and Communion, my entrance into the Society was the principal and strongest, for in it I have found examples of piety more frequent than mention of it, and, far otherwise than is commonly the case in this world, I have found men who cultivate a goodness to outnumber those who preach it.

Now with regard to my faith and considered religious principles, although the description of 'Catholic' has adequately indicated them, yet I desire to explain them more clearly, if possible. Let Your Worships then know that *as a young man I had for long been led hither*

and thither by the misleading utterances of false preachers, and this
was accentuated after I had come to the University. There for many
years I desired to accept the attitude newly adopted by my country
and by degrees to reconcile my conscience which was very opposed
to it; for I perceived that all promotion in the service of the kingdom
had been made to depend on this. I have to thank God, however,
that He never allowed my wavering soul, though I was daily listen-
ing to and reading the new teachers, to adhere to them so obstinately
as to be infected with this plague which it was God's will to keep
from me. Yet the more I kept reading, ever the more uncertain and
restless I seemed to become. But after I had begun to peruse the
sacred writings of the Fathers, I perceived that everything they contained was so repugnant to this new doctrine that I was ashamed
any longer to tempt God and do violence to my own convictions.
For in those writings not only was I finding almost every line quite
contrary to the new doctrine of our times, but, when I looked at the
titles of their works, I discovered also that what is now being
impiously taught is condemned by entire volumes written by the
Fathers of the primitive Church. For what else is to be inferred from
that book by the disciple of Paul on the use and institution of those
very sacraments which are universally rejected by the Protestants, in
which the manner of consecrating the oil is prescribed! And after
this I noticed that others of the Fathers in whole volumes build up
the Catholic position. And of these, one writes about virgins taking
the veil, another about the life, rule and dress of monks, another
composes a treatise on free will, and on the care that should be had
for the dead. Finally when I perused very carefully those wonderful
books against Vigilantius and Jovinianus, of whom the former held
that Saints should neither be honoured nor invoked, the latter put
matrimony on the same plane as virginity, I immediately made this
deduction, to wit, that either all those Fathers, who had as it were
the first fruits of the Holy Ghost, had erred, or that our teachers were
liars. So when I had compared the teaching and piety of the former
with the latters' blindness combined with impiety, I had been of no
discernment if I had had any further doubts which of them should
be followed. Discovering in this way and by greater intercourse with
Catholics that all precedent, authority, weight of argument, erudi-
tion, reason and right thinking were on their side, thereafter I began
to devote myself with constancy to that faith, and I have persevered
in it indeed up to now and I hope to die in it. And so be it known to

you that I firmly believe all that which the Catholic Church of Christ in any way proposes for belief. And I mean by this that church which has always been acknowledged as the visible church of Christ on earth. Of this I hold the Roman church is to be the most honoured part, and I hold the holy Bishop of that See to have been constituted by God, next after Himself, as the universal Pastor and supreme Governor of the whole of it; and all heretics, both ancient and modern, who have left the Church or shall leave it in the time to come, inventing some new form of belief, I hate to the death, and especially the heresiarchs of our day, *Luther, Zwingli, Calvin, Beza* and men of the same kidney, as for instance all the congregations and sects of the Puritans, the Family of Love, the Family of Charity, the Adamites, and any other fantastic inventions which the devil shall introduce into England hereafter; for I am firmly convinced that there can no more be a new faith or religion than there can be some new God, or a Christ other than Him in whom we conscientiously believe.

And now I will set down openly and truthfully what has been the motive of my coming to these parts at this time. It is not unknown to you, I imagine, that there is a certain Society called, from its imitating in a special way the life of our Saviour, the Society of Jesus; and you have heard perhaps that by its profession it incurs the liability of being sent to any part of the whole world to preach the gospel of Christ, without taking any account of danger. It is with this end in view that so many men in these last few years have flocked to it through the various Colleges, in which they arm themselves with the weapons necessary for so great a conflict. Here they spend their time partly in giving earnest attention to letters, partly also in taking stock of the strength for so great a labour as this; thereby fulfilling the counsel of Christ, who exhorts him who will build a tower to reckon the expense necessary for it, and so too him who is entering on a battle, especially when it is a most bloody one, to hold an inspection of his forces. And when this has been done and they perceive that they have laid aside all sensual love and have won a complete victory over themselves, so as to be resolved to despise for Christ's sake even the greatest advancement in this world and to give up their own liberty and yield themselves wholly to the disposition of their superiors, holding no danger to be an excuse from carrying out their commands, then at length, when they have put off all earthly affections, whatever mission may be assigned to them, they welcome it invariably for the honour of God (always after the customary outpouring of prayer) without any dread at all, nay more, subjugating to the service of Christ their intellects and all their inclinations, and promising themselves the favour and help of Him for whose sake they are undertaking this enterprise. And that God has not failed them up to now, the many glorious deeds they have done in nearly all parts of the world bear witness.

I have explained to you thus far the principles of this Society in order that you may realize (as is the truth) that in entering this kingdom I had by no means followed my own inclinations, but had performed an act of obedience to which I had bound myself by vow, and I could not refuse to go to this province any more than if I had been sent to India or Turkey, as comrades of mine have been sent. And to these latter places I should have had no right to refuse to go nor would I have done so on any account. Hence clearly it is in singular hatred of truth that our adversaries most falsely pretend that we are come to stir up rebellion and I know not what unholy plots in our peaceful kingdom; for there is nothing that is less our aim. For we have been sent by men who have practically no knowledge of your secular conditions here, and so far is it from being their wish to be involved in them, that not even the Catholic Princes, though they pressed them very strongly in the matter, were able to induce them to mix themselves in any way in their secular government. Not only therefore is this the end for which they have now sent us, but they have banned all conversation about your politics and have been unwilling to listen to any who made mention of them.

This then I call God Himself to witness (though it is not my habit lightly to take an oath) that what I have said is the absolute truth. Whatever therefore shall eventually happen to me, on my word as a priest I repudiate on behalf of myself and all my comrades this most unjust suspicion. For we are proposing to do here nothing more than our comrades are doing in other parts of the world, viz. to teach those Christians who shall receive us, the rudiments of the Catholic faith and to make their habits conform to the most holy commandments of God. And that obedience which they owe to their Sovereign we inculcate not less but truly much more than does any of the Protestants. For we preach that Princes should be obeyed not merely for fear of punishment or for the sake of avoiding scandal but for conscience's sake as well; and that he may be condemned who does not obey his Prince even in the utmost secrecy of his closet, where no fear of punishment or scandal exists. Whereas on the contrary the

Protestants would have no law, which if broken does not give rise to scandal, to be kept for any reason of conscience; so that a Prince may command abstinence from meat as much as he likes, yet these libertines of ours will eat it in secret and have no suspicion that they have hurt their consciences by doing so. And though this holds good in the case of penal laws, yet in other cases we maintain clearly the opposite. We preach to the people that a salutary observance of the commandments of God is so essential that, lacking it, bare faith will be of little value. And so whosoever has not determined from his heart to amend both in word and deed the irregularities of his life, who is not willing to put away once for all stealing, licentiousness, bribery and other sins of that kind, such a one can nowise live a healthy life in our Church or obtain any absolution for his sins (which the Catholic Church has power to give by reason of that authority to bind and loose left her by Christ). We restore to you your friends and servants instilled with much higher principles of conduct than when they first approached us. Through our intervention not a few hundreds of pounds *have been secretly given back even to the Protestants themselves* by men who listen to us. We exhort those who command large incomes to repair secretly the injuries they have done to men and henceforward to use greater charity towards them. If any one is inclined to be unyielding in such matters, we do not admit him to the bosom of the Church. In fine we incline your people to patience in all things and counsel them to endure any punishment, which Your Worships may yourselves inflict, without resentment, taking comfort only in the testimony of a good conscience. And so far are we from encouraging resistance in any way to any person's authority, that we exhort them much to pray God for us all in Christ our Lord, who, though for our sakes He suffered far more, was willing to endure it all with such patience that He would not open His mouth. This is the evil, if evil indeed it be, which the men of our profession are bringing on your commonwealth; and if you shall wish to condemn it as malice, we nowise decline to pay the penalty due to it.

For myself indeed I assert boldly, that I am so well disposed to this realm or rather to you who are now its rulers, that even at the price of my life and with the shedding of my blood for that end I would procure the salvation of the soul of any one of you. It remains to speak of a certain humble petition to Parliament, viz. that you will refuse to form your judgment concerning me, and my having come here, otherwise than fairly; for I have had in view this purpose only which I have stated and none other. *Well then, since it is on account of my confessing to the Catholic faith that I have been brought by divine permission before your Court here,* although I acknowledge myself to be inferior to many thousands in the Church, and so also in the Society of which I am an insignificant member, yet, trusting in divine assistance and greatly encouraged by the very truth of my cause, I demand to be allowed to defend this faith; and this I do relying, if not on your zeal for truth — and nothing should be dearer to you than that, since the salvation of your souls depends on it — at least on your wish to counteract that invidious report of which I have made mention before, which has become insistent in the ears of men: *that your ignorant Ministers have never dared to submit to the test of any disputation.* For this reason I say, I beg most earnestly that either here or elsewhere at your pleasure I may join battle in some kind of disputation with some of your ministers or prelates. I bar none of them, but in this cause I challenge the lot of them, knowing full well that when they have been stripped of a certain sort of parade and pretence, they can make no defence of their perversions of the truth. For I have no doubt that, when a few small withered flowers of oratory have been lopped off, Your Worships will perceive clearer than light the complete nakedness of these men and the fullness of their ignominy. And if you shall not consent to allow me this contest, still by the fact of the petition we shall give abundant testimony of confidence on our part and on theirs of exceeding incompetence. Finally I ask, with all the earnestness I am capable of, that you will not attribute my petition to arrogance or obstinacy or any suchlike humour, for it proceeds from obedience, a sense of duty, and a certain conscientious zeal.

Those dangers to which I am exposed now had been long anticipated and pondered over; and had they been greater they ought nowise to have hindered this enterprise committed to me by my Superiors, in whom I reverence the person of God. Nor is it possible for anything to happen to me of so bloodthirsty a nature as to intimidate in any way either them from sending men or other men from coming if sent; so entirely ready are they to suffer death for the sake of the Catholic faith. In truth I ought to tell you that five hundred men more or less, belonging to that holy Society, among whom I find myself rather like a fly among eagles, have firmly resolved to assist this holy cause in its necessities.

For my own part I have one life only, which I must yield one day to God from whom I received it, and I can never offer it in a better cause than this, if you wish to deprive me of it. I hope, however, that Your Worships are not going to put in use against us a tyrannical severity of this sort and stain your hands in the blood of men who wish you no evil whatsoever but are very well disposed to you in every way. But if the divine Majesty shall permit you to make void this hope of ours, we must indeed bear it with such strength as God gives us, whatever may be the degree of cruelty that you will to inflict on us; for we know that it will all eventually bear fruit to the honour of God and the confusion of His enemies. In the meantime know this: that if your intentions are bloodthirsty (from which evil may God defend you) there will be no lack of scope for them. For you are persecuting a corporation that will never die, and sooner will your hearts and hands, sated with blood, fail you, than will there be lacking men, eminent for virtue and learning, who will be sent by this Society and allow their blood to be shed by you for this cause.

For the rest then I entreat God Almighty to deign to enlighten you by his grace, so that you may have regard for the divine glory and for the salvation of your souls. And you will do this especially by clemency, for you have no other cause for indignation with us except the defence we must necessarily make of our conscience and faith. This faith we cannot make void at will; and it is for this reason that *Protestants in other kingdoms* have been willing for it to be free. After a few years, or possibly even a few days hence, most noble Lords, we shall all be standing together before that most strict tribunal of God, just as now I stand before this court of yours, where no longer will man be his own judge, and where we shall get more comfort from the mercy we have shown to our neighbours than from severity; for from the former we shall derive some hope of the divine clemency. Now this kindly consideration towards those who are of a different religion, just as I have wished to find it always in others, so according to the slight opportunity I have had, I have quite often practised. Witness to this is the protection we give to my fellow Englishmen who are Protestants in Catholic countries where heresy is persecuted by law. And I know of such men, by no means of the lowest station, if I liked to name them, men of position without any exception; but I beg for no favour in return for this graciousness to them; I urge only the equity and worthiness of my cause and the consideration due from Christians, especially from those of noble birth. For indeed I am most content to await whatever determination you shall come to about me; and if God shall turn it all to His honour, from that aspect it will be most welcome to me. May He make you, who are nobles in this life, more noble still in the life that is to come.

17

A Scientist of the Sixteenth Century

PHILIPP THEOPHRAST VON HOHENHEIM, called Aureolus Bombastus Paracelsus, was born in Switzerland and attended the universities of Vienna
and Ferrara, where he took the doctorate in medicine. It is too easy to
dismiss him for his vanity and superstition: Paracelsus spent his life in a
noble effort to heal others and to discover the secrets of nature, and,
while he traded in occultism, he also held a number of ideas which
pointed in the right direction for the development of a science of
medicine. Consider, for example, his attempt to formulate a doctrine of
empirical research. Underlying all he had a philosophy of progress and
of man which was worthy of the leading Renaissance thinkers.

Paracelsus (1493–1541), Credo and Man and Works

Credo

*   *   *

I AM resolved to pursue the noblest and highest philosophy and
to let nothing divert me from it. . . . I shall not be concerned
with the mortal part of man, and I shall meditate only upon that
within him which does not die; for that is what we hold to be the
highest philosophy.

Ever since my childhood I have pursued these things and learned
them from good teachers, who were thoroughly grounded in *adepta
philosophia* and well versed in the arts. First, from Wilhelmus von
Hohenheim, my father, who has never forsaken me, and later from
a great number of others whom I shall not name here, also from
many writings of ancients and moderns of diverse lands, who laboured mightily.

From Paracelsus, SELECTED WRITINGS (London, 1951), pp. 78–79, 82,
182–186, 194–202, 211–212. Edited by Jolande Jacobi. Translation by
Norbert Guterman. Reprinted by permission of The Bollingen Foundation.

For many years I studied at the universities of Germany, Italy, and France, seeking to discover the foundations of medicine. However, I did not content myself with their teachings and writings and books, but continued my travels to Granada and Lisbon, through Spain and England, through Brandenburg, Prussia, Lithuania, Poland, Hungary, Wallachia, Transylvania, Croatia, the Wendian Mark, and yet other countries which there is no need to mention here, and wherever I went I eagerly and diligently investigated and sought after the tested and reliable arts of medicine. I went not only to the doctors, but also to barbers, bathkeepers, learned physicians, women, and magicians who pursue the art of healing; I went to alchemists, to monasteries, to nobles and common folk, to the experts and the simple. . . . I have oftentimes reflected that medicine is an uncertain and haphazard art scarcely honourable to practise, curing one, and killing ten. . . . Many times I abandoned medicine and followed other pursuits, but then again I was driven back to it. Then I remembered Christ's saying: The healthy need not a physician, but only the sick. And so I made a new resolve, interpreting Christ's words to mean that the art of medicine is true, just, certain, perfect, and whole, and there is nothing in it that should be attributed to the deception of spirits or chance, but that it is an art tested in need, useful to all the sick and beneficial in restoring their health.

This is my vow: To perfect my medical art and never to swerve from it so long as God grants me my office, and to oppose all false medicine and teachings. Then, to love the sick, each and all of them, more than if my own body were at stake. Not to judge anything superficially, but by symptoms, nor to administer any medicine without understanding, nor to collect any money without earning it. Not to trust any apothecary, nor to do violence to any child. Not to guess, but to know. . . .

* * *

I am not an apostle or anything like an apostle, but a philosopher in the German manner.

Here I have no wish to philosophize or speak of the afterlife, except in so far as this can be done in the light of nature. I await the consummation of my hope; let me first achieve my own salvation through my faith in the Saviour, and then it will be time to impart it to others.

Although I have spoken here in a heathen way, as many might

think, although I called man an animal, it is not concealed from me and I know full well that the difference between man and animal lies solely in the countenance and the spirit. To this I must bear witness before God.

Man and Works

*   *   *

Not will alone, only will and deed make for perfect achievement.

All things on earth have been given into the hands of man. And they are given into his hands in order that he may bring them to the highest development, just as the earth does with all that it brings forth. But this highest should be for man the lowest — a beginning; it is a seed which he is beholden to shape into something greater.

Nothing created is beyond man's fathoming. And everything has been created to the end that man may not remain idle, but walk in the path of God, that is to say, in His works and not in vice, not in fornication, not in gambling and not in drinking, not in robbing, not in the acquisition of goods, nor in the accumulation of treasures for the worms. To the end that he may experience God's spirit, His light, and His angelic ways in all things which are of divine nature. It is more blessed to write about nymphs than about the ecclesiastical hierarchy, more blessed to write about the origin of the giants than about court etiquette, more blessed to praise Melusina than cavalry and artillery, and more blessed to speak of miners under the earth than of tournaments and chivalry. For in the former the spirit deals in divine works, while in the latter it is busied in worldly things, to please the world in vanity and impurity.

Behold the herbs! Their virtues are invisible and yet they can be detected. Behold the beasts which can neither speak nor explain anything, and yet nothing is so hidden in them that man cannot learn of it. Thus there is no thing on earth or in the sea, in chaos or in the firmament, that does not become manifest at the appointed time. It is God's will that nothing remain unknown to man as he walks in the light of nature; for all things belonging to nature exist for the sake of man. And since they have been created for his sake, and since it is he who needs them, he must explore everything that lies in nature.

It is not God's will that His secrets should be visible; it is His will that they become manifest and knowable through the works of man who has been created in order to make them visible. Thus Christ, whom no one recognized as the second person of the Trinity, was considered by everyone a man, because what He actually was remained invisible. . . . For God is the revealer of that which is hidden in all things. . . . And it is no different with man. No one sees what is hidden in him, but only what his works reveal. Therefore man should work continually to discover what God has given him. . . . We too should make manifest that which He has put in us, to the end that the unbelievers may see what God can achieve through man.

*　　　*　　　*

Christ charged us with a task which must guide us all, which we must forever strive to perform. His commandments and teachings apply not only to the eternal light but also to the light of nature. He enjoined us: "Seek, and ye shall find." It is our task to seek art, for without seeking it we shall never learn the secrets of the world. Who can boast that a roast squab flies into his mouth? Or that a grapevine runs after him? You must go to it yourself. We can seek in various ways: . . . but the seeking that is needed here concerns the occult things. When the goal of the seeking is hidden, the manner of seeking is also occult; and because knowledge is inherent in the art, he who seeks the art also finds knowledge in it.

All things are given into the hands of man though he make no effort to obtain them; they grow without his help. The ore takes its shape without human aid, and the flowers likewise. But if he wants to use or enjoy them, he must expend labour upon them. For although iron is iron, it is not of itself a plowshare or a carpenter's ax. Although corn means bread, it is not ready to be consumed as bread. So is it with all products; God has given them to us that through them we may preserve ourselves, and He has also given us the arts that we need to this end. Therefore we must be versed not only in all the plants of nature, but also in the art with which God has endowed us for the purpose of preparing them. In this practice we must withstand the test, and being natural bodies, we must during our stay on earth be guided by the light of nature. Let us not be idlers or dreamers, but always at work, both physically and spiritually, so that no part of us remains inactive. Such work in the sweat of our brow may even drive away the devil and his pack, for where man is at work none of them can abide.

*   *   *

Everything that is within can be known by what is without.

It is not God's will that all He has created for the benefit of man and has given him as his own should remain hidden. . . . And even if He did conceal some things, He left nothing unmarked, but provided all things with outward, visible marks, with special traits — just as a man who has buried a treasure marks the spot in order that he may find it again.

We men discover everything that lies hidden in the mountains by external signs and correspondences, and thus also do we find all the properties of herbs and everything that is in the stones. There is nothing in the depths of the seas, nothing on the heights of the firmament, that man is unable to discover. No mountain, no cliff, is so vast as to hide or conceal what is in it from the eyes of man; it is revealed to him by corresponding signs. . . . For each fruit is a sign, and through it we discover what is contained in that from which it stems. Similarly there is nothing in man that is not marked in his exterior, so that by the exterior one may discover what is in the individual who bears the sign. . . . There are four ways by which the nature of man and of all living things can be discovered. . . . First, chiromancy; it concerns the extreme parts of man's limbs, namely the hands and feet. . . . Second, physiognomics; it concerns the face and the whole head. . . . Third, the *substantina,* which refers to the whole shape of the body. . . . And fourth, the customs and usages, that is to say, manners and gestures in which man appears and shows himself. . . . These four belong together; they provide us with a complete knowledge of the hidden, inward man, and of all things that grow in nature. . . . Nature is the sculptor: she endows everything with the form which is also the essence, and thus the form reveals the essence.

There is nothing that nature has not signed in such a way that man may discover its essence. . . . The stars have their orbits by which they are known. The same is true of man. As you can see, each herb is given the form that befits its nature; similarly, man is endowed with a form corresponding to his inner nature. And just as the form shows what a given herb is, so the human shape is a sign which indicates what a given man is. This does not refer to the name, sex, or similar characteristics, but to the qualities inherent in the man. The art of signs teaches us to give each man his true name in accordance with his innate nature. A wolf must not be called a sheep, a dove must not be called a fox; each being should be given the name that belongs to its essence. . . . Since nothing is so secret or hidden that it cannot be revealed, everything depends on the discovery of those things which manifest the hidden. . . . The nature of each man's soul accords with the design of his lineaments and arteries. The same is true of the face, which is shaped and formed according to the content of his mind and soul, and the same is again true of the proportions of the human body. For the sculptor of Nature is so artful that he does not mould the soul to fit the form, but the form to fit the soul; in other words, the shape of a man is formed in accordance with the manner of his heart. . . . Artists who make sculptures proceed no differently. . . . And the more accomplished an artist would be, the more necessary it is that he master the art of signs. . . . No artist can paint or carve, no one can produce an accomplished work, without such knowledge. . . . Only he who has some knowledge of this can be a finished artist.

Behold the *Satyrion* root, is it not formed like the male privy parts? No one can deny this. Accordingly magic discovered it and revealed that it can restore a man's virility and passion. And then we have the thistle; do not its leaves prickle like needles? Thanks to this sign, the art of magic discovered that there is no better herb against internal prickling. The *Siegwurz* root is wrapped in an envelope like armour; and this is a magic sign showing that like armour it gives protection against weapons. And the *Syderica* bears the image and form of a snake on each of its leaves, and thus, according to magic, it gives protection against any kind of poisoning. The chicory stands under a special influence of the sun; this is seen in its leaves, which always bend toward the sun as though they wanted to show it gratitude. Hence it is most effective while the sun is shining, while the sun is in the sky. As soon as the sun sets, the power of chicory dwindles. Why, do you think, does its root assume the shape of a bird after seven years? What has the art of magic to say about this? If you know the answer, keep silent and say nothing the scoffers; if you do not know it, try to find out; investigate, and do not be ashamed to ask questions.

*   *   *

Through the art of chiromancy and the art of physiognomics . . . it is possible to tell by the shape, form, and colour, and nothing more, the qualities and virtues of each herb and root; these are their signs. And for this we need no other test or long study. For God has carefully differentiated all His creation from the beginning, and has never given to different things the same shape and form.

Physiognomics is the art of discovering what is within and hidden in man. . . . It tells us in what relation his heart stands to God and his neighbour, what eyes are those of a rogue and what eyes are not, which tongue is cunning and which is not, which ears are open to evil and which to good. By it we know a man's temperament and his attitude toward God and his fellow men. . . . For his conduct toward God, his ways of acting, hearing, and seeing, all these are signs by which his heart can be known. That which fills the heart overflows in the mouth; and what a man's heart desires, that is what his ears hear, and his eyes seek after. The physiognomics of the heavens provides us with exactly similar insights. . . . For it is written: by their fruits ye shall know them!

*   *   *

There are many kinds of chiromancy; not only the chiromancy of man's hands, from which it is possible to infer and discover his inclinations and his fate, to ascertain what good or evil will befall him; there are yet other kinds of chiromancy, for example, that of herbs, of tree leaves, of wood, of rocks, of mines, or the chiromancy of landscapes, of their roads and rivers, and so on. . . . All this must be studied and well understood, and the physician should also study the lines of the herbs and the leaves, and by the application of chiromancy, he should discover their efficacy and virtues. Those who work wood, such as carpenters, cabinet-makers, and the rest, must estimate the quality of wood by means of chiromancy, and discover its uses, what it is good for. Similarly, a miner should study mines with the help of chiromancy, in order to know what ores and metals a mine contains and whether they are deposited close to the surface or deep below it. And in the same way the cosmographer should study the chiromancy of landscapes, countries, and streams.

Customs are innate in us, and we are brought up in certain customs. Our manners and customs depend on the way in which we are brought up. By finding out whether or not these customs serve God and our fellow man, whether we observe them steadily or whether we waver like reeds in the wind, we obtain a clear picture of our nature. Therefore you can discern man's immortal part in his visible, innate, characteristic signs, and you can know him even by his appearance; for the outer reveals the inner.

God gives us no art that does not bear in itself the necessity of its fulfilment.

Human nature is different from all other animal nature. It is endowed with divine wisdom, endowed with divine arts. Therefore we are justly called gods and the children of the Supreme Being. For the light of nature is in us, and this light is God. Our mortal bodies are vehicles of the divine wisdom. Within our power there are arts that we owe to no one but God; they are given us in the hour of our conception. For this reason there is no justification for the skeptical question: "Is man able to see the future and is he able to know it?" Such doubts imply that not man, but only God, is capable of this knowledge. But since God has created the art, He is not alone to have the knowledge, it is also inherent in his art . . . and this art He has entrusted to man. Who conferred the word upon the prophets? God alone. Who taught the arts? Again God alone. And if everything comes from God, why should art be incapable of something that God is capable of? Therefore, study without respite, that the art may become perfect in us.

Who gives man all the arts, all the skills that he achieves? Man does not give them to himself. No more than an ass becomes a lute-player does man by himself become something he is not. Since man is more gifted than an ass, it follows that he can learn lute-playing and even more difficult things. But not from the firmament. For who is there that can play the lute? No one. But how could someone teach it if he did not know it himself? What we can do must come to us from another who can do it; for nothing can be learned from someone who knows nothing. And although we speak of heavenly songs and symphonies, they are produced neither by harps nor lutes, but are a noise in the clouds, an echo from the earth. Thus all things come from God, and God plants all things in us according to His will.

In the stars all skills are arts, all crafts are hidden, and also all wisdom, all reason, as well as foolishness and what belongs to it; for there is nothing in man that does not flow into him form the light of nature. But what is in the light of nature is subject to the influence of the stars. The stars are our school in which everything must be learned.

* * *

Magic is the most secret of the arts and the highest wisdom concerning the supernatural on earth. . . .

Magic has power to experience and fathom things which are inaccessible to human reason. For magic is a great secret wisdom, just as reason is a great public folly. Therefore it would be desirable and good for the doctors of theology to know something about it and to understand what it actually is, and cease unjustly and unfoundedly to call it witchcraft.

After all, God has permitted magic, and this is a sign that we may use it; it is also a sign of what we are; but we must not interpret this sign as a summons to practise magic. For if a man practises false magic, he tempts God. . . . And if he tempts God, woe to his soul!

All skills and arts come from God, and nothing comes from any other source . . . and therefore no one may vilify astronomy, alchemy, or medicine, or philosophy, or theology, acting, poetry, music, geomancy . . . or any other high art. Why not? What then does man invent of himself? Not even the slightest rag with which to patch his breeches. What new thing can the devil invent? Nothing on earth, nothing pure and simple; not even so much as is needed to catch and kill a louse on your head. But as soon as something is kindled in us by the light of nature, the devil pretends to be our guide and makes bold to falsify all things that God has given us, to slander them, and to make them deceptive, and thus does he spoil everything. . . . The devil makes bold to brand God's works as lies, in order to abuse Him; he seduces those who are weak in their faith and leads them astray in order to make them desert God and cultivate false arts and grievously affront Him. They spend their time in lies, and although they too brood, and inquire and explore, they nevertheless must die without finding the truth.

18

The Turks through Western Eyes

THE IRON CURTAIN between Latin Christendom and the empire of the Ottoman Turks was repeatedly penetrated by Western diplomats, businessmen, and missionaries. One of the most informative of the mid-sixteenth century travelers was Ogier de Busbecq, who spent several years in the lands of the Sultan as an envoy of the Emperor Ferdinand I (1556–1564) and wrote lively, detailed accounts of his observations. Busbecq viewed the Turks with a mixture of wonder, puzzlement, and respect, and, like all good travelers, found that his experiences in strange lands gave him a new perspective on his own society. The comparison of West and East was not altogether favorable to the former: Busbecq was fearful of the outcome of what he believed was an inevitable confrontation. He did not know that the Turks were reaching the limits of a century of expansion.

Ogier Ghiselin de Busbecq (1522–1592), Turkish Letters

... A MESSENGER was despatched to Solyman, with a letter announcing my arrival. During the interval, while we were waiting for his answer, I had an opportunity of seeing Constantinople at my leisure. My chief wish was to visit the Church of St. Sophia; to which, however, I only obtained admission as a special favour, as the Turks think that their temples are profaned by the entrance of a Christian. It is a grand and massive building, well worth visiting. There is a huge central cupola, or dome, lighted only from a circular opening at the top. Almost all the Turkish mosques are built after the pattern of St. Sophia. Some say it was formerly much bigger, and that there were several buildings in connection with it, covering a great extent of ground, which were

From Charles Thornton Forster and F. H. Blackburne Daniell, eds., LIFE AND LETTERS OF OGIER GHISELIN DE BUSBECQ, 2 vols. (London, 1881), I, pp. 123–126, 128–130, 153–156, 219–221.

pulled down many years ago, the shrine in the middle of the church alone being left standing.

As regards the position of the city, it is one which nature herself seems to have designed for the mistress of the world. It stands in Europe, Asia is close in front, with Egypt and Africa on its right; and though these last are not, in point of distance, close to Constantinople, yet, practically, the communication by sea links them to the city. On the left, are the Black Sea and the Sea of Azoff. Many nations live all round the coasts of these seas, and many rivers pour into them; so that, through the length and breadth of these countries, which border on the Black Sea, there is nothing grown for man's use, which cannot, with the greatest ease, be brought to Constantinople by water. On one side the city is washed by the Sea of Marmora, on the other the creek forms a harbour which, from its shape, is called by Strabo 'the Golden Horn.' On the third side it is united to the mainland, so that its position may be described as a peninsula or promontory formed by a ridge running out between the sea on one side, and the frith on the other. Thus from the centre of Constantinople there is a most exquisite view over the sea, and of Mount Olympus in Asia, white with perpetual snow. The sea is perfectly crowded with shoals of fish making their way, after the manner of their kind, from the Sea of Azoff and the Black Sea through the Bosphorus and the Sea of Marmora into the Ægean and Mediterranean, or again returning to the Black Sea. The shoals are so big, and so closely packed, that sometimes fish can be caught with the hand. Mackerel, tunnies, bigheads, bream, and sword-fish are to be had in abundance. The fishermen are, for the most part, Greeks, as they take to this occupation more readily than the Turks, although the latter do not despise fish when brought to table, provided they are of the kinds which they consider clean; as for the rest, they would as lief take a dose of poison as touch them. I should tell you, by the way, that a Turk would sooner have his tongue or teeth torn out, than taste anything which he considers unclean, as, for instance, a frog, a snail, or a tortoise. The Greeks are subject to the same superstition. I had engaged a lad of the Greek Church as purveyor for my people. His fellow-servants had never been able to induce him to eat snails; at last they set a dish of them before him, cooked and seasoned in such a way that he fancied it was some kind of fish, and helped himself to it most liberally. But when the other servants, laughing and giggling, produced the snail shells, and showed him that he had been taken in, his distress was such as to baffle all description. He rushed to his chamber, where there was no end to his tears, misery, and sickness. He declared that it would cost him two months' wages, at the least, to obtain absolution for his sin; it being the custom of Greek priests to charge those who come for confession a price varying with the nature and extent of the offence, and to refuse absolution to those who do not comply with their demand.

At the end of the promontory I mentioned, stands the palace of the Turkish Sultan, which, as far as I can see — for I have not yet been admitted within its walls — has no grandeur of design or architectural details to make it worth a visit. Below the palace, on lower ground near the shore, lie the Sultan's gardens fringing the sea. This is the quarter where people think that old Byzantium stood. You must not expect here to have the story of why in former days the people of Chalcedon were called blind, who lived opposite Byzantium — the very ruins of Chalcedon have now well nigh disappeared; neither must you expect to hear of the peculiar nature of the sea, in that it flows downwards with a current that never stops nor changes; nor about the pickled condiments which are brought to Constantinople from the Sea of Azoff, which the Italians call moronellas, botargas, and caviare. Such matters would be out of place here; indeed, I think I have already exceeded the limits of a letter; besides, they are facts which can be read both in ancient and modern authors.

I now return to Constantinople. Nothing could exceed the beauty or the commercial advantages of its situation. In Turkish cities it is, as I told you before, useless to expect handsome buildings or fine streets; the extreme narrowness of the latter renders a good effect impossible. In many places are to be found interesting remains of ancient works of art, and yet, as regards number, the only marvel is that more are not in existence, when we remember how many Constantine brought from Rome. I do not intend to describe each of them separately, but I will touch on a few. On the site of the ancient hippodrome are a pair of bronze serpents, which people go to see, and also a remarkable obelisk. There are besides two famous pillars at Constantinople, which are considered among the sights. One of them is opposite the caravanserai where we were entertained, and the other is in the market-place which the Turks call 'Avret Bazaar,' i.e. the female slave market. It is engraven from top to bottom with the history of the expedition of Arcadius, who built it, and by whose statue it was long surmounted. It would be more correct to call it a spiral staircase than a column, for there is inside it a set of steps, by ascending which one can reach the top.

*　　*　　*

If I had not visited the Black Sea, when I had an opportunity of sailing thither, I should have deserved to be blamed for my laziness, since the ancients held it to be quite as great an exploit to have visited the Black Sea, as to have sailed to Corinth. Well, we had a delightful voyage, and I was allowed to enter some of the royal kiosks. On the folding doors of one of these palaces I saw a picture of the famous battle between Selim and Ismael, King of the Persians, executed in masterly style, in tesselated work. I saw also a great many pleasure-grounds belonging to the Sultan, situated in the most charming valleys. Their loveliness was almost entirely the work of nature; to art they owed little or nothing. What a fairyland! What a landscape for waking a poet's fancy! What a retreat for a scholar to retire to! I do declare that, as I said just now, these spots seem to grieve and ask for Christian help and Christian care once more; and still truer are these words of Constantinople, or rather of the whole of Greece. That land was once most prosperous; today it is subject to an unnatural bondage. It seems as if the country, which in ancient times discovered the fine arts and every liberal science, were demanding back that civilisation which it gave to us, and were adjuring us, by the claim of a common faith, to be its champion against savage barbarism. But it is all in vain. The princes of Christendom have other objects in view; and, after all, the Greeks are not under heavier bondage to the Turks, than we are to our own vices — luxury, intemperance, sloth, lust, pride, ambition, avarice, hatred, envy, malice. By these our souls are so weighed down and buried, that they cannot look up to heaven, or entertain one glorious thought, or contemplate one noble deed. The ties of a common faith, and the duty we owe our brethren ought to have drawn us to their assistance, even though glory and honour had no charm for our dull hearts; at any rate, self-interest, which is the first thing men think of nowadays, should have made us anxious to rescue lands so fair, with all their great resources and advantages, from the hand of the barbarian, that we might hold them in his stead. At present we are seeking across the wide seas the Indies and Antipodes.

And why? It is because in those lands there are simple, guileless creatures from whom rich booty may be torn without the cost of a single wound. *For these expeditions religion supplies the pretext and gold the motive.*

This was not the fashion with our ancestors. They scorned to place themselves on the level of a trader by seeking those lands where gold was most plentiful, but deemed that land most desirable which gave them the best opportunity of proving their valour and performing their duty. They, too, had their toil; they, too, had their dangers; they, too, had their distant expeditions; but honour was the prize they sought, not profit. When they came home from their wars, they came home not richer in *wealth,* but richer in *renown.*

These words are for your private ear, for perhaps some may hold it foul wrong for a man to suggest that the moral tone of the present day leaves aught to be desired. However that may be, I see that the arrows are being sharpened for our destruction; and I fear it will turn out that if we *will* not fight for glory, we shall be *compelled* to fight for existence.

*   *   *

On our arrival at Amasia we were taken to call on Achmet Pasha (the chief Vizier) and the other pashas — for the Sultan himself was not then in the town — and commenced our negotiations with them touching the business entrusted to us by King Ferdinand. The Pashas, on their part, apparently wishing to avoid any semblance of being prejudiced with regard to these questions, did not offer any strong opposition to the views we expressed, and told us that the whole matter depended on the Sultan's pleasure. On his arrival we were admitted to an audience; but the manner and spirit in which he listened to our address, our arguments, and our message, was by no means favourable.

The Sultan was seated on a very low ottoman, not more than a foot from the ground, which was covered with a quantity of costly rugs and cushions of exquisite workmanship; near him lay his bow and arrows. His air, as I said, was by no means gracious, and his face wore a stern, though dignified, expression.

On entering we were separately conducted into the royal presence by the chamberlains, who grasped our arms. This has been the Turkish fashion of admitting people to the Sovereign ever since a

Croat, in order to avenge the death of his master, Marcus, Despot of Servia, asked Amurath for an audience, and took advantage of it to slay him. After having gone through a pretence of kissing his hand, we were conducted backwards to the wall opposite his seat, care being taken that we should never turn our backs on him. The Sultan then listened to what I had to say; but the language I held was not at all to his taste, for the demands of his Majesty breathed a spirit of independence and dignity, which was by no means acceptable to one who deemed that his wish was law; and so he made no answer beyond saying in a tetchy way, 'Giusel, giusel,' i.e. well, well. After this we were dismissed to our quarters.

The Sultan's hall was crowded with people, among whom were several officers of high rank. Besides these there were all the troopers of the Imperial guard, Spahis, Ghourebas, Ouloufedgis, and a large force of Janissaries; but there was not in all that great assembly a single man who owed his position to aught save his valour and his merit. No distinction is attached to birth among the Turks; the deference to be paid to a man is measured by the position he holds in the public service. There is no fighting for precedence; a man's place is marked out by the duties he discharges. In making his appointments the Sultan pays no regard to any pretensions on the score of wealth or rank, nor does he take into consideration recommendations or popularity; he considers each case on its own merits, and examines carefully into the character, ability, and disposition of the man whose promotion is in question. It is by merit that men rise in the service, a system which ensures that posts should only be assigned to the competent. Each man in Turkey carries in his own hand his ancestry and his position in life, which he may make or mar as he will. Those who receive the highest offices from the Sultan are for the most part the sons of shepherds or herdsmen, and so far from being ashamed of their parentage, they actually glory in it, and consider it a matter of boasting that they owe nothing to the accident of birth; for they do not believe that high qualities are either natural or hereditary, nor do they think that they can be handed down from father to son, but that they are partly the gift of God, and partly the result of good training, great industry, and unwearied zeal; arguing that high qualities do not descend from a father to his son or heir, any more than a talent for music, mathematics, or the like; and that the mind does not derive its origin from the father, so that the son should necessarily be like the father in character, but emanates from heaven, and is thence infused into the human body. Among the Turks, therefore, honours, high posts, and judgeships are the rewards of great ability and good service. If a man be dishonest, or lazy, or careless, he remains at the bottom of the ladder, an object of contempt; for such qualities there are no honours in Turkey!

This is the reason that they are successful in their undertakings, that they lord it over others, and are daily extending the bounds of their empire. These are not our ideas, with us there is no opening left for merit; birth is the standard for everything; the prestige of birth is the sole key to advancement in the public service. But on this head I shall perhaps have more to say to you in another place, and you must consider what I have said as strictly private.

For the nonce, take your stand by my side, and look at the sea of turbaned heads, each wrapped in twisted folds of the whitest silk; look at those marvellously handsome dresses of every kind and every colour; time would fail me to tell how all around is glittering with gold, with silver, with purple, with silk, and with velvet; words cannot convey an adequate idea of that strange and wondrous sight: it was the most beautiful spectacle I ever saw.

With all this luxury great simplicity and economy are combined; every man's dress, whatever his position may be, is of the same pattern; no fringes or useless points are sewn on, as is the case with us, appendages which cost a great deal of money, and are worn out in three days. In Turkey the tailor's bill for a silk or velvet dress, even though it be richly embroidered, as most of them are, is only a ducat. They were quite as much surprised at our manner of dressing as we were at theirs. They use long robes reaching down to the ankles, which have a stately effect and add to the wearer's height, while our dress is so short and scanty that it leaves exposed to view more than is comely of the human shape; besides, somehow or other, our fashion of dress seems to take from the wearer's height, and make him look shorter than he really is.

I was greatly struck with the silence and order that prevailed in this great crowd. There were no cries, no hum of voices, the usual accompaniments of a motley gathering, neither was there any jostling; without the slightest disturbance each man took his proper place according to his rank. The Agas, as they call their chiefs, were seated, to wit, generals, colonels (bimbaschi), and captains (soubaschi). Men of a lower position stood. The most interesting sight in this assembly was a body of several thousand Janissaries, who were drawn up in a long line apart from the rest; their array was so steady and motionless that, being at a little distance, it was some time before I could make up my mind as to whether they were human beings or statues; at last I received a hint to salute them, and saw all their heads bending at the same moment to return my bow. On leaving the assembly we had a fresh treat in the sight of the household cavalry returning to their quarters; the men were mounted on splendid horses, excellently groomed, and gorgeously accoutred. And so we left the royal presence, taking with us but little hope of a successful issue to our embassy.

*   *   *

The Turkish monarch going to war takes with him over 40,000 camels and nearly as many baggage mules, of which a great part, when he is invading Persia, are loaded with rice and other kinds of grain. These mules and camels also serve to carry tents and armour, and likewise tools and munitions for the campaign. The territories, which bear the name of Persia, and are ruled by the Sophi, or Kizilbash as the Turks call him, are less fertile than our country, and even such crops as they bear are laid waste by the inhabitants in time of invasion in hopes of starving out the enemy, so that it is very dangerous for an army to invade Persia, if it be not furnished with abundant supplies. The invading army carefully abstains from encroaching on its magazines at the outset; as they are well aware that, when the season for campaigning draws to a close, they will have to retreat over districts wasted by the enemy, or scraped as bare by countless hordes of men and droves of baggage animals, as if they had been devastated by locusts; accordingly they reserve their stores as much as possible for this emergency. Then the Sultan's magazines are opened, and a ration just sufficient to sustain life is daily weighed out to the Janissaries and other troops of the royal household. The rest of the army are badly off, unless they have provided some supplies at their own expense. And this is generally the case, for the greater number, and especially the cavalry, having from their long experience in war already felt such inconveniences, lead with them a sumpter horse by a halter, on which they carry many of the necessaries of life; namely, a small piece of canvas which they use as a tent, for protection against sun and rain, with the addition of some clothes and bedding; and as provisions for their private use, a leathern bag or two of the finest flour, with a small pot of butter, and some spices and salt, on which they sustain life when they are hard pressed. On such occasions they take out a few spoonfuls of flour and put them into water, adding some butter, and seasoning the mess with salt and spices; these ingredients are boiled, and a large bowl of gruel is thus obtained. Of this they eat once or twice a day, according to the quantity they have, without any bread, unless they have brought some biscuit with them. In this way they are able to support themselves from their own supplies for a month, or if necessary longer. Some fill a bladder with beef, dried and reduced to powder, which forms a highly nutritious food and expands greatly in the cooking, like the flour of which I spoke above. Sometimes too they have recourse to horseflesh; dead horses are of course plentiful in their great hosts, and such beasts as are in good condition when they die furnish a meal not to be despised by famished soldiers. I must not forget to tell you of the men who have lost their horses. When the Sultan moves his camp they stand in a long line by the side of the road with their saddles on their heads, as a sign that they have lost their steeds and need assistance for the purchase of others. An allowance is then made to them by the Sultan at his discretion.

From this you will see that it is the patience, self-denial, and thrift of the Turkish soldier that enable him to face the most trying circumstances, and come safely out of the dangers that surround him. What a contrast to our men! Christian soldiers on a campaign refuse to put up with their ordinary food, and call for thrushes, beccaficos, and such like dainty dishes! If these are not supplied they grow mutinous and work their own ruin; and, if they are supplied, they are ruined all the same. For each man is his own worst enemy, and has no foe more deadly than his own intemperance, which is sure to kill him, if the enemy be not quick. It makes me shudder to think of what the result of a struggle between such different systems must be; one of us must prevail and the other be destroyed, at any rate we cannot both exist in safety. On their side is the vast wealth of their empire, unimpaired resources, experience and practice in arms, a veteran soldiery, an uninterrupted series of victories, readiness to endure hardships, union, order, discipline, thrift, and watchfulness. On ours are found an empty exchequer, luxurious habits, exhausted resources, broken spirits, a raw and insubordinate soldiery, and greedy generals; there is no regard for discipline, license runs riot, the men indulge in drunkenness and debauchery, and, worst of all, the enemy are accustomed to victory, we, to defeat. Can we doubt what the result must be? The only obstacle is Persia, whose position on his rear forces the invader to take precautions. The fear of Persia gives us a respite, but it is only for a time. When he has secured himself in that quarter, he will fall upon us with all the resources of the East. How ill prepared we are to meet such an attack it is not for me to say.

19

Rabelais Lampoons Contemporary Education

RABELAIS was one of those men of the Renaissance — Erasmus was another — whose thirst for learning and for knowledge of the world drew him out of the monastery where he had first learned to love the classics. Everything Rabelais learned and saw in his travels he poured into his comic masterpiece about the giant Gargantua and his son Pantagruel, which he began publishing in sections in 1532. Usually bawdy, almost always satirical, sometimes idealistic, it is an encyclopedia of French life in the sixteenth century. Like Erasmus in The Praise of Folly Rabelais sides with nature against art and with instinct against reason; but he also believed, as did Erasmus, in the value of liberal education. In this selection he expresses his views on the contemporary educational scene in France, when humanism had already begun to make headway against scholasticism.

Francois Rabelais (ca. 1494–1553), Pantagruel

Chapter v, of the acts of the noble Pantagruel in his youthful age

THUS GREW Pantagruel from day to day, and to every one's eye waxed more and more in all his dimensions, which made his father to rejoice by a natural affection. Therefore caused he to be made for him, whilst he was yet little, a pretty cross-bow, wherewith to shoot at small birds, which now they call the great cross-bow at Chantelle. Then he sent him to the school to learn, and to spend his youth in virtue. In the prosecution of which design he came

From Sir Thomas Urquhart and Peter Anthony Motteux, trans., THE WORKS OF FRANCIS RABELAIS, 2 vols. (London, rev. ed., 1863), II, pp. 304–310, 314–316, 344–348.

first to Poictiers, where, as he studied and profited very much, he saw that the scholars were oftentimes at leisure, and knew not how to bestow their time, which moved him to take such compassion on them, that one day he took from a long ledge of rocks, called there Passelourdin, a huge great stone, of about twelve fathom square, and fourteen handfuls thick, and with great ease set it upon four pillars in the midst of a field, to no other end, but that the said scholars, when they had nothing else to do, might pass their time in getting up on that stone, and feast it with store of gammons, pasties, and flagons, and carve their names upon it with a knife; in token of which deed till this hour the stone is called the lifted stone. And in remembrance hereof there is none entered into the register and matricular book of the said university, or accounted capable of taking any degree therein, till he have first drunk in the Caballine fountain of Croustelles, passed at Passelourdin, and got up upon the lifted stone.

Afterwards, reading the delectable Chronicles of his Ancestors, he found that Geoffrey of Lusinian, called Geoffrey with the great tooth, grandfather to the cousin-in-law of the eldest sister of the aunt of the son-in-law of the uncle of the good daughter of his stepmother, was interred at Maillezais; therefore one day he took campos, (which is a little vacation from study to play a while,) that he might give him a visit as unto an honest man. And going from Poictiers with some of his companions, they passed by Legugé, visiting the noble Abbot Ardillon: then by Lusignan, by Sansay, by Celles, by Colonges, by Fontenay le Comte, saluting the learned Tiraqueau, and from thence arrived at Maillezais, where he went to see the sepulchre of the said Geoffrey with the great tooth; which made him somewhat afraid, looking upon the picture, whose lively draughts did set him forth in the representation of a man in extreme fury, drawing his great Malchus faulchion half-way out of his scabbard. When the reason hereof was demanded, the canons of the said place told him, that there was no other cause of it, but that *Pictoribus atque poetis, &c.,* that is to say, that painters and poets have liberty to paint and devise what they list after their own fancy. But he was not satisfied with their answer, and said, He is not thus painted without a cause, and I suspect that at his death there was some wrong done him, whereof he requireth his kindred to take revenge. I will inquire further into it, and then do what shall be reasonable. Then he returned not to Poictiers, but would take a view of the other Universities of France. Therefore, going to Rochelle, he took shipping and arrived at Bordeaux, where he found no great exercise, only now and then he would see some mariners and lightermen a wrestling on the quay or strand by the river side. From thence he came to Thoulouse, where he learned to dance very well, and to play with the two-handed sword, as the fashion of the scholars of the said University is to bestir themselves in games, whereof they may have their hands full: but he stayed not long there, when he saw that they did cause burn their regents alive, like red herrings, saying, Now God forbid that I should die this death! for I am by nature sufficiently dry already, without heating myself any further.

He went then to Montpellier, where he met with the good wives of Mirevaux, and good jovial company withal, and thought to have set himself to the study of physic; but he considered that that calling was too troublesome and melancholic, and that physicians did smell of glisters like old devils. Therefore he resolved he would study the laws; but seeing that there were but three scauld, and one bald-pated legist in that place, he departed from thence, and in his way made the bridge of Guard, and the amphitheatre of Nismes, in less than three hours, which nevertheless seems to be a more divine than human work. After that he came to Avignon, where he was not above three days before he fell in love; for the women there take great delight in playing at the close buttock-game, because it is papal ground. Which his tutor and pedagogue Epistemon perceiving, he drew him out of that place, and brought him to Valence in the Dauphiny, where he saw no great matter of recreation, only that the lubbards of the town did beat the scholars, which so incensed him with anger, that when, upon a certain very fair Sunday, the people being at their public dancing in the streets, and one of the scholars offering to put himself into the ring to partake of that sport; the foresaid lubberly fellows would not permit him the admittance into their society, he taking the scholar's part, so belaboured them with blows, and laid such load upon them, that he drove them all before him, even to the brink of the river Rhone, and would have there drowned them, but they did squat to the ground like moles, and there lay close a full half league under the river. The hole is to be seen there yet.

After that he departed from thence, and in three strides and one leap, came to Angiers, where he found himself very well, and would have continued there some space, but that the plague drove them away. So from thence he came to Bourges, where he studied a good long time, and profited very much in the faculty of the laws, and would sometimes say, that the books of the civil law were like unto a wonderfully precious, royal, and triumphant robe of gold, edged with dirt; for in the world are no goodlier books to be seen, more ornate, nor more eloquent than the texts of the Pandects, but the bordering of them, that is to say, the gloss of Accursius, is so scurvy, vile, base, and unsavoury, that it is nothing but filthiness and villany.

Going from Bourges, he came to Orleans, where he found store of swaggering scholars that made him great entertainment at his coming, and with whom he learned to play at tennis so well, that he was a master at that game. For the students of the said place make a prime exercise of it; and sometimes they carried him unto Cupid's houses of commerce, (in that city termed islands, because of their being most ordinarily environed with other houses, and not contiguous to any,) there to recreate his person at the sport of poussevant, which the wenches of London call the ferkers in and in. As for breaking his head with over-much study, he had an especial care not to do it in any case, for fear of spoiling his eyes. Which he the rather observed, for that it was told him by one of his teachers, there called regents, that the pain of the eyes was the most hurtful thing of any to the sight. For this cause when he one day was made a licentiate, or graduate in law, one of the scholars of his acquaintance, who of learning had not much more than his burden, though instead of that he could dance very well, and play at tennis, made the blazon and device of the licentiates in the said university, saying,

> So you have in your hand a racket,
> A tennis-ball in your cod-placket,
> A Pandect law in your cap's tippet,
> And that you have the skill to trip it
> In a low dance, you will be allowed
> The grant of the licentiate's hood.

Chapter vii, how Pantagruel came to Paris, and of the choice books of the library of St. Victor

After that Pantagruel had studied very well at Orleans, he resolved to see the great University at Paris; but, before his departure, he was informed, that there was a huge big bell at St. Anian, in the said town of Orleans, under the ground, which had been there above two hundred and fourteen years, for it was so great that they could not by any device get it so much as above the ground, although they used all the means that are found in Vitruvius *de Architectura,* Albertus *de Re Ædificatoria,* Euclid, Theon, Archimedes, and Hero *de Ingeniis:* for all that was to no purpose. Wherefore, condescending heartily to the humble request of the citizens and inhabitants of the said town, he determined to remove it to the tower that was erected for it. With that he came to the place where it was, and lifted it out of the ground with his little finger, as easily as you would have done a hawk's bell, or bell-weather's tingle tangle; but, before he would carry it to the foresaid tower or steeple appointed for it, he would needs make some music with it about the town, and ring it along all the streets, as he carried it in his hand, wherewith all the people were very glad. But there happened one great inconveniency, for with carrying it so, and ringing it about the streets, all the good Orleans wine turned instantly, waxed flat, and was spoiled, which nobody there did perceive till the night following; for every man found himself so altered, and a-dry with drinking these flat wines, that they did nothing but spit, and that as white as Maltha cotton, saying, We have got the Pantagruel, and our very throats are salted. This done, he came to Paris with his retinue. And at his entry every one came out to see him, — as you know well enough, that the people of Paris is sottish by nature, by B. flat, and B. sharp, — and beheld him with great astonishment, mixed with no less fear, that he would carry away the palace into some other country, *à remotis,* and far from them, as his father formerly had done the great peal bells at our Lady's church, to tie about his mare's neck. Now after he had stayed there a pretty space, and studied very well in all the seven liberal arts, he said it was a good town to live in, but not to die; for that the grave-digging rogues of St. Innocent used in frosty nights to warm their bums with dead men's bones. In his abode there he found the library of St. Victor, a very stately and magnificent one, especially in some books which were there, of which followeth the Repertory and Catalogue, *Et primo,*

The two-horse tumbrel of Salvation.
The Codpiece of the Law.
The slippers or Pantofles of the Decretals.
The Pomegranate of Vice.

The Clew-bottom of Theology

The Duster or Foxtail-flap of Preachers, composed by Turlupin.

The Churning Ballock of the Valiant.

The Henbane of the Bishops.

Marmotretus de baboonis et apis, cum Commento Dorbellis.

Decretum Universitatis Parisiensis super gorgiasitate muliercularum ad placitum.

The Apparition of Sanct Geltrude to a Nun of Poissy, being in travail, at the bringing forth of a child.

Ars honeste fartandi in societate, per Marcum Ortuinum.

The Mustard-pot of Penance.

The Gamashes, alias the Boots of Patience.

Formicarium artium.

De brodiorum usu, et honestate chopinandi, per Sylvestrem Prioratem Jacobinum

The Cuckold in Court.

*   *   *

[The list continues with 124 more titles of the same kind.]

Chapter viii, how Pantagruel, being at Paris, received letters from his father Gargantua, and the copy of them

Pantagruel studied very hard, as you may well conceive, and profited accordingly; for he had an excellent understanding, and notable wit, together with a capacity in memory, equal to the measure of twelve oil budgets, or butts of olives. And, as he was there abiding one day, he received a letter from his father in manner as followeth.

Most dear Son, — Amongst the gifts, graces, and prerogatives with which the sovereign plasmator God Almighty hath endowed and adorned human nature at the beginning, that seems to me most singular and excellent, by which we may in a mortal estate attain to a kind of immortality, and in the course of this transitory life perpetuate our name and seed, which is done by a progeny issued from us in the lawful bonds of matrimony. Whereby that in some measure is restored unto us, which was taken from us by the sin of our first parents, to whom it was said, that, because they had not obeyed the commandment of God their Creator, they should die; and by death should be brought to nought that so stately frame and plasmature, wherein the man at first had been created.

... And, therefore, not without just and reasonable cause do I give thanks to God my Saviour and Preserver, for that he hath enabled me to see my bald old age reflourish in thy youth; for when, at his good pleasure, who rules and governs all things, my soul shall leave this mortal habitation, I shall not account myself wholly to die, but to pass from one place unto another, considering that, in and by thee, I continue in my visible image living in the world, visiting and conversing with people of honour, and other my good friends, as I was wont to do. Which conversation of mine, although it was not without sin, (because we are all of us trespassers, and therefore ought continually to beseech his divine majesty to blot our transgressions out of his memory,) yet was it by the help and grace of God, without all manner of reproach before men.

Wherefore, if those qualities of the mind but shine in thee, wherewith I am endowed, as in thee remaineth the perfect image of my body, thou wilt be esteemed by all men to be the perfect guardian and treasure of the immortality of our name. But, if otherwise, I shall truly take but small pleasure to see it, considering that the lesser part of me, which is the body, would abide in thee, and the best, to wit, that which is the soul, and by which our name continues blessed amongst men, would be degenerate and abastardized. This I do not speak out of any distrust that I have of thy virtue, which I have heretofore already tried, but to encourage thee yet more earnestly to proceed from good to better. And that which I now write unto thee is not so much that thou shouldest live in this virtuous course, as that thou shouldest rejoice in so living and having lived, and cheer up thyself with the like resolution in time to come; to the prosecution and accomplishment of which enterprize and generous undertaking thou mayest easily remember how that I have spared nothing, but have so helped thee as if I had no other treasure in this world, but to see thee once in my life completely well bred and accomplished, as well in virtue, honesty, and valour, as in all liberal knowledge and civility, and so to leave thee after my death as a mirror representing the person of me thy father, and if not so excellent, and such indeed as I do wish thee, yet such in my desire.

But although my deceased father of happy memory, Grangousier, had bent his best endeavours to make me profit in all perfection and political knowledge, and that my labour and study was fully correspondent to, yea, went beyond his desire, nevertheless, as thou mayest well understand, the time then was not so proper and fit for learning as it is at present, neither had I plenty of such good masters as thou hast had. For that time was darksome, obscured with clouds of ignorance, and savouring a little of the infelicity and calamity of the Goths, who had, wherever they set footing, destroyed all good literature, which in my age hath by the divine goodness been restored unto its former light and dignity, and that with such amendment and increase of knowledge, that now hardly should I be admitted unto the first form of the little grammar-school boys. I say, I, who in my youthful days was, and that justly, reputed the most learned of that age. Which I do not speak in vain boasting, although I might lawfully do it in writing unto thee, — in verification whereof thou hast the authority of Marcus Tullius in his book of old age, and the sentence of Plutarch, in the book intituled, How a man may praise himself without envy: — but to give thee an emulous encouragement to strive yet further.

Now it is, that the minds of men are qualified with all manner of discipline, and the old sciences revived, which for many ages were extinct. Now it is, that the learned languages are to their pristine purity restored, viz., Greek, without which a man may be ashamed to account himself a scholar, Hebrew, Arabic, Chaldæan, and Latin. Printing likewise is now in use, so elegant and so correct, that better cannot be imagined, although it was found out but in my time by divine inspiration, as by a diabolical suggestion on the other side, was the invention of ordnance. All the world is full of knowing men, of most learned schoolmasters, and vast libraries; and it appears to me as a truth, that neither in Plato's time, nor Cicero's, nor Papinian's, there was ever such conveniency for studying, as we see at this day there is. Nor must any adventure henceforward to come in public, or present himself in company, that hath not been pretty well polished in the shop of Minerva. I see robbers, hangmen, freebooters, tapsters, ostlers, and such like, of the very rubbish of the people, more learned now than the doctors and preachers were in my time.

What shall I say? The very women and children have aspired to this praise and celestial manna of good learning. Yet so it is, that at the age I am now of, I have been constrained to learn the Greek tongue, — which I contemned not like Cato, but had not the leisure in my younger years to attend the study of it, — and I take much delight in the reading of Plutarch's Morals, the pleasant Dialogues of Plato, the Monuments of Pausanias, and the Antiquities of Athenæus, in waiting on the hour wherein God my Creator shall call me, and command me to depart from this earth and transitory pilgrimage. Wherefore, my son, I admonish thee to employ thy youth to profit as well as thou canst, both in thy studies and in virtue. Thou are at Paris, where the laudable examples of many brave men may stir up thy mind to gallant actions, and hast likewise for thy tutor and pedagogue the learned Epistemon, who by his lively and vocal documents may instruct thee in the arts and sciences.

I intend, and will have it so, that thou learn the languages perfectly; first of all, the Greek, as Quintilian will have it; secondly, the Latin; and then the Hebrew, for the Holy Scripture-sake; and then the Chaldee and Arabic likewise, and that thou frame thy style in Greek in imitation of Plato; and for the Latin, after Cicero. Let there be no history which thou shalt not have ready in thy memory; — unto the prosecuting of which design, books of cosmography will be very conducible, and help thee much. Of the liberal arts of geometry, arithmetic and music, I gave thee some taste when thou wert yet little, and not above five or six years old. Proceed further in them, and learn the remainder if thou canst. As for astronomy, study all the rules thereof. Let pass, nevertheless, the divining and judicial astrology, and the art of Lullius, as being nothing else but plain abuses and vanities. As for the civil law, of that I would have thee to know the texts by heart, and then to confer them with philosophy.

Now, in matter of the knowledge of the works of nature, I would have thee to study that exactly; that so there be no sea, river, nor fountain, of which thou dost not know the fishes; all the fowls of the air; all the several kinds of shrubs and trees, whether in forest or orchards; all the sorts of herbs and flowers that grow upon the ground; all the various metals that are hid within the bowels of the earth; together with all the diversity of precious stones, that are to be seen in the orient and south parts of the world. Let nothing of all these be hidden from thee. Then fail not most carefully to peruse the books of the Greek, Arabian, and Latin physicians, not despising the Talmudists and Cabalists; and by frequent anatomies get thee the perfect knowledge of that other world, called the microcosm, which is man. And at some of the hours of the day apply thy mind to the study of the Holy Scriptures; first, in Greek, the New Testament, with the Epistles of the Apostles; and then the Old Testament in

Hebrew. In brief, let me see thee an abyss, and bottomless pit of knowledge: for from henceforward, as thou growest great and becomest a man, thou must part from this tranquillity and rest of study, thou must learn chivalry, warfare, and the exercises of the field, the better thereby to defend my house and our friends, and to succour and protect them at all their needs, against the invasion and assaults of evil doers.

Furthermore, I will that very shortly thou try how much thou hast profited, which thou canst not better do, than by maintaining publicly theses and conclusions in all arts, against all persons whatsoever, and by haunting the company of learned men, both at Paris and otherwhere. But because, as the wise man Solomon saith, Wisdom entereth not into a malicious mind, and that knowledge without conscience is but the ruin of the soul; it behoveth thee to serve, to love, to fear God, and on him to cast all thy thoughts and all thy hope, and, by faith formed in charity, to cleave unto him, so that thou mayst never be separated from him by thy sins. Suspect the abuses of the world. Set not thy heart upon vanity, for this life is transitory, but the Word of the Lord endureth for ever. Be serviceable to all thy neighbours, and love them as thyself. Reverence thy preceptors: shun the conversation of those whom thou desirest not to resemble; and receive not in vain the graces which God hath bestowed upon thee. And, when thou shalt see that thou hast attained to all the knowledge that is to be acquired in that part, return unto me, that I may see thee, and give thee my blessing before I die. My son, the peace and grace of our Lord be with thee, Amen.

Thy father, GARGANTUA.

From Utopia the 17th day of the
month of March.

20

Montaigne, Seeker of the Golden Mean

AMID THE DIN of the Wars of Religion in France Montaigne retired from public service and the practice of law to think and to write his essays. His subject was himself—man thinking, doubting, feeling—and his object was to work out a way to live, not only for himself, but for all men as well. Montaigne dissociated himself from the humanist optimism of the Renaissance as well as from the fanaticism of the Reformation; yet both these movements influenced him. It is fascinating to pick out the threads of thought which bind him to this double heritage as well as to trace those elements which mark a fresh point of view.

Michel Eyquem de Montaigne (1553–1592), Of Managing One's Will

FEW THINGS, in comparison of what commonly affect other men, move, or, to say better, possess me; for 'tis but reason they should concern a man, provided they do not take possession of him. I am very solicitous, both by study and reasoning, to enlarge this privilege of insensibility, which is naturally raised to a pretty high degree in me; so that consequently I espouse or am very much moved with very few things. I have my sight clear enough, but I fix it upon very few objects; my sense delicate and tender enough, but an apprehension and application stubborn and negligent. I am very unwilling to engage myself; as much as in me lies, I employ myself wholly upon myself; and in this very subject should rather choose to curb and restrain my affection from plunging itself over head and ears into it, it being a subject that I possess at the mercy of others, and over which fortune has more right than I; so that even

From William Hazlitt, ed. and trans., THE COMPLETE WORKS OF MICHAEL DE MONTAIGNE (Philadelphia, 1879), pp. 490–501.

so much as to health, which I so much value, it were necessary for me not so passionately to covet and desire it as to find diseases insupportable. A man ought to moderate himself betwixt the hatred of pain and the love of pleasure, and Plato sets down a middle path of life betwixt both. But against such affections as wholly carry me away from myself and fix me elsewhere, against these, I say, I oppose myself with my utmost force and power. 'Tis my opinion that a man should lend himself to others, and only give himself to himself. Were my will easy to lend itself out, and to be swayed, I should not stick there; I am too tender, both by nature and custom:

> "Born and bred up in negligence and ease,
> I fly from business as from disease." [Ovid]

The hot and obstinate disputes wherein my adversary would at last have the better, the issue that would render my heat and obstinacy disgraceful, would perhaps vex me to the last degree. Should I set myself to it at the rate that others do, my soul would never have the force to bear the emotions and alarms that attend those who pursue and grasp at so much; it would immediately be disordered by this inward agitation. If sometimes I have been put upon the management of other men's affairs, I have promised to take them in hand, but not into my lungs and liver; to take them upon me, not to incorporate them; to take pains for, but not to be impassioned about, them. I have a care of them, but I will not brood upon them. I have enough to do to order and govern the domestic tumults that I have in my own veins and bowels, without introducing a crowd of other men's affairs, and am sufficiently concerned about my own proper and natural business, without meddling with the concerns of others. Those who know how much they owe to themselves, and how many offices they are bound to of their own, find that nature has given them this commission, full enough to keep them from being ever idle: "Thou hast business enough at home, look to that."

Men let themselves out to hire; their faculties are not for themselves, but to be employed for those to whom they have enslaved themselves: their hirers are in their houses, not themselves. This common humour pleases not me. We must be thrifty of the liberty of our souls, and never let them out but upon just occasions, which are very few, if we judge aright. Do but observe such as have accustomed themselves to be at every one's call, they do it indifferently upon all, as well upon little as upon great occasions, in that which nothing concerns them, as much as in what imports them most; they intrude themselves indifferently wherever there is business and obligation, and are without life, when not in the bustle of affairs: "they only seek business for business sake" [Seneca]. It is not so much that they will go, as that they cannot stand still: like a rolling stone that does not stop till it can go no farther. Business, by a certain sort of men, is thought a mark of capacity and honour; their souls seek repose in motion, as children do by being rocked in a cradle; they may pronounce themselves as serviceable to their friends, as troublesome to themselves. No one distributes his money to others, but every one distributes his time and his life. There is nothing of which we are so prodigal as of these two things, of which to be thrifty would be both commendable and useful. I am of a quite contrary humour; I look to myself, and commonly covet with no great ardour what I do desire, and desire little, and employ and busy myself but rarely and temperately in the same way. Whatever they take in hand, they do it with their utmost power and vehemence. There are so many dangerous steps, that, for the more safety, we must a little lightly and superficially slide through the world, and not rush through it. Pleasure itself is painful in its depth:

> "Thou upon glowing coals dost tread,
> Under deceitful ashes hid." [Horace]

The citizens of Bordeaux chose me mayor of their city at a time when I was at a distance from France, and still more remote from any such thought. I begged to be excused, but I was told that I had committed an error in so doing, and the greater because the king had moreover interposed his command in the affair. 'Tis an office that ought to be looked upon so much more honourable, as it has no other pay nor advantage than the bare honour of its execution. It continues two years, but may be extended by a second election, which very rarely happens. It was so to me, and had never been so but twice before, some years ago to Monsieur Lanssac, and lately to Monsieur de Biron, marshal of France, in whose place I succeeded, and left mine to Monsieur de Matignon, marshal of France also. Proud of so noble a fraternity,

> "Both fit for governing in peace and war." [Virgil]

Fortune would have a hand in my promotion, by this particular circumstance, which she put in of her own, not altogether vain; for

Alexander disdained the ambassadors of Corinth, who came to make him a tender of the burgess-ship of their city; but when they proceeded to lay before him that Bacchus and Hercules were also in the register, he thankfully accepted the offer.

At my arrival, I faithfully and conscientiously represented myself to them for such as I find myself to be; a man without memory, without vigilance, without experience, and without vigour; but withal without hatred, without ambition, without avarice, and without violence. That they might be informed and know what they were to expect from my service, and being that the knowledge they had had of my father, and the honour they had for his memory, had been the only motives to confer this upon me, I plainly told them that I should be very sorry any thing should make so great an impression upon me, as their affairs and the concerns of their city had done upon him, whilst he had the same government to which they had preferred me. I very well remember, when a boy, to have seen him in his old age, tormented with and solicitous about the public affairs, neglecting the soft repose of his own house, to which the declension of his age had attached him for several years before, the management of his own affairs, and his health, and certainly despising his own life, which was in great danger of being lost, by being engaged in long and painful journeys on their behalf. Such was he, and this humour of his proceeded from a marvelous goodness of nature. Never was there a more charitable and popular spirited man. Yet this which I commend in others, I do not love to follow myself, and am not without excuse.

He had heard that a man must forget himself for his neighbour, and that particular individuals were in no manner of consideration in comparison with the general concern. Most of the rules and precepts of this world run this way, to drive us out of ourselves into the world, for the benefit of public society: they thought to do a great feat, to divert us from ourselves, presuming we were but too much fixed at home, and by a too natural inclination, and have said all they could to that purpose; for 'tis no new thing for wise men to preach things as they serve, not as they are. Truth has its obstructions, inconveniences, and incompatibilities with us: we must be often deceived, that we may not deceive ourselves, and shut our eyes, and stupefy our understandings, to redress and amend them: "For the ignorant judge, and therefore are oft to be deceived, lest they should err" [Quintilian]. When they prescribe us to love three, four, fifty degrees of things above ourselves, they do like archers, who, to hit the mark, take their aim a great deal higher than the butt: to set a crooked stick straight, we bend it the contrary way.

I take it that in the temple of Pallas, as we see in all other religions, there were apparent mysteries to be shown to the people, and others, more secret and high, that were only to be shown to such as were professed: 'tis likely that in these the true point of friendship that every one owes to himself is to be found; not a false friendship, that makes us embrace glory, knowledge, riches, and the like, with a principal and immoderate affection, as members of our being, nor an indiscreet and effeminate friendship, wherein it happens, as with ivy, that decays and ruins the walls it embraces; but a sound and regular friendship, equally useful and pleasant. Who knows the duties of this friendship, and practises them, is truly of the cabinet council of the muses, and has attained the summit of human wisdom and our happiness: such a one, exactly knowing what he owes to himself, will in his part find that he ought to apply the use of the world and of other men to himself, and, to do this, to contribute to the public society the duties and offices appertaining to him. Who does not in some sort live to others, does not live much to himself: "He who is his own friend is a friend to every body else" [Seneca]. The principal charge we have is, to every one his own conduct, and 'tis for this that we are here. As he who should forget to live a virtuous and holy life, and should think he acquitted himself of his duty in instructing and training up others to it, would be a fool; even so he who abandons his own particular healthful and pleasant living to serve others, takes, in my opinion, a wrong and an unnatural course.

I would not that men should refuse, in the employments they take upon them, their attention, pains, their eloquence, and their sweat and blood, in time of need:

> "And for his friend or country's good
> Would never fear to spill his blood." [Horace]

but 'tis only as a loan, and incidentally; his mind being always in repose and in health not without action, but without vexation, without passion. To be simply doing costs him so little that he acts even sleeping; but he must set on the motion with discretion; for the body receives the offices imposed upon it, just according to what they are;

the mind often extends, and makes them heavier at its own expense, giving them what measure it pleases. Men perform like things with several sorts of endeavour, and different contentions of the will: the one does well enough without the other; for how many people hazard themselves every day in war, without any concern which way it goes, and thrust themselves into the dangers of battles, the loss of which will not break their next night's sleep? And such a man may be at home, out of danger, which he durst not have looked upon, who is more passionately concerned for the issue of this war, and whose soul is more anxious about events, than the soldier who stakes his life and blood in the quarrel. I could have engaged myself in public employments, without quitting myself a nail's breadth, and have given myself to others without abandoning myself. This sharpness and violence of desires more hinders than it advances the execution of what we undertake, fills us with impatience against slow or contrary events, and with heat and suspicion against those with whom we have to do. We never carry on that thing well by which we are prepossessed and led:

"For over heat doth carry on things ill." [Statius]

He who therein employs only his judgment and address proceeds more cheerfully: he counterfeits, he gives way, he defers all things at his ease, according to the necessities of occasions; he fails in his attempts, without trouble and affliction, ready and entire for a new effort; he always rides bridle in hand. In him who is drunk with violent and tyrannic intention, we see of necessity much imprudence and injustice: the impetuosity of his desire carries him away; these are rash motions, and, if fortune does not very much assist, of very little fruit. Philosophy wills that in the revenge of injuries received we should strip ourselves of choler, not that the chastisement should be less, but, on the contrary, that the revenge may be the better and more heavy, which it conceives will be by this impetuosity hindered. For anger does not only trouble, but of itself does also weary, the arm of those who chastise; this fire benumbs and wastes their force: as in precipitation, "haste fetters itself" [Quintus Curtius, Seneca]. For example, according to what I commonly see, avarice has no greater impediment than itself; the more bent and vigorous it is, the less it rakes together, and commonly sooner grows rich, when disguised in a vizor of liberality.

A very honest gentleman, and a particular friend of mine, had like to have cracked his brains by a too passionate attention and affection to the affairs of a certain prince, his master; which master has thus set himself out to me: — "That he foresees the weight of accidents as well as another; but that in those for which there is no remedy he presently resolves upon suffering; in others, having taken all the necessary precaution, which, by the vivacity of his understanding, he can presently do, he quietly awaits what may follow." And, in truth, I have accordingly seen him maintain a great nonchalance and liberty of action, and serenity of countenance, in very great and difficult affairs; I find him much greater and of greater capacity in adverse than prosperous fortune; his losses are to him more glorious than his victories, and his mourning than his triumph.

Do but consider that, even in vain and frivolous actions, as at chess, tennis, and the like, this eager and ardent engaging with an impetuous desire immediately throws the mind and members into indirection and disorder; a man confounds and hinders himself: he that carries himself the most moderately, both towards gain and loss, has always his wits about him; the less peevish and passionate he is at play, he plays much more advantageously and surely.

As to the rest, we hinder the mind's seizure and hold, in giving it so many things to seize upon: some things we are only to offer to it, to tie others to it, and others to incorporate with it: it can feel and discern all things, but ought to feed on nothing but itself, and should be instructed in what properly concerns itself, that is properly of its own having and substance. The laws of nature teach us exactly what we need. After the sages have told us that, according to nature, no one is indigent, and that every one is so according to opinion, they very subtly distinguish betwixt the desires that proceed from her and those that proceed from the disorder of our own fancy: those of which we can see the end are hers; those that fly before us, and of which we can see no end, are our own. Want of goods is easily repaired; poverty of soul is irreparable:

> "If what's for man enough enough could be
> It were enough: but as we plainly see
> That won't suffice, how can I e'er believe
> That any wealth my mind content can give?"
>   [Lucilius in *Novius Marcellus*]

Socrates seeing a great quantity of riches, jewels, and furniture of great value, carried in pomp through the city: "How many things," said he, "do I not desire!" Metrodorus lived on twelve ounces a day; Epicurus upon less; Metrocles slept in winter abroad among sheep; in summer in the cloisters of churches. "Nature provides for its own exigences" [Seneca]. Cleanthes lived by the labour of his own hands, and boasted, "That Cleanthes, if he would, could maintain yet another Cleanthes."

If that which nature exactly and originally requires of us for the conservation of our being be too little (as, in truth, what it is and how very cheap life may be maintained cannot be better made out than by this consideration; that it is so little that by its littleness it escapes the gripe and shock of fortune), let us dispense with a little more; let us call every one of our habits and conditions nature; let us tax and treat ourselves by this measure; let us stretch our appurtenances and accounts so far; for so far I fancy we have some excuse. Custom is a second nature, and no less powerful. What is wanting to my custom I hold to be wanting to me; and I should be almost as well content that they took away my life, as take me far from the way wherein I have so long lived. I am no more in a condition for any great change, nor to put myself into a new and unwonted course, though never so much to my advantage. 'Tis past the time for me to become other than what I am; and as I should complain of any great adventure that should now befall me, that it came not in time to be enjoyed:

> "For what are fortune's gifts, if I'm denied
> Their cheerful use?" [Horace]

so should I complain of any inward acquest. It were almost better never, than so late, to become an honest man, and well understanding in living, when a man has no longer to live. I, who am going, would readily resign to any new-comer all the wisdom I have acquired for the world's commerce: "after meat comes mustard." I want no goods of which I can make no use; of what use is knowledge to him that has lost his head? 'Tis adding insult to injury for fortune to offer us presents that will only inspire us with a just despite that we had them not in their due season. Guide me no more, I can no longer go. Of so many parts as make a perfect man, patience suffices. Give an excellent treble to a chorister that has rotten lungs, and eloquence to a hermit exiled in the deserts of Arabia. There needs no art to further a fall; the end finds itself of itself, at the conclusion of every affair. My world is at an end, my form expired;

I belong to the past, and am bound to authorise it, and to conform my end to it. I will here mention, by way of example, that the recent eclipse by the pope of ten days, has taken me so low that I cannot well get used to it; I belong to the years wherein we kept another kind of account. So ancient and so long a custom challenges and calls me back to it; I am constrained to be somewhat heretical in this point: impatient of any, even though a corrective innovation. My imagination, in spite of my teeth, always pushes me ten days forward or backward, and is ever murmuring in my ears, "This rule concerns those who are going to be." If health itself, sweet as it is, returns to me by fits, 'tis rather to give me cause of regret than fruition of itself; I have no place left to keep it in. Time leaves me, without which nothing can be possessed. Oh, what little account should I make of those great elective dignities that I see in such esteem in the world, that are never conferred but upon men who are taking leave of it, in whom they do not so much regard how well he will discharge his trust, as how short his administration will be; from the very entry they look at the exit. In short, I am about to finish this man, and not to rebuild another. By long habit this form is, in me, turned into substance, and fortune into nature.

I say, therefore, that every one of us feeble creatures is excusable in thinking that to be his own which is comprised under this measure; but withal, beyond these limits, 'tis nothing but confusion; 'tis the largest extent we can grant to our own claim. The more business we create ourselves, the more we amplify our possession, so much more do we expose ourselves to the blows and adversities of fortune. The career of our desires ought to be circumscribed, and restrained to a short limit of near and contiguous conveniences; and ought moreover, to perform their course, not in a right line, that ends elsewhere, but in a circle, of which the two points by a short wheel meet and terminate in ourselves. Actions that are carried on without this reflection (a near and essential reflection I mean), such as those of ambitious and avaricious men, and many more who run point blank, and whose career always carries them before themselves, such actions, I say, are erroneous and sickly.

Most of our business is farce: "All the world's a stage, and all the men and women merely players" [Petronius]. We must play our part well, but withal as the part of a borrowed personage; we must not make a real essence of a mask and outward appearance, nor of a strange person our own; we cannot distinguish the skin from the shirt; 'tis enough to meal the face without mealing the breast. I see some who transform and transubstantiate themselves into as many new shapes and new beings as they undertake employments, and who prelate themselves even to the heart and liver, and carry their office along with them, even to the close stool; I cannot make them distinguish the salutations that are made to them from those made to their commission, their train, or their mule: "They so much give themselves up to fortune as even to forget nature" [Petronius]; they swell and puff up their souls and their natural way of speaking, according to the height of their magisterial place. The mayor of Bordeaux and Montaigne have ever been two by very manifest separation. To be an advocate or a treasurer, a man must not be ignorant of the knavery of such callings; an honest man is not accountable for the vice or folly of his business, and yet ought not to refuse to take the calling upon him; 'tis the custom of his country, and there is money to be got by it; a man must live by the world, and make his best of it, such as it is. But the judgment of an emperor ought to be above his empire, and view and consider it as an accident; and he ought to know how to enjoy himself apart from it, and to communicate himself as James and Peter, to himself at least.

I cannot engage myself so deep and so entire; when my will gives me to a party, 'tis not with so violent an obligation that my judgment is infected with it. In the present broils of this kingdom, my interest in the one side has not made me forget either the laudable qualities of some of our adversaries, nor those that are reproachable in my own party. People generally adore all of their own side; for my part I do not so much as excuse most things in those of mine; a good book has never the worse grace for being written against me. The knot of the controversy excepted, I have always kept myself in equanimity and pure indifference: "And have no express hatred beyond the necessity of war" [Quintus Curtius]; for which I am pleased with myself, and the more, because I see others commonly fail in the contrary way. Such as extend their anger and hatred beyond the dispute in question, as most men do, show that they spring from some other occasion and particular cause; like one who, being cured of an ulcer, has yet a fever remaining, by which it appears that the ulcer had another more concealed beginning. It is because they are not concerned in the common cause, because it is wounding to the state and common interest, but are only nettled by reason of their private and particular concern: this is why they are so especially animated, beyond justice and public reason: "Every one was not so much angry against things in general as against those that particularly concerned himself" [Livy]. I would have matters go well on our side; but if they do not, I shall not run mad. I am heartily for the right party; but I do not affect to be taken notice of for an especial enemy to others, and beyond the general quarrel. I am a mortal enemy to this vicious form of censure: "He is of the league because he admires the Duke of Guise. He is astonished at the king of Navarre's valour and diligence, and therefore he is a Huguenot. He finds such and such faults in the king, and therefore he is seditious in his heart;" and I would not grant to the magistrate that he did well in condemning a book, because it had placed a heretic among the best poets of the time. Shall we not dare to say of a thief that he has a handsome leg? Because a woman is a strumpet, must it needs follow that she has a stinking breath? Did they, in the wiser ages, revoke the proud title of Capitolinus, they had before bestowed upon Marcus Manlius as the preserver of religion and the public liberty; did they damn the memory of his liberality, his feats of arms, and the military recompense granted to his virtue, because he afterwards aspired to the sovereignty, to the prejudice of the laws of his country? If they take a hatred against an advocate, he will not be allowed the next day to be eloquent. I have elsewhere spoken of the zeal that pushes on worthy men to the like faults. For my part I can say: "such an one does this ill, and that well and virtuously." So, in the prognostics or sinister events of affairs, they will have every one, in his own party, blind or a blockhead; and our persuasion and judgment be subservient, not to truth, but to the project of our desires. I should rather incline towards the other extreme, so much do I fear being suborned by my desire; to which may be added, that I am a little tenderly distrustful of things that I wish.

I have in my time seen wonders in the way of an indiscreet and prodigious facility in people to suffer their hopes and belief to be led and governed which way has best pleased and served their leaders, through a hundred mistakes one upon another, and through dreams and phantasms. I no more wonder at those who have been blinded and led by the nose by the ape's tricks of Apollonius and Mahomet. Their sense and understanding is absolutely taken away by their passion: their discretion has no longer any other choice than that which smiles upon them, and supports their cause. I principally observed that in the beginning of our intestine distempers: this other, which is sprung up since, in imitation, has surpassed it: by which I am satisfied that it is a quality inseparable from popular errors; after the first that sets out, opinions drive on one another like waves with the wind; you are not part of the body, if you utter a word of objection, and do not follow the common run. But doubtless they wrong the just side, when they go about to assist it with fraud; I have ever been against that practice: 'tis only fit to work upon weak heads; for the sound, there are surer and more honest ways to keep up their courage, and to excuse adverse accidents.

Heaven never saw a greater animosity than that between Cæsar and Pompey, nor ever will; and yet I observe, methinks, in those fine souls a great moderation towards one another; it was a jealousy of honour and command, which did not transport them to a furious and indiscreet hatred, and that was without malignity and detraction: in their hottest exploits upon one another, I discover some traces of respect and good-will; and therefore am of opinion that, had it been possible, each of them would rather have done his business without the ruin of the other, than with it. Take notice how different matters were with Marius and Sylla.

We must not precipitate ourselves so headlong after our affections and interest. As, when I was young, I opposed the progress of love, which I perceived to advance too fast upon me, and had a care lest it should at last become so pleasing as to force, captivate, and wholly reduce me to its mercy, so I do the same upon all other occasions, where my will is running on with too warm an appetite; I lean opposite to the side it inclines to, as I find it going to plunge and make itself drunk with its own wine: I evade nourishing its pleasure so far, that I cannot recover it without infinite loss. Souls that, through their own stupidity, only discern things by halves, have this happiness, that they smart the less with hurtful things: 'tis a spiritual leprosy that has some show of health, and such a health as philosophy does not altogether contemn; but yet we have no reason to call it wisdom, as we often do. And after this manner a man mocked Diogenes, who, in the depth of winter, and stark naked, went hugging an image of snow for a trial of his patience; seeing him in this exercise: "Art thou very cold?" said he; "Not at all," replied Diogenes; "Why, then," said the other, "what great and exemplary thing dost thou think thou art doing now?" To estimate a man's firmness, we must know what his suffering is.

But souls that are to meet with adverse events, and the injuries of fortune in their depth and sharpness, that are to weigh and taste them according to their natural weight and sharpness, let such show their skill in avoiding the causes and diverting the blow. What did King Cotys do? He paid liberally for the rich and beautiful service of porcelain that had been brought him; but, seeing it was exceedingly brittle he immediately broke it, in order to prevent so easy a matter of displeasure against his servants. In like manner, I have willingly avoided all confusion in my affairs, and never coveted to have my estate contiguous to those of my relations, and those with whom I coveted a strict friendship; whence matter of unkindness and fallings-out often proceed. I formerly loved cards and dice, but have long since left them off, only for this reason, that though I carry my losses as handsomely as another, I was not quiet within. Let a man of honour, who ought to be sensible of the lie, and who will not take a scurvy excuse for satisfaction, avoid occasions of dispute. I shun melancholic and sour-natured men as I would the plague; and in matters I cannot talk of without emotion and concern, I never meddle, if not compelled by duty: "Tis better not to begin, than to desist" [Seneca]. The surest way, then, is to prepare one's-self before the occasion.

I know very well that some wise men have taken another way, and have not feared to grapple and engage to the utmost upon several subjects: these are confident of their own strength, under cover of which they protect themselves in all ill successes, making their patience wrestle and contend with disaster:

> "He, like a solid rock by seas inclosed,
> To raging winds and roaring waves opposed,
> From his proud summit, looking down, disdains
> Their empty menace, and unmoved remains." [Virgil]

Let us never attempt these examples; we shall never come up to them. They set themselves resolutely, and without trouble, to behold the ruin of their country, to which all the good they can contrive or perform is due: this is too much and too rude for our common souls to undergo. Cato gave up the noblest life that ever was upon this account; but it is for us smaller men to fly from the storm as far as we can; we ought to shun pain, instead of cultivating patience, and dip under the blows we cannot parry. Zeno seeing Chremonides, a young man whom he loved, draw near to sit down by him, suddenly started up, and Cleanthes asking him the reason why he did so: "I hear," said he, "that physicians especially order repose, and forbid emotion, in all excitements." Socrates does not say: "Do not surrender to the charms of beauty; stand your ground, and do your utmost to oppose it." "Fly it," says he, "shun the sight and encounter of it, as of a powerful poison, that darts and wounds at a distance" [Xenophon]. And his good disciple, either feigning or reciting, but in my opinion rather reciting than feigning, the rare perfections of that great Cyrus, makes him distrustful of his own strength to resist the charms of the divine beauty of the illustrious Panthea, his captive, and commiting the visiting and keeping of her to another, who could not have so much licence as himself. And the Holy Spirit, in like manner: "Lead us not into temptation" [Matt. 6:13]. We do not pray that our reason may not be combated and overcome by concupiscence, but that it should not be so much as tried by it; that we should not be brought into a state wherein we should have so much as to suffer the approaches, solicitations, and temptations of sin; and we beg of Almighty God to keep our consciences quiet, fully and perfectly delivered from all commerce of evil.

Such as say that they have reason for their avenging passion, or any other sort of troublesome agitation of mind, do often say true, as things now are, but not as they were; they speak to us when the causes of their error are nourished and advanced by themselves: but look back, recall these causes to their beginning, and there you will put them to a nonplus. Will they have their fault less, for being of longer continuance; think they of an unjust beginning the sequel can be just? Whoever desires the good of his country, as I do, without fretting and pining, will be troubled, but will not swoon to see it threatened either with its own ruin, or a not less ruinous continuance: poor vessel, that the waves, the wind, and the pilot toss and steer to so contrary designs! He who does not gape after the favour of princes, as after a thing he cannot live without, does not much concern himself at the coldness of their reception and countenance, nor at the inconstancy of their wills. He who does not brood over his children or his honours with a slavish propension, ceases not to live commodiously enough after their loss. He who does good principally for his own satisfaction will not be much troubled to see men judge of his actions contrary to his merit. A quarter of an ounce of patience will provide sufficiently against such inconveniences. I find ease in this receipt, redeeming myself in the beginning as cheap as I can; and find that by this means I have escaped much trouble and many difficulties. With very little effort I stop the first sally of my emotions, and quit the subject that begins to be troublesome, before it carries one away. He who stops not the start will hardly ever be able to stop the career: he who cannot keep them out will never get them out, when they are once in; he who cannot crush them at the beginning, will never do it after; nor ever keep himself from falling, if he cannot recover himself when first he begins to totter: "For they throw themselves headlong, when once they lose their reason; and frailty so far indulges itself that it is unawares carried out into the deep, and can find no port wherein to come to an anchor" [Cicero]. I am betimes sensible of the little breezes that begin to sing and whistle in the shrouds, the forerunners of a storm:

> "So winds, when yet unfledged in woods they lie,
> In whispers first their tender voices try;
> Then issue on the main with bellowing rage,
> And storms to trembling mariners presage." [Virgil]

How often have I done myself a manifest injustice, to avoid the hazard of having yet a worse done me by the judges, after an age of vexations, dirty and vile practices, more enemies to my nature than fire or the rack? "A man should be an enemy to all contention as much as he lawfully may, and I know not whether or not something more: for 'tis not only handsome, but sometimes also advantageous too, a little to recede from one's right" [Cicero]. Were we wise, we ought to rejoice and boast, as I one day heard a young gentleman of a good family very innocently do, that his mother had lost her suit, as if it had been a cough, a fever, or something very troublesome to keep. Even the favours that fortune might have given me through relationship, or acquaintance with those who have sovereign authority in our affairs, I have conscientiously waived, and very carefully avoided employing them to the prejudice of others, and of advancing my pretensions above their true right. In fine, I have so much prevailed by my endeavours (happy 'tis for me I can say), that I am to this day a virgin from all suits at law, though they have made me very fair offers, and with very just ground, would I have hearkened to them; and a virgin from quarrels too; I have almost passed over a long life without any offence of moment, either active or passive, or without ever hearing myself called by a worse word than my own name; a rare favour of heaven!

Our greatest agitations have ridiculous motives and causes; what ruin did our last Duke of Burgundy run into about a cart-load of sheepskins! And was not the engraving of a seal the first and principal cause of the greatest commotion that this machine of the world ever underwent? for Pompey and Cæsar were but the off-sets and continuation of the two others; and I have in my time seen the wisest heads in this kingdom assembled with great ceremony, and at the public expense, about treaties and agreements, of which the real decision in the mean time absolutely depended upon the ladies' cabinet council, and the inclination of some woman body. The poets very well understood this, when they put all Greece and Asia to fire and sword for an apple. Enquire why that man hazards his life and honour upon the fortune of his rapier and dagger: let him acquaint you with the occasion of the quarrel; he cannot do it without blushing, 'tis so idle and frivolous!

A little thing will engage you in't, but being once embarked, all cords draw; greater considerations are then required, more hard and more important. How much easier is it not to enter in, than it is to get out? We should proceed contrary to the reed, which at its first spring produces a long and straight shoot, but afterwards, as if tired and out of breath, runs into thick and frequent joints and knots, as so many pauses, which demonstrate that it has no more its first vigour and constancy: 'twere better to begin fair and calmly, and to keep a man's breath and vigour for the height and stress of the business. We guide and govern affairs in their beginnings, and have them then in our own power; but afterwards, when they are once at work, 'tis they that guide and govern us, and we have to follow them.

Yet do I not pretend by this to say that this plan has relieved me of all difficulty, and that I have not often had enough to do to curb and restrain my passions; they are not always to be governed according to the measure of occasions, and often have their entries very sharp and violent. Yet good fruit and profit may thence be reaped, except by those who in well-doing are not satisfied with any benefit, if reputation be wanting; for, in truth, such an effect is of no account, but by every one in himself; you are better contented, but no more esteemed, seeing you reformed yourself before you came into play, or that any vice was discovered in you. Yet not in this only, but in all other duties of life also, the way of those who aim at honour is very different from that they proceed by, who propose to themselves order and reason. I find some who rashly and furiously rush into the lists, and cool in the race. As Plutarch says, that as those who, through awkwardness, are soft and facile to grant whatever is desired of them, are afterwards as frail to break their word and to recant; so likewise he who enters lightly into a quarrel, is subject to run as lightly out of it. The same difficulty that keeps me from entering into it would, when once hot and engaged in it, incite me to maintain it with resolution. 'Tis, perhaps, wrong; but when a man is once engaged, he must go through with it or die. "Undertake coldly," said Bias, "but pursue with ardour" [Laertius]. For want of prudence, men fall into want of courage, which is still more intolerable.

Most accommodations of our quarrels now-a-days are discreditable and false: we only seek to save appearances, and in the mean time betray and disavow our true intentions; we salve over the fact. We know very well how we said the thing, and in what sense we spoke it, and all the company, and all our friends with whom we would appear to have the advantage, understand it well enough too; 'tis at the expense of our frankness, and the honour of our courage, that we disown our thoughts, and seek subterfuge in falsehood to make friends; we give ourselves the lie, to excuse the lie we have given another. You are not to consider whether your word or action may admit of another interpretation; 'tis your own real and sincere interpretation, your real meaning, that you are thenceforward to maintain, whatever it cost you. Men address themselves to your virtue and your conscience, which are neither of them to be disguised: let us leave these pitiful ways and expedients to the tricksters of the law. The excuses and satisfactions that I see every day made and given to repair indiscretion, seem to me more scandalous than the indiscretion itself. It were better to affront your adversary a second time, than to offend yourself by giving him such satisfaction. You have braved him in your heat and anger and you go to appease him in your cooler and better sense; and by that means lay yourself lower, and at his feet, whom before you pretended to overtop. I do not find any thing a gentleman can say so rude and vicious in him, as unsaying what he has said is infamous, when that unsaying is authoritatively extracted from him; forasmuch as obstinacy is more excusable in him than pusillanimity. Passions are as easy for me to evade, as they are hard for me to moderate: "'Tis easier to tear them altogether from the mind, than to moderate them" [Seneca]. He who cannot attain unto that noble stoical impassibility, let him secure himself in the bosom of this popular stupidity of mine: what those great souls performed by their virtue, I inure myself to do by complexion. The middle region harbours storms and tempests; the two extremes of philosophers and rustics concur in tranquillity and happiness:

> "How blest the sage! whose mind can pierce each cause
> Of changeful nature, and her wond'rous laws;
> Who tramples fear beneath his foot, and braves
> Fate, and stern death, and hell's resounding waves!
> Blest too, who knows each god that guards the swain,
> Pan, old Sylvanus, and the Dryad train." [Virgil]

The birth of all things is weak and tender; and therefore we are to have an eye to beginnings; for as then, in their infancy, the danger is not perceived, so, when it is grown up, neither is the remedy to be found. I had every day encountered a million of crosses, harder to digest, in the progress of ambition, than it has been difficult for me to curb the natural propension that inclined me to it:

> "For well might I be shy,
> To raise my head so high." [Horace]

All public actions are subject to various and uncertain interpretations, for too many heads judge of them. Some say of this city employment of mine (and I am willing to say a word of it, not that it is worth so much, but to exhibit my conduct in such things), that I have behaved myself in it like a man not easy to be moved, and with a languishing affection; and they have some colour for what they say. I endeavour to keep my mind and my thoughts in repose; "As being always quiet by nature, so also now by age" [Cicero]; and if they sometimes lash out on some rude and sensible impression, 'tis, in truth, without my advice. Yet, from this natural heaviness of mine, men ought not to conclude a total inability in me (for want of care and want of sense are two very different things), and much less any ingratitude towards that city, who employed the utmost means they had in their power to oblige me, both before they knew me and after, and did much more for me in choosing me anew, than conferring that honour upon me at first. I wish them all the good that can befall them, and certainly, had occasion offered, there is nothing I would have spared for their service. I did for them as I would have done for myself. 'Tis a good, warlike, and generous people, but capable of obedience and discipline, and of whom the best use may be made, if well guided. They say also that my administration was passed over without mark or thing worthy of record. Very good! They accuse my cessation in a time when every body almost was convicted of doing too much. I am impatient to be doing where my will spurs me on; but this point is an enemy to perseverence. Let whoever will make use of me according to my own way, employ me in affairs where vigour and liberty are required; where a direct, short, and moreover a hazardous conduct is necessary; I may do something: but if it must be long, subtle, laborious, artificial, and intricate, they would do better to call in somebody else. All important offices are not hard: I came prepared to work a little more, had there been great occasion; for it is in my power to do something more than I do, or than I love to do; I did not to my knowledge omit any thing that my duty really required. I easily forget those offices that ambition mixes with duty, and shelters under that title; these are they that, for the most part, fill the eyes and ears, and give men the most satisfaction: not the thing, but the appearance contents them; they think men sleep, if they hear no noise. My humour is no friend to tumult; I could appease a riot without emotion, and chastise a disorder without alteration. If I stand in need of anger and inflammation, I borrow it and put it on; my manners are heavy, rather faint than sharp. I do not condemn a magistrate that sleeps, provided the people under his charge sleep as well as he: the laws in that case sleep too. For my part I commend a gliding, quiet, and silent life, "Neither abject nor overbearing:" my fortune will have it so. I am descended from a family that has lived without lustre or tumult, and time out of mind, particularly ambitious of the character of truth and honesty.

Our people now-a-days are so bred up to bustle and ostentation, that goodness, moderation, equability, and such quiet and obscure qualities, are no more regarded: rough bodies make themselves felt, the smooth are imperceptibly handled; sickness is felt; health little, or not at all; no more than the oils that foment us, in comparison of the pain for which we are fomented. 'Tis acting for a man's reputation and particular profit, not for the public good, to refer that to be done in the public place which a man may as well do in the council-chamber, and to noon-day what might have been done the night before; and to be jealous to do that himself which his colleague can do as well as he. So some surgeons of Greece used to perform their operations upon scaffolds, in the sight of the people, to draw more practice and profit. They think that good orders cannot be understood but by the sound of trumpet. Ambition is not a vice of little people, and of so mean abilities as ours. One said to Alexander: "Your father will leave you a great dominion, easy and pacific;" but this youth was envious of his father's victories, and the justice of his government, and would not have enjoyed the empire of the world in ease and peace. Alcibiades, in Plato, had rather die young, beautiful, rich, noble, and learned, and all this *par excellence,* than stop in the state of such a condition; this disease is perhaps excusable in so strong and so full a soul. When these wretched and dwarfish little souls gull and deceive themselves, and think to spread their fame, for having given right judgment in some affair, or kept up the discipline of the guard of the city gate, the more they think to exalt their heads, the more they show their tails. This little well-doing has neither body nor life; it vanishes in the first mouth, and goes no farther than from one street to another. Talk of it, in God's name, to your son or your servant; like that old fellow who, having no other auditor of his praises, nor approver of his valour, boasted to his chambermaid, crying out: "O, Peretta, what a brave man hast thou to thy master!" At the worst, talk of it to yourself; like a counsellor of my acquaintance, who, having disgorged a whole cart-load of paragraphs with great heat, and as great folly, coming out of the council-chamber to make water, was heard very conscientiously to mutter betwixt his teeth: "Not unto us, O Lord, not unto us, but unto thy name, be the glory." — *Psalm* 113. He who can get it of nobody else, let him pay himself out of his own purse.

Fame is not prostituted at so cheap a rate; rare and exemplary actions, to which it is due, would not endure the company of this prodigious crowd of little every-day performances. Marble may exalt your titles as much as you please, for having repaired a rod of a ruinous wall, or cleansed a public sewer, but not men of sense. Renown does not follow all good deeds, if novelty and difficulty be not conjoined; nay, so much as mere estimation, according to the Stoics, is not due to every action that proceeds from virtue; neither will they allow him bare thanks who, out of temperance, forbears to meddle with any old blear-eyed hag. Such as have known the admirable qualities of Scipio Africanus deny him the glory that Panætius attributes to him, of being abstinent from gifts, as a glory not so much his as that of the age he lived in. We have pleasures suitable to our fortunes; let us not usurp those of grandeur. Our own are more natural, and by so much more solid and sure, as they are more low. If not for that of conscience, yet at least for ambition's sake, let us reject ambition; let us disdain that thirst of honour and renown, so low and mendicant, that it makes us beg it of all sorts of people "What praise is that which is to be got in the market?" [Cicero] by abject means, and at what cheap rate soever. 'Tis dishonour to be so honoured. Let us learn to be no more greedy of honour than we are capable of it. To be puffed up with every action that is innocent, or of use, is only for such with whom such things are extraordinary and rare; they will value it as it costs them. How much the more a good effect makes a noise, so much I abate of the goodness of it, as I enter into suspicion that it was more performed for noise than upon the account of goodness: being exposed upon the stall, it is half sold. Those actions have much more grace and lustre that slip from the hand of him that does them negligently and without noise, and that some honest man after chooses out and raises from the shade, to produce it to the light upon its own account: "All things, truly, seem more laudable to me that are performed without ostentation and without the testimony of the people," says the most vain-glorious man in the world [Cicero].

I had no care but to conserve and to continue, which are silent and insensible effects. Innovation is of great lustre, but 'tis interdicted in this time, when we are pressed upon, and have nothing to defend ourselves from but novelties. To forbear doing is often as noble as to do; but 'tis less in the light: and the little good I have in me is almost all of this kind. In fine, occasions in this employment of mine have been confederate with my humour, and I thank them for it. Is there any one who desires to be sick that he may see his physician at work? And would not that physician deserve to be whipped who should wish the plague amongst us, that he might put his art in practice? I have never been of that wicked, though common enough, humour, to desire that the trouble and disorders of this city should elevate and honour my government: I have ever willingly contributed all I could to their tranquillity and ease. He who will not thank me for the order, gentle and silent calm, that has accompanied my administration, cannot, however, deprive me of the share that belongs to me by the title of my good fortune. And I am of such a composition that I would as willingly be happy as wise; and had rather owe my successes purely to the favour of Almighty

God than to any industry or operation of my own. I had sufficiently published to the world my unfitness for such public offices. But I have something in me yet worse than incapacity, which is that I am not much displeased at it, and that I do not much go about to cure it, considering the course of life that I have proposed to myself. Neither have I satisfied myself in this employment, but I have very near arrived at what I expected from myself, and have much surpassed what I promised them with whom I had to do; for I am apt to promise something less than what I am able to do, and than what I hope to make good. I am sure that I have left no impressions of offence or hatred behind me; and as to leaving regret or desire of me amongst them, I at least know very well that I never much affected it:

> "Wouldst thou I should a quiet sea believe,
> To this inconstant monster credit give?" [Virgil]

21

Jean Bodin Defines Sovereignty

LIKE HIS COUNTRYMAN, Montaigne, Bodin was a lawyer and public servant who lived at the time of the Wars of Religion in France. Like Montaigne also, he deplored the fanaticism of those terrible years. But while Montaigne's thoughts turned inward, to problems of the mind and the private life, Bodin's turned to the problems of his country, and he searched for solutions by studying history, economics, and political theory. He has been described as a conservative, in the constitutional tradition of the Middle Ages, and as a radical advocate of monarchical sovereignty who helped prepare for the royal absolutism of the next century. He was both: he aimed to preserve those traditions which he thought indispensable to the common good and at the same time to cut away outmoded feudal notions of government in order to formulate a clear idea of the power necessary to preserve the state. He brought all these problems into focus in his conception of sovereignty.

This selection is taken from the Knolles translation of 1606. Spelling and punctuation have been modernized.

Jean Bodin (ca. 1529–1596), The Six Books of a Commonweal

SEEING THAT nothing upon earth is greater or higher, next unto God, than the majesty of kings and sovereign princes, for that they are in a sort created his lieutenants for the welfare of other men, it is meet diligently to consider of their majesty and power, as also who and of what sort they be; that so we may in all obedience respect and reverence their majesty, and not to think or speak of them otherwise than of the lieutenants of the most mighty and immortal God. For that he which speaketh evil of his prince unto whom he oweth all duty, doth injury unto the majesty of God him-

From Richard Knolles, trans., THE SIX BOOKS OF A COMMONWEAL (London, 1606), pp. 153–182.

self, whose lively image he is upon earth. As God speaking unto Samuel, of whom the people of Israel had unadvisedly asked a king, "It is not thee," saith God, "but me whom they have despised."

Now to the end that one may know him that is such an one (that is to say a sovereign prince) we must know the marks, which are not common unto other subjects also; for if they were common unto others, then should there be no sovereign prince. And yet they which have writ best of or concerning a Commonweal, have not sufficiently and as it ought, manifested this point, than which none is more plentiful or more profitable in the discourse of a Commonweal: whether it were by them for flattery, for fear, for hatred, or by forgetfulness omitted. For when Samuel had denounced him king whom God had before chosen, and consecrated him before the people, as if he had but come by chance, he is reported to have writ a book of the power and sovereignty of a king, which the Hebrew priests have written to have been by their kings suppressed and rent, that so they might more freely tyrannize over their subjects.

*   *   *

And amongst the Greeks there are none who have anything written concerning the laws of sovereignty, except Aristotle, Polybius, and Dionysius Halicarnasus, who have writ with so great brevity and obscurity, as that they seem rather to have propounded the question than to have declared what was to be thought thereof, as not therein well resolved themselves.

*   *   *

For who is there that would not deem him to be a sovereign, which giveth laws unto his subjects, which maketh peace and war, which appointeth all the officers and magistrates of his country, which imposeth tributes, and at his pleasure easeth whom he seeth good, which hath power of life and death, and in brief to dispose of the whole Commonweal? All which they before rehearsed have power to do: and what more can a man desire in a sovereign prince? For all these are the marks of sovereignty. And yet nevertheless we have before showed that the dukes of Milan, of Savoy, of Ferrara, of Florence, and of Mantua, hold all of the Empire, . . . we have also said that they have their investiture from the Empire and that they yield their fealty and homage unto the Empire; in brief that they are natural subjects of the Empire, and borne in the territories subject unto the Empire. Then how can they be absolute sovereigns? For how should he be a sovereign which acknowledgeth the jurisdiction of another greater than himself, of one which reverseth his judgements, which correcteth his laws, which chastiseth himself if he commit abuse?

* * *

. . . For that he only is a sovereign which hath none his superior or companion with himself in the same kingdom. For as the great sovereign God cannot make another God equal unto himself, considering that He is of infinite power and greatness, and that there cannot be two infinite things, as is by natural demonstrations manifest, so also may we say that the prince whom we have set down as the image of God cannot make a subject equal unto himself but that his own sovereignty must thereby be abased; which if it be so, it followeth that the administration of justice, which Aristotle maketh the third part of a Commonweal, is not the true mark of sovereignty; for that it indifferently agreeth almost to all magistrates as well as to the prince neither in like sort to make or displace officers; for that the prince and the subject have both this power, not only in appointing the officers' servants at home, and in time of war, but even of the officers and magistrates themselves, which command in peace or in war.

* * *

As for that which Dionysius Halicarnasus saith of Marcus Valerius the Consul in the oration which he made unto the people of Rome for the appeasing of the troubles then risen betwixed the Senate and them, that the people ought to content themselves to have the power to make laws and magistrates, that is not sufficient to declare a sovereignty of power in them, as I have before declared concerning the magistrates. Yea the power to make laws is not the proper marks of sovereignty, except we understand thereby the sovereign prince's law; for that the magistrate may also give laws unto them that are within the compass of his jurisdiction, so that nothing be by him decreed contrary to the edicts and laws of his sovereign prince. And to manifest this point we must presuppose that this word Law, without any other addition, signifieth *the right command of him or them, which have sovereign power over others, without exception of person,* be it that such commandment concern the subjects in general or in particular; except him or them which have given the law. Howbeit to speak more properly, *A law is the command of a sovereign concerning all his subjects in general,* or else concerning general things, as saith Festus Pompeius, as a privilege concerneth someone, or some few. Which law if it be made by the Privy Council, or Senate of a Commonweal, it is called *senatus consultum,* . . . But if the vulgar people made any such command it was called *Plebiscitum.* . . .

*   *   *

Wherefore let this be the first and chief mark of a sovereign prince, to be of power to give laws to all his subjects in general and to every one of them in particular, (yet is not that enough, but that we must join thereunto) without consent of any other greater, equal, or lesser than himself. For if a prince be bound not to make any law without consent of a greater than himself, he is then a very subject; if not without his equal, he then hath a companion; if not without the consent of his inferiors, whether it be of his subjects, of the Senate, or of the people, he is then no sovereign. And as for the names of lords and senators, which we oftentimes see joined unto laws, they are not thereunto set as of necessity to give thereunto force or strength, but to give unto them testimony and weight, as made by the wisdom and discretion of the chief men, so to give them the better grace, and to make them to be the better received; and not for any necessity at all.

*   *   *

Under this same sovereignty of power for the giving and abrogating of the law are comprised all the other rights and marks of sovereignty, so that, to speak properly, a man may say that there is but this only mark of sovereign power, considering that all other the rights thereof are contained in this, *viz.* to have power to give laws unto all and every one of the subjects, and to receive none from them. For to denounce war unto the enemy, or to make peace with him, although it seem to be a thing different from the name of the law, yet is it manifest these things to be done by the law, that is to say by the commandment of the sovereign power. So also is it proper unto sovereign majesty to receive the subjects' appeals from other, and the greatest magistrates, to place and displace the greatest officers, charge or exempt the subjects from taxes and subsidies, to grant pardons and dispensations against the rigor of the law, to have power of life and death, to increase or diminish the valor and weight of the coin, to give it title, name, and figure, to cause all subjects and liegemen to swear for the keeping of their fidelity without exception, unto him to whom such oath is due; which are the true marks of sovereignty, comprised under the power of being able to give a law to all in general, and to everyone in particular, and not to receive any law or command from any other, but from almighty God only. For a prince or duke who hath power to give laws unto all his subjects in general, and to every one of them in particular is yet no sovereign, if he receive his power from the Emperor, the Pope, or the King, or any other greater than himself, or yet have a companion in his government, a companion I say, for that he seemeth in a manner to have a superior or master, which hath a companion, without whose help and consent he can command and do nothing. Much less is he a sovereign, if he be another man's lieutenant or deputy.

But forasmuch as the word *Law* is too general a mark, it is the more expedient particularly to specify the rights of sovereignty comprised (as I have said) under that sovereign law, as to denounce war, or treat of peace, one of the greatest points of sovereign majesty; for that oftentimes it draweth after it the ruin or assurance of a Commonweal; which is to be verified not only by the law of the Romans, but of all other nations. And for that there was more danger to be feared from war than from peace, it was lawful for the common people of Rome to command peace, but if question were for making of war, it might not be decreed but in the greatest assembly of all the states together, until such time as that the menial people had also full power to make laws. And therefore was it that war was decreed against Mithridates by the law Manilia against the pirates by the law Gabinia, against Philip the Second, king of Macedon, by the law Sulpitia Peace was also made with the Carthaginians by the law Martia. And for because Caesar had without command of the people made wars in France, Cato Uticensis was of opinion in the Senate that the army was to be called home and Caesar for his presumption delivered unto the enemy. In like case the estates of the people of Athens determined of war and peace, as a man may see by the war by them decreed against the Megarians, against the Syracusans, and against the kings of Macedon. I here but briefly set down certain examples of two of the greatest and most famous popular Commonweals that ever yet were; for in a regal state there is none (as I suppose) which doubt all the power of peace and war to be in the king, insomuch as that for any man to attempt even the least thing therein without the king's command is unto the doer thereof dangerous if the king might thereof have before been advertised. And what charge soever that they give unto their deputies or commissioners to entreat of peace or of alliance, yet consent they unto nothing without the advertising of the king; as was to be seen in the last treaty of Cambray, betwixt the French king and the king of Spain, the commissioners on the King's behalf writ to him from hour to hour the whole proceedings both of the one part and of the other. But in popular or aristocratical estate we oft times see that after the war is once denounced it is then managed by the advice of the Senate or Privy Council only: yea, and sometimes by the advice of one only captain also; for that nothing is more dangerous in war than to have the secret policies thereof revealed: which must needs be if the people have therein to do.

*   *   *

The third mark of sovereign majesty is to be of power to create and appoint magistrates, than which no more certain sign can be; especially the principal officers which are not under the command of other magistrates. This was the first law that Publius Valerius made after the expulsion of the kings out of Rome, that the magistrates should be chosen and appointed by the people. Which self same law was published also by the Venetians, at such time as they first assembled into the Gulf, for the establishing of their state, as Contarinus writeth; than which law there is none more religiously kept by the Senate and the Venetian people. Yet much better is it kept in monarchies, where all is governed by one, and where the greatest, the meaner, yea and the least offices of all, as of porters, sergeants, clerks, trumpeters, criers, which in the Roman state were placed and displaced by the Roman magistrates, are provided for by order from the prince, even unto the meanest offices. I have said the appointing of princes' officers, that is to say, of the chief magistrates, for there is no Commonweal where it is not permitted unto greater magistrates, as also to many corporations and colleges, to make certain menial officers under them, as I have before showed of the Romans. But yet that they do by virtue of the office which they hold, and as proctors created with power to substitute other their deputies under them. We see also that clients and vassals, albeit that they hold their jurisdiction of some sovereign prince in fealty and homage, have nevertheless power to establish judges and officers in their jurisdiction; but yet this power is given them by some sovereign prince. For no doubt dukes, marquises, counties, barons, and lieutenants of countries were no other of their first institution but judges and officers, as we shall in due place declare.

* * *

But now let us speak of the fourth mark of sovereignty, that is to wit, of the Last Appeal, which is and always hath been one of the most principal rights of sovereignty. As a man may see, after that the Romans had driven out their kings, not only the Last Appeal, but even all appeals from the magistrates, were by the Law Valeria reserved unto the people. And for that the consuls and other magistrates oftentimes gave small ear unto them that did appeal unto them, the same law was often times renewed, and by the Tribunitial Law Duilia the pain of death adjoined thereunto for him that should oppose himself against the same; which law Livy calleth the foundation of the popular liberty, albeit that it were evil executed. The same law was yet more straitly kept in Athens, where the Last Appeal was reserved unto the people, not only from the magistrates of the city, but even from the magistrates of their allies and fellows also, as the writings of Xenophon and Demosthenes do right well declare. The same law Contarinus writeth to have been the first that was by the Venetians made for the establishing of their Commonweal, *viz.* that all men might freely appeal from the magistrates unto the Grand Council of the people. Neither was Francis Valory, duke of Florence, for any other cause slain than for not having given way unto the appeal made from him unto the Great Council of the people by three Florentines by him condemned to die, and so, notwithstanding their appeal, by him executed. But some may say that not only this duke at Florence, but at Rome the dictators and other magistrates also oftentimes put to death condemned citizens, notwithstanding their appeal made unto the people, as is in many histories to be seen. . . . Whereunto in brief I answer as did Papinian, that we ought not to rest ourselves upon that they do at Rome, but on that which ought to be there done.

* * *

Wherefore the best and most expedient way for the preservation of a state is never to give any mark or right of sovereignty unto a subject, and much less unto a stranger, for that is one step and degree to mount unto his sovereign majesty. And therefore it was long doubted in the Council whether power and authority without appeal should be granted unto Francis, duke of Alencon (who made me Master of the Requests and one of his Council) in that his dukedom as had before been granted unto the ancient dukes there. And although he were the King's best and most loving brother, yet one of the Attorneys General was so bold as to say in full Council that it were better to bring in twelve Courts of Parliament than to suffer that; albeit that that jurisdiction was for a short time granted, and extraordinary judges by the king appointed, with reservation of appeals in many cases and causes, as also with exception of fealty and homage. Wherein our ancestors much offended, who with too much facility (should I say, or necessity) granted the same jurisdiction unto the dukes of Normandy. For by this means the dukes of Brittany and Burgundy revolted from our kings unto the kings of England; for that such judges were denied them as had been granted unto the dukes of Alencon, taking it grievously themselves in the name of their magistrates to be summoned unto the court at Paris, there to have those things reversed which their magistrates had unjustly determined; although sometime they were things of right small weight and importance. Whereof the dukes of Brittany complained both unto King Philip the Fair and Philip the Long, who by their Letters Patent sent unto the Court of Parliament in February, 1306, and in October, 1316, declared that their meeting was not that the Duke of Brittany or his officers should be called before them into the Court but in question of sovereignty, or in case they should deny to do justice, or else had given false judgment.

*   *   *

From this mark of majesty and benefit of supreme appeal dependeth also the power to grant grace and pardon unto the condemned, contrary to judgment given and to the rigor of the laws, be it for life, be it for goods, be it for honor, or recalling from banishment; for it is not in the power of the magistrates or judges, how great soever that they be, to grant the least of these things unto the condemned person, or of themselves to alter anything of the judgments by them once given. And albeit that the proconsuls and governors of provinces had as much power in their jurisdiction as had all the magistrates of Rome together, yet so it was, that it was not lawful for them so much as to restore him whom they had but for a time banished (as we read in the letters of Pliny the Younger, governor of Asia unto Trajan the Emperor) and much less give pardon unto men condemned to die, which is most straitly forbidden all magistrates in every Commonweal, be it well or evil ordered or governed.

*   *   *

As for the right and power to coin money, it is of the same nature with the law, and there is none but he which hath power to make a law which can appoint the value, weight, and stamp of the coin; which is well to be understood by the Greek and Latin word; for the Latin word *numus* seemeth well to have been derived of the Greek word *nomos*. For nothing is in a Commonweal of greater consequence, next unto the law, than the value, weight, and stamp of the coin, as we have in a special treatise declared, and in every well ordered Commonweal none but the sovereign prince hath power to appoint the same. As we read they did in Rome, when the value of the Victoriat was appointed and set down, it was done by an express law of the people.

*   *   *

As for the right to impose taxes or imposts upon the subjects, [it] is as proper unto sovereign majesty as is the law itself; not for that a Commonweal cannot stand without taxes and tallages, as the president the M. [Gilles le Maistre] hath well noted, that taxes were not levied in this realm but since the time of Saint Louis the king. But if it must needs be that they must for the public necessity be levied or taken away, it cannot be done but by him that hath the sovereign power, as it hath been judged by a decree of parliament against the duke of Burgundy and many times since, as well in the High Court of Parliament as also in the Privy Council. And for that divers particular lords, cities, and corporations, under show of the common good, have imposed divers taxes and payments upon their people, King Charles IX, by a general edict by him made in the Parliament at Orleans, expressly forbideth them so to do without leave; albeit that for the common necessity they be borne withal in so doing without commission, so that they exceed not the sum of twenty-five pounds.

And afterward the same edict was more straitly again renewed at Moulins, well agreeing both the law and equity. And although that the Roman Senate in time of wars, yea and the censors themselves impose certain taxes and payments, which could hardly have been extorted from the body of the whole commonalty; yet so it was, that that still passed by the sufferance of the Tribunes of the People, who oft times also opposed themselves against the same. Yea and that in such sort, that they presented a request unto the people that from that time forward no man upon pain of his head should be so hardy as to cause any law to be passed in the camp; for that the Senate by subtle means had there in the camp at Sutrium caused to be published that notable imposition, which they called *Vicesima Manumissorum,* that is to say, the twentieth part of the goods of them that were manumitted; under color that it was to pay the army withal. Which thereunto right willingly agreed and so suffered the law to pass. And in the Second Carthaginian War at such time as there was great want of coin in the common treasury, there was by a law made a tax generally imposed upon every man, which was by another contrary law again repealed. After the return of Paulus Emilius, who with the spoils of Perseus, king of Macedon so filled the city and every private man also with wealth, as that the people was from that time discharged of all taxes and payments until the Triumvirate civil war, about an hundred years after, until that such new taxes and tributes as by the power or covetousness of former tyrants had been imposed upon the people, were by the good Emperor Pertinax again eased and taken away.

But here might some say, divers particular lords here and there, to exact not only customs but tributes also, not only in France, where (as Caesar had most truly written) nothing is more contemptible than the vulgar people, but in England and Germany, and much more straitly in Denmark, Polonia and Norway. Which impositions and tributes are confirmed and grown strong both by long prescription of time and use of judgments. Yea and that to be lawful, even unto such as have neither sovereignty nor any jurisdiction at all, the Court of Paris hath adjudged. Whereunto I answer that the thing having begun by abuse and by long continuance of time inveterate hath well some color of prescription; but yet an abuse can never be so overgrown but that the law shall ever be a greater force than it; whereby the abuse is to be reformed. And for that cause it was forbidden by an edict of Moulins that any tribute should be exacted of the subjects under the color of prescription; for that many lawyers and judges have exposed all the strength and force of judgments only in prescription alone, not regarding whether that which is in question can of right be prescribed or not.

22

A Huguenot for Representative Government

MUCH OF THE ARGUMENT that Calvinism inspired resistance to political authority and hence to the development of doctrines of popular sovereignty rests upon the evidence of such works as the Vindiciae Contra Tyrannos. Published under the pseudonym Junius Brutus in 1579, it was an important representative of a group of Huguenot, or French Calvinist, writings against the repressive policies of King Henry III. It is interesting to see how the author of the Vindiciae makes the transition from the religious question to the question of the nature of government generally. In his definition of the relation between the king and his subjects and of the function of each in the commonwealth, the author stood foursquare against the authoritarianism of his contemporary countryman Jean Bodin.

A Defence of Liberty against Tyrants

The First Question, WHETHER SUBJECTS ARE BOUND AND OUGHT TO OBEY PRINCES, IF THEY COMMAND THAT WHICH IS AGAINST THE LAW OF GOD

THIS QUESTION happily may seem at the first view to be altogether superfluous and unprofitable, for that it seems to make a doubt of an axiom always held infallible amongst Christians, confirmed by many testimonies in Holy Scripture, divers examples of the histories of all ages, and by the death of all the holy martyrs. For it may be well demanded wherefore Christians have endured so many afflictions, but that they were always persuaded that God must be obeyed simply and absolutely, and kings with this exception, that

From VINDICIAE CONTRA TYRANNOS: A DEFENCE OF LIBERTY AGAINST TYRANTS OR OF THE LAWFUL POWER OF THE PRINCE OVER THE PEOPLE, AND OF THE PEOPLE OVER THE PRINCE (London, 1689), pp. 65–66, 87–88, 89–90, 96–97, 109–111, 117–119, 124–125, 133–137, 150–151, 158–160.

they command not that which is repugnant to the law of God. Otherwise wherefore should the apostles have answered, that God must rather be obeyed than men, and also seeing that the only will of God is always just, and that of men may be, and is, oftentimes unjust, who can doubt but that we must always obey God's commandments without any exception, and men's ever with limitation?

But for so much as there are many princes in these days, calling themselves Christians, which arrogantly assume an unlimited power, over which God himself hath no command, and that they have no want of flatterers, which adore them as gods upon earth, many others also, which for fear, or by constraint, either seem, or else do believe, that princes ought to be obeyed in all things, and by all men. And withal, seeing the unhappiness of these times is such, that there is nothing so firm, certain, or pure, which is not shaken, disgraced, or polluted; I fear me that whosoever shall nearly and thoroughly consider these things, will confess this question to be not only most profitable, but also, the times considered, most necessary. For my own part, when I consider the cause of the many calamities wherewith Christendom hath been afflicted for these late years, I cannot but remember that of the prophet Hosea, "the princes of Judah were like them that remove the bounds: wherefore I will pour out myself like water. Ephraim is oppressed, and broken in judgment, because he willingly walked after the commandments." Here you see the sin of the princes and people dispersed in these two words. The princes exceed their bounds, not contenting themselves with that authority which the almighty and all good God hath given them, but seek to usurp that sovereignty, which he hath reserved to himself over all men, being not content to command the bodies and goods of their subjects at their pleasure, but assume licence to themselves to enforce the consciences, which appertains chiefly to Jesus Christ. Holding the earth not great enough for their ambition, they will climb and conquer heaven itself. The people on the other side walk after the commandment, when they yield to the desire of princes, who command them that which is against the law of God, and as it were to burn incense, and adore these earthly gods; and instead of resisting them, if they have means and occasion, suffer them to usurp the place of God, making no conscience to give that to Cæsar, which belongs properly and only to God.

*　　*　　*

The Second Question, WHETHER IT BE LAWFUL TO RESIST A PRINCE WHO DOTH INFRINGE THE LAW OF GOD, OR RUIN HIS CHURCH: BY WHOM, HOW, AND HOW FAR IT IS LAWFUL

This question seems at the first view to be of a high and difficult nature, for so much as there being small occasion to speak to princes that fear God. On the contrary, there will be much danger to trouble the ears of those who acknowledge no other sovereign but themselves, for which reason few or none have meddled with it, and if any have at all touched it, it has been but as it were in passing by. The question is, If it be lawful to resist a prince violating the law of God, or ruinating the church, or hindering the restoring of it? If we hold ourselves to the tenure of the Holy Scripture it will resolve us. For, if in this case it had been lawful to the Jewish people (the which may be easily gathered from the books of the Old Testament), yea, if it had been enjoined them, I believe it will not be denied, that the same must be allowed to the whole people of any Christian kingdom or country whatsoever. In the first place it must be considered, that God having chosen Israel from amongst all the nations of the earth, to be a peculiar people to Him, covenanted with them, that they should be the people of God. This is written in divers places of Deuteronomy: the substance and tenor of this alliance was, "That all should be careful in their several lines, tribes, and families in the land of Canaan, to serve God purely, who would have a church established amongst them for ever," which may be drawn from the testimony of divers places, namely, that which is contained in the twenty-seventh chapter of Deuteronomy; there Moses and the Levites covenanting as in the name of God, assembled all the people, and said unto them: "This day, O Israel, art thou become the people of God, obey you therefore His voice," etc. And Moses said, "When thou hast passed the River of Jordan, thou shalt set six tribes on the mountain of Gerizzim on the one side, and the six others on the mountain of Eball, and then the Levites shall read the law of God, promising the observers all felicity, and threatening woe and destruction to the breakers thereof, and all the people shall answer, Amen." The which was afterwards performed by Joshua, at his entering into the land of Canaan, and some few days before his death. We see by this that all the people is bound to maintain the law of God to perfect His church, and on the contrary to exterminate the idols of the land of Canaan: a covenant which can no ways appertain to particulars, but only to the whole body of the people. To which it also seems the encamping of all the tribes round about the ark of the Lord to have reference; to the end that all should look to the preservation of that which was committed to the custody of all.

*   *   *

Now after that kings were given unto the people, there was so little purpose of disannulling or disbanding the former contract, that it was renewed and confirmed for ever. We have formerly said at the inaugurating of kings, there was a double covenant treated of, to wit "between God and the king"; and "between God and the people." The agreement was first passed between "God, the king, and the people." Or between the "high priest, the people" (which is named in the first place in the twenty-third chapter of the second book of the Chronicles) "and the king." The intention of this was, that the "people should be the people of God" (which is as much as to say) "that the people should be the church of God." We have shewed before to what end God contracted covenants with the king.

Let us now consider wherefore also He allies Himself with the people. It is a most certain thing, that God has not done this in vain, and if the people had not "authority to promise, and to keep promise," it were vainly lost time to contract or covenant with them. It may seem then that God has done like those creditors, which having to deal with not very sufficient borrowers, take divers jointly bound for one and the same sum, insomuch as two or more being bound one for another and each of them apart, for the entire payment of the total sum, he may demand his whole debt of which of them he pleases. There was much danger to commit the custody of the church to one man alone, and therefore God did recommend, and put it in trust "to all the people." The king being raised to so slippery a place might easily be corrupted: for fear lest the church should stumble with him, God would have the people also to be respondents for it. In the covenant of which we speak, God, or (in His place) the High Priest are stipulators, the king and all the people, to wit, Israel, do jointly and voluntarily assume, promise, and oblige themselves for one and the same thing. The High Priest demands if they promise, that the people shall be the people of God, that God shall always have His temple, His church amongst them, where He shall be purely served. The king is respondent, so also are the people (the whole body of the people representing, as it were, the office and place of one man) not severally, but jointly, as the words themselves make clear, being incontinent, and not by intermission or distance of time, the one after the other.

* * *

It is then lawful for Israel to resist the king, who would overthrow the law of God and abolish His church; and not only so, but also they ought to know that in neglecting to perform this duty, they make themselves culpable of the same crime, and shall bear the like punishment with their king.

If their assaults be verbal, their defence must be likewise verbal; if the sword be drawn against them, they may also take arms, and fight either with tongue or hand, as occasion is: yea, if they be assailed by surprisals, they may make use both of ambuscades and countermines, there being no rule in lawful war that directs them for the manner, whether it be by open assailing their enemy, or by close surprising; provided always that they carefully distinguish between advantageous stratagems, and perfidious treason, which is always unlawful.

But I see well, here will be an objection made. What will you say? That a whole people, that beast of many heads, must they run in a mutinous disorder, to order the business of the commonwealth? What address or direction is there in an unruly and unbridled multitude? What counsel or wisdom, to manage the affairs of state?

When we speak of all the people, we understand by that, only those who hold their authority from the people, to wit, the magistrates, who are inferior to the king, and whom the people have substituted, or established, as it were, consorts in the empire, and with a kind of tribunitial authority, to restrain the encroachments of sovereignty, and to represent the whole body of the people. We understand also, the assembly of the estates, which is nothing else but an epitome, or brief collection of the kingdom, to whom all public affairs have special and absolute reference; such were the seventy ancients in the kingdom of Israel, amongst whom the high priest was as it were president, and they judged all matters of greatest importance, those seventy being first chosen by six out of each tribe, which came out of the land of Egypt, then the heads or governors of provinces. In like manner the judges and provosts of towns, the captains of thousands, the centurions and others who commanded over families, the most valiant, noble, and otherwise notable personages, of whom was composed the body of the states, assembled divers times as it plainly appears by the word of the holy scripture. At the election of the first king, who was Saul, all the ancients of Israel assembled together at Kama. In like manner all Israel was assembled, or all Judah and Benjamin, etc. Now, it is no way probable, that all the people, one by one, met together there. Of this rank there are in every well governed kingdom, the princes, the officers of the crown, the peers, the greatest and most notable lords, the deputies of provinces, of whom the ordinary body of the estate is composed, or the parliament or the diet, or other assembly, according to the different names used in divers countries of the world; in which assemblies, the principal care is had both for the preventing and reforming either of disorder or detriment in church or commonwealth.

Whether private men may resist by arms

It remains now that we speak of particulars who are private persons. First, particulars or private persons are not bound to take up arms against the prince who would compel them to become idolaters. The covenant between God and all the people who promise to be the people of God, does not in any sort bind them to that; for as that which belongs to the whole universal body is in no sort proper to particulars, so, in like manner, that which the body owes and is bound to perform cannot by any sensible reason be required of particular persons: neither does their duty anything oblige them to it; for every one is bound to serve God in that proper vocation to which he is called. Now private persons, they have no power; they have no public command, nor any calling to unsheathe the sword of authority; and therefore as God has not put the sword into the hands of private men, so does He not require in any sort that they should strike with it. It is said to them, "put up thy sword into thy scabbard." On the contrary the apostles say of magistrates, they carry not the sword in vain. If particular men draw it forth they make themselves delinquents. If magistrates be slow and negligent to use it when just occasion is offered, they are likewise justly blameable of negligence in performing their duties, and equally guilty with the former.

But you will say unto me, has not God made a covenant, as well with particular persons as with the generality, with the least as well as the highest? To what purpose was circumcision and baptism ordained? What means that frequent repetition of the covenant in so many passages of holy writ? All this is true, but the consideration hereof is diverse in their several kinds. For as all the subjects of a good and faithful prince, of what degree soever they be, are bound to obey him; but some of them, notwithstanding, have their particular duty, as magistrates must hold others in obedience; in like manner all men are bound to serve God; but some are placed in a higher rank, have received greater authority, in so much as they are accountable for the offences of others, if they attend not the charges of the commonalty carefully.

The kings, the commonalties of the people, the magistrates into whose hands the whole body of the commonwealth has committed the sword of authority, must and ought to take care that the church be maintained and preserved; particulars ought only to look that they render themselves members of this church. Kings and popular estates are bound to hinder the pollution or ruin of the temple of God, and ought to free and defend it from all corruption within, and all injury from without. Private men must take order, that their bodies, the temples of God, be pure, that they may be fit receptacles for the Holy Ghost to dwell in them. If any man defile the temple of God, saith the apostle, him shall God destroy; for the temple of God is holy, which temple ye are; to the former He gives the sword which they bear with authority; to the other He recommends the sword of the Spirit only, to wit, the word of God, wherewith Saint Paul arms all Christians against the assaults of the devil. What shall then private men do, if the king will constrain them to serve idols? If the magistrates into whose hands the people have consigned their authority, or if the magistrates of the place, where these particulars dwell, do oppose these proceedings of the king, let them in God's name obey their leaders, and employ all their means (as in the service of God) to aid the holy and commendable enterprises of those who oppose themselves lawfully against his wicked intention. Amongst others they have the examples of the centurions, and men at arms, who readily and cheerfully obeyed the princes of Judah, who, stirred up by Jehoidas, purged the church from all profanation, and delivered the kingdom from the tyranny of Athaliah. But if the princes and magistrates approve the course of an outrageous and irreligious prince, or if they do not resist him, we must lend our ears to the counsel of Jesus Christ, to wit, retire ourselves into some other place.

*　　*　　*

The Third Question, WHETHER IT BE LAWFUL TO RESIST
A PRINCE WHO DOTH OPPRESS OR RUIN A PUBLIC STATE,
AND HOW FAR SUCH RESISTANCE MAY BE EXTENDED:
BY WHOM, HOW, AND BY WHAT RIGHT OR LAW IT IS
PERMITTED

For so much as we must here dispute of the lawful authority of a
lawful prince, I am confident that this question will be the less acceptable to tyrants and wicked princes; for it is no marvel if those
who receive no law, but what their own will and fancy dictate unto
them, be deaf unto the voice of that law which is grounded upon
reason. But I persuade myself that good princes will willingly entertain this discourse, insomuch as they sufficiently know that all magistrates, be they of never so high a rank, are but an inanimated and
speaking law. Neither though anything be pressed home against the
bad, can it fall within any inference against the good kings or princes,
as also good and bad princes are in a direct diameter opposite and
contrary: therefore, that which shall be urged against tyrants, is so
far from detracting anything from kings, as on the contrary, the more
tyrants are laid open in their proper colours, the more glorious does
the true worth and dignity of kings appear; neither can the vicious
imperfections of the one be laid open, but it gives addition of perfections and respect to the honour of the other.

But for the tyrants let them say and think what they please, that
shall be the least of my care; for it is not to them, but against them
that I write; for kings I believe that they will readily consent to that
which is propounded, for by true proportion of reason they ought
as much to hate tyrants and wicked governors, as shepherds hate
wolves, physicians, poisoners, true prophets, false doctors; for it must
necessarily occur that reason infuses into good kings as much hatred
against tyrants, as nature imprints in dogs against wolves, for as the
one lives by rapine and spoil, so the other is born or bred to redress
and prevent all such outrages. It may be the flatterers of tyrants will
cast a supercilious aspect on these lines; but if they were not past
all grace they would rather blush for shame. I very well know that
the friends and faithful servants of kings will not only approve and
lovingly entertain this discourse, but also, with their best abilities,
defend the contents thereof. Accordingly as the reader shall find himself moved either with content or dislike in the reading hereof, let

him know that by that he shall plainly discover either the affection or hatred that he bears to tyrants. Let us now enter into the matter.

Kings are made by the people

We have shewed before that it is God that does appoint kings, who chooses them, who gives the kingdom to them: now we say that the people establish kings, puts the sceptre into their hands, and who with their suffrages, approves the election. God would have it done in this manner, to the end that the kings should acknowledge, that after God they hold their power and sovereignty from the people, and that it might the rather induce them, to apply and address the utmost of their care and thoughts for the profit of the people, without being puffed with any vain imagination, that they were formed of any matter more excellent than other men, for which they were raised so high above others; as if they were to command our flocks of sheep, or herds of cattle. But let them remember and know, that they are of the same mould and condition as others, raised from the earth by the voice and acclamations, now as it were upon the shoulders of the people unto their thrones, that they might afterwards bear on their own shoulders the greatest burdens of the commonwealth. Divers ages before that, the people of Israel demanded a king. God gave and appointed the law of royal government contained in the seventeenth chapter, verse fourteen of Deuteronomy, when, says Moses, "thou art come unto the land which the Lord thy God giveth thee, and shalt possess it, and shalt dwell therein, and shalt say, I will set a king over me like as all the nations that are about me, thou shalt in any wise set him whom the Lord thy God shall choose from amongst thy brethren, etc." You see here, that the election of the king is attributed to God, the establishment to the people: now when the practice of this law came in use, see in what manner they proceeded.

The whole body of the people is above the king

Now, seeing that the people choose and establish their kings, it follows that the whole body of the people is above the king; for it is a thing most evident, that he who is established by another, is accounted under him who has established him, and he who receives his authority from another, is less than he from whom he derives his power. Potiphar the Egyptian sets Joseph over all his house; Nebuchadnezar, Daniel over the province of Babylon; Darius the six score governors over the kingdom. It is commonly said that masters establish their servants, kings their officers. In like manner, also, the people establish the king as administrator of the commonwealth. Good kings have not disdained this title; yea, the bad ones themselves have affected it; insomuch, as for the space of divers ages, no Roman emperor (if it were not some absolute tyrant, as Nero, Domitian, Caligula) would suffer himself to be called lord. Furthermore, it must necessarily be, that kings were instituted for the people's sake, neither can it be, that for the pleasure of some hundreds of men, and without doubt more foolish and worse than many of the other, all the rest were made, but much rather that these hundred were made for the use and service of all the other, and reason requires that he be preferred above the other, who was made only to and for his occasion: so it is, that for the ship's sail, the owner appoints a pilot over her, who sits at the helm, and looks that she keeps her course, nor run not upon any dangerous shelf; the pilot doing his duty, is obeyed by the mariners; yea, and of himself who is owner of the vessel, notwithstanding, the pilot is a servant as well as the least in the ship, from whom he only differs in this, that he serves in a better place than they do.

*   *   *

The assembly of the three estates

Besides all this, anciently every year, and since less often, to wit, when some urgent necessity required it, the general or three estates were assembled, where all the provinces and towns of any worth, to wit, the burgesses, nobles and ecclesiastical persons, did all of them send their deputies, and there they did publicly deliberate and conclude of that which concerned the public state. Always the authority of this assembly was such that what was there determined, whether it were to treat peace, or make war, or create a regent in the kingdom, or impose some new tribute, it was ever held firm and inviolable; nay, which is more by the authority of this assembly, the kings convinced of loose intemperance, or of insufficiency, for so great a charge or tyranny, were disthronized; yea, their whole races were for ever excluded from their succession to the kingdom, no more nor less, as their progenitors were by the same authority formerly called to that administration of the same kingdom. Those whom the consent and approbation of the estates had formerly raised, were by the dissent and disallowing of the same afterwards cast down. Those who tracing in the virtuous steps of their ancestors, were called to that dignity, as if it had been their inheritance, were driven out and disinherited for their degenerate ingratitude, and for that being tainted with insupportable vices, they made themselves incapable and unworthy of such honour.

This shews that succession was tolerated to avoid practices, close and underhand canvassing, discontents of persons refused, contentions, interreigns, and other discommodities of elections. But on the other part, when successions brought other mischiefs more pernicious, when tyranny trampled on the kingdom, and when a tyrant possessed himself of the royal throne, the medicine proving much worse than the disease, then the estates of the kingdom lawfully assembled in the name of all the people, have ever maintained their authority, whether it were to drive out a tyrant, or other unworthy king, or to establish a good one in his place. The ancient French had learned that of the Gauls, as Cæsar shews in his commentaries. For Ambiorix, king of the Eburons, or Leigeons confesses, "That such were the condition of the Gaulish empire, that people lawfully assembled had no less power over the king, than the king had over the people." The which appears also in Vercingetorix, who gives an account of his actions before the assembly of the people.

In the kingdoms of Spain, especially Aragon, Valentia, and Catalonia, there is the very same. For that which is called the Justitia Major in Aragon has the sovereign authority in itself. And there, the lords who represent the people proceed so far, that both at the inauguration of the king, as also at the assembly of the estates, which is observed every third year, they say to the king in express words that which follows, "We who are as much worth as you, and have more power than you, choose you king upon these and these conditions, and there is one between you and us who commands over you, to wit, the Justitia Major of Aragon, who oftentimes refuses that which the king demands, and forbids that which the king enjoins."

In the kingdoms of England and Scotland the sovereignty seems to be in the parliament, which heretofore was held almost every year. They call parliaments the assembly of the estates of the kingdom, in the which the bishops, earls, barons, deputies of towns and

provinces deliver their opinions, and resolve with a joint consent of
the affairs of state. The authority of this assembly has been so sacred
and inviolable, that the king dare not abrogate or alter that which
had been there once decreed.

It was that which heretofore called and installed in their charges
all the chief officers of the kingdom; yea, and sometimes the ordinary
councillors of that which they call the king's privy council. In some,
the other Christian kingdoms, as Hungary, Bohemia, Denmark, Swe-
den, and the rest, they have their officers apart from the kings; and
histories, together with the examples that we have in these our times,
sufficiently demonstrate that these officers and estates have known
how to make use of their authority, even to the deposing and driving
out of the tyrannous and unworthy kings.

*   *   *

Kings receive laws from the people

These may be sufficiently verified by examples. Before there was
a king in Israel, God by Moses prescribed to him both sacred and
civil ordinances, which he should have perpetually before his eyes;
but after that Saul was elected and established by the people, Samuel
delivered it to him written, to the end, he might carefully observe it;
neither were the succeeding kings received before they had sworn to
keep those ordinances.

The ceremony was this, that together with the setting of the
crown on the king's head, they delivered into his hands the Book of
the Testimony, which some understand to be the right of the people
of the land, others, the law of God according to which he ought to
govern the people. Cyrus, acknowledging himself conservator of his
country's laws, obliges himself to oppose any man who would offer
to infringe them; and at his inauguration, ties himself to observe
them, although some flatterers tickled the ears of his son Cambises,
that all things were lawful for him.

The kings of Sparta, whom Aristotle calls lawful princes, did
every month renew their oaths, promising in the hands of the
ephori, procures for the kingdom, to rule according to those laws
which they had from Lycurgus.

Hereupon, it being asked Archidamus, the son of Zeuxidamus,

who were the governors of Sparta, he answered, "The laws, and the lawful magistrates."

* * *

For neither the emperor, the king of France, nor the kings of Spain, England, Polander, Hungary, and all other lawful princes; as the archdukes of Austria, dukes of Brabante, earls of Flanders, and Holland, nor other princes, are not admitted to the government of their estates, before they have promised to the electors, peers, palatines, lords, barons, and governors, that they will render to every one right according to the laws of the country, yea, so strictly that they cannot alter or innovate anything contrary to the privileges of the countries, without the consent of the towns and provinces; if they do it, they are no less guilty of rebellion against the laws than the people are in their kind, if they refuse obedience, when they command according to law. Briefly, lawful princes receive the laws from the people as well as the crown, in lieu of honour, and the sceptre, in lieu of power, which they are bound to keep and maintain and therein reposes their chiefest glory.

* * *

If the prince may make new laws

What then? Shall it not be lawful for a prince to make new laws and abrogate the old? seeing it belongs to the king, not only to advise that nothing be done neither against, nor to defraud the laws, but also that nothing be wanting to them, nor anything too much in them: briefly, that neither age nor lapse of time do abolish or entomb them; if there be anything to abridge, to be added or taken away from them, it is his duty to assemble the estates, and to demand their advice and resolution, without presuming to publish anything before the whole have been, first, duly examined and approved by them, after the law is once enacted and published, there is no more dispute to be made about it, all men owe obedience to it, and the prince in the first place, to teach other men their duty, and for that all men are easier led by example than by precepts, the prince must necessarily express his willingness to observe the laws, or else by what equity can he require obedience in his subjects, to that which he himself contemns.

For the difference which is between kings and subjects ought not to consist in impunity, but in equity and justice. And therefore, although Augustus was esteemed to be exempt by the decree of the senate, notwithstanding, reproving of a young man who had broken the Julian law concerning adultery, he boldly replied to Augustus, that he himself had transgressed the same law which condemns adulterers. The emperor acknowledged his fault, and for grief forbore too late. So convenient a thing it is in nature, to practise by example that which we would teach by precept.

The lawgiver Solon was wont to compare laws to money, for they maintain human societies, as money preserves traffic; neither improperly, then, if the king may not lawfully, or at the least heretofore could not, mannace or embase good money without the consent of the commonwealth, much more less can he have power to make and unmake laws, without the which, nor kings, nor subjects, can cohabit in security, but must be forced to live brutishly in caves and deserts like wild beasts, wherefore also the emperor of Germany, esteeming it needful to make some law for the good of the empire, first he demands the advice of the estates. If it be there approved, the princes, barons, and deputies of the towns sign it, and then the law is satisfied, for he solemnly swears to keep the laws already made, and to introduce no new ones without a general consent.

There is a law in Polonia, which has been renewed in the year 1454, and also in the year 1538, and by this it is decreed, that no new laws shall be made, but by a common consent, nor nowhere else, but in the general assembly of the estates.

For the kingdom of France, where the kings are thought to have greater authority than in other places; anciently all laws were only made in the assembly of the estates, or in the ambulatory parliament. But since this parliament has been sedentary, the king's edicts are not received as authentical, before the parliament has approved them.

Whereas on the contrary, the decrees of this parliament, where the law is defective, have commonly the power and effect of law. In the kingdoms of England, Spain, Hungary, and others, they yet enjoy in some sort their ancient privileges.

For, if the welfare of the kingdom depends on the observation of the laws, and the laws are enthralled to the pleasure of one man, is it not most certain, that there can be no permanent stability in that government? Must it not then necessarily come to pass, that if the king (as some have been) be infected with lunacy, either continually, or by intervals, that the whole state fall inevitably to ruin? But if the laws be superior to the king, as we have already proved, and that the king be tied in the same respect of obedience to the laws as the servant is to his master, who will be so senseless, who will not rather obey the law than the king or will not readily yield his best assistance against those who seek to violate or infringe them? Now seeing that the king is not lord over the laws, let us examine how far his power may be justly extended in other things.

*   *   *

Whether the goods of the people belong to the king

But to proceed let us now see whether the king, whom we have already proved has not power to the lives of his subjects, is not at the least lord over their goods. In these days there is no language more common in the courts of princes, than of those who say all is the king's. Whereby it follows, that in exacting any thing from his subjects, he takes but his own, and in that which he leaves them, he expresses the care he has that they should not be altogether destitute of means to maintain themselves, and this opinion has gained so much power in the minds of some princes, that they are not ashamed to say that the pains, sweat and industry of their subjects is the proper revenue, as if their miserable subjects only kept beasts to till the earth for their insolent master's profit and luxury. And indeed, the practice at this day is just in this manner, although in all right and equity it ought to be contrary. Now we must always remember that kings were created for the good and profit of the people, and that these (as Aristotle says) who endeavour and seek the commodity of the people, are truly kings: whereas those who make their own private ends and pleasures the only butt and aim of their desires, are truly tyrants.

It being then so that every one loves that which is his own, yea, that many covet that which belongs to other men, is it anything probable that men should seek a master to give him frankly all that they had long laboured for, and gained with the sweat of their brows? May we not rather imagine, that they chose such a man on whose integrity they relied for the administering of justice equally both to the poor and rich, and who would not assume all to himself, but rather maintain every one in the fruition of his own goods? or who, like an unprofitable drone, should suck the fruit of other men's labours, but rather preserve the house, for those whose industry justly deserved it? Briefly, who, instead of extorting from the true owners their goods, would see them defended from all ravening oppressors? What, I pray you matters it, says the poor country man, whether the king or the enemy make havoc of my goods, since through the spoil thereof I and my poor family die for hunger? What imports it whether a stranger or home-bred caterpillar ruin my estate, and bring my poor fortune to extreme beggary? Whether a foreign soldier, or a sycophant courtier, by force or fraud, make me alike miserable? Why shall he be accounted a barbarous enemy, if thou be a friendly patriot? Why he a tyrant if thou be king? Yea, certainly by how much parricide is greater than manslaughter, by so much the wickedness of a king exceeds in mischief the violence of an enemy.

If then, therefore, in the creation of kings, men gave not their own proper goods unto them, but only recommended them to their protection; by what other right then, but that of freebooters, can they challenge the property of other men's goods to themselves? Wherefore the kings of Egypt were not (according to law) at the first the lords of particular men's estates, but only then when they were sold unto them for corn, and yet may there well be question made of the validity of that contract. Ahab, king of Israel, could not compel Naboth to sell him his vineyard; but rather if he had been willing, the law of God would not permit it. The Roman emperors who had an unreasonable power, could neither by right have done it. At this day there is with much difficulty any kingdom to be found, where the meanest subject may not suit the king, and where many times the king is not cast in the suit, which succeeding, he must as well as others satisfy the judgment. And to this is not contrary, although at the first view it seem so, that which some of their most familiars have written of the emperors. That by the civil law all things were the king's, and that Cæsar was absolute lord of all things, they themselves expound this their opinion in this manner, that the dominion of all things belongs to the king, and the propriety to particular persons, in so much as the one possesses all by the right of commanding, the other by the law of inheritance. We know that it is a common saying amongst the civilians, that if any make claim to a house or a ship, it follows not therefore that he can extend his right to all the furniture or lading. And therefore, a king may challenge and gain right to the kingdom of Germany, France and England: and yet, notwithstanding, he may not lawfully take any honest man's estate from him, but by a manifest injustice, seeing that they are things diverse, and by law distinguished, to be possessors of the whole, and of all the particular parts.

23

The Way to Wealth

THOMAS MUN WROTE England's Treasure around 1630, so it falls a few years beyond our terminal date. However, it shows what men had been learning from a century of expanding world trade. Mun himself had made a fortune in the Mediterranean trade, and he was a member of the committee on England's East India Company. He had also pondered the lessons to be learned from the meteoric career of Spain during her "Golden Century." His theory of the balance of trade and his analysis of the fruitful ways to employ national resources contributed to the development of mercantilist economics.

Thomas Mun (1571–1641), England's Treasure by Forraign Trade

Chapter ii, the means to enrich this kingdom, and to encrease our treasure

ALTHOUGH A KINGDOM may be enriched by gifts received, or by purchase taken from some other Nations, yet these are things uncertain and of small consideration when they happen. The ordinary means therefore to encrease our wealth and treasure is by *Forraign Trade,* wherein wee must ever observe this rule; to sell more to strangers yearly than wee consume of theirs in value. For suppose that when this Kingdom is plentifully served with the Cloth, Lead, Tinn, Iron, Fish and other native commodities, we doe yearly export the overplus to forraign Countries to the value of twenty two hundred thousand pounds; by which means we are enabled beyond the Seas to buy and bring in forraign wares for our use and Consumptions, to the value of twenty hundred thousand pounds; By this order duly kept in our trading, we may rest assured

From Thomas Mun, ENGLAND'S TREASURE BY FORRAIGN TRADE OR THE BALLANCE OF OUR FORRAIGN TRADE IS THE RULE OF OUR TREASURE (London, 1664), pp. 5–23.

that the Kingdom shall be enriched yearly two hundred thousand pounds, which must be brought to us in so much Treasure; because that part of our stock which is not returned to us in wares must necessarily be brought home in treasure.

For in this case it cometh to pass in the stock of a Kingdom, as in the estate of a private man; who is supposed to have one thousand pounds yearly revenue and two thousand pounds of ready money in his Chest: If such a man through excess shall spend one thousand five hundred pounds *per annum,* all his ready mony will be gone in four years; and in the like time his said money will be doubled if he take a Frugal course to spend but five hundred pounds *per annum;* which rule never faileth likewise in the Commonwealth, but in some cases (of no great moment) which I will hereafter declare, when I shall shew by whom and in what manner this ballance of the Kingdoms account ought to be drawn up yearly, or so often as it shall please the State to discover how much we gain or lose by trade with forraign Nations. But first I will say something concerning those ways and means which will encrease our exportations and diminish our importations of wares; which being done, I will then set down some other arguments both affirmative and negative to strengthen that which is here declared, and thereby to shew that all the other means which are commonly supposed to enrich the Kingdom with Treasure are altogether insufficient and meer fallacies.

Chapter iii, the particular ways and means to encrease the exportation of our commodities, and to decrease our consumption of forraign wares

The revenue or stock of a Kingdom by which it is provided of forraign wares is either *Natural* or *Artificial.* The Natural wealth is so much only as can be spared from our own use and necessities to be exported unto strangers. The Artificial consists in our manufactures and industrious trading with forraign commodities, concerning which I will set down such particulars as may serve for the cause we have in hand.

1] First, although this Realm be already exceeding rich by nature, yet might it be much encreased by laying the waste grounds (which are infinite) into such employments as should no way hinder the present revenues of other manured lands, but hereby to supply our selves and prevent the importations of Hemp, Flax, Cordage, Tobacco, and divers other things which now we fetch from strangers to our great impoverishing.

2] We may likewise diminish our importations, if we would soberly refrain from excessive consumption of forraign wares in our diet and rayment, with such often change of fashions as is used, so much the more to encrease the waste and charge; which vices at this present are more notorious amongst us than in former ages. Yet might they easily be amended by enforcing the observation of such good laws as are strictly practised in other Countries against the said excesses; where likewise by commanding their own manufactures to be used, they prevent the coming in of others, without prohibition, or offence to strangers in their mutual commerce.

3] In our exportations we must not only regard our own super-fluities, but also we must consider our neighbours necessities, that so upon the wares which they cannot want, nor yet be furnished thereof elsewhere, we may (besides the vent of the Materials) gain so much of the manufacture as we can, and also endeavour to sell them dear, so far forth as the high price cause not a less vent in the quantity. But the superfluity of our commodities which strangers use, and may also have the same from other Nations, or may abate their vent by the use of some such like wares from other places, and with little inconvenience; we must in this case strive to sell as cheap as possible we can, rather than to lose the utterance of such wares. For we have found of late years by good experience, that being able to sell our Cloth cheap in Turkey, we have greatly en-creased the vent thereof, and the *Venetians* have lost as much in the utterance of theirs in those Countreys, because it is dearer. And on the other side a few years past, when by the excessive price of Wools our Cloth was exceeding dear, we lost at the least half our clothing for forraign parts, which since is no otherwise (well neer) recovered again than by the great fall of price for Wools and Cloth. We find that twenty five in the hundred less in the price of these and some other Wares, to the loss of private mens revenues, may raise above fifty upon the hundred in the quantity vented to the benefit of the publique. For when Cloth is dear, other Nations doe presently practise clothing, and we know they want neither art nor materials to this performance. But when by cheapness we drive them from this employment, and so in time obtain our dear price again, then do they also use their former remedy. So that by these alterations we learn, that it is in vain to expect a greater revenue of our wares than their condition will afford, but rather it concerns us to apply our endeavours to the times with care and diligence to help our selves the best we may, by making our cloth and other manufactures without deceit, which will encrease their estimation and use.

4] The value of our exportations likewise may be much advanced when we perform it our selves in our own Ships, for then we get only not the price of our wares as they are worth here, but also the Merchants gains, the charges of ensurance, and fraight to carry them beyond the seas. As for example, if the *Italian* Merchants should come hither in their own shipping to fetch our Corn, our red Herrings or the like, in this case the Kingdom should have ordinarily but 25. s. for a quarter of Wheat, and 20. s. for a barrel of red herrings, whereas if we carry these wares our selves into *Italy* upon the said rates, it is likely that wee shall obtain fifty shillings for the first, and forty shillings for the last, which is a great difference in the utterance or vent of the Kingdoms stock. And although it is true that the commerce ought to be free to strangers to bring in and carry out at their pleasure, yet nevertheless in many places the exportation of victuals and munition are either prohibited, or at least limited to be done onely by the people and shipping of those places where they abound.

5] The frugal expending likewise of our own natural wealth might advance much yearly to be exported unto strangers; and if in our rayment we will be prodigal, yet let this be done with our own materials and manufactures, as Cloth, Lace, Imbroderies, Cutworks and the like, where the excess of the rich may be the employment of the poor, whose labours notwithstanding of this kind, would be more profitable for the Commonwealth, if they were done to the use of strangers.

6] The Fishing in his Majesties seas of *England, Scotland* and *Ireland* is our natural wealth, and would cost nothing but labour, which the *Dutch* bestow willingly, and thereby draw yearly a very great profit to themselves by serving many places of Christendom with our Fish, for which they return and supply their wants both of forraign Wares and Mony, besides the multitude of Mariners and Shipping, which hereby are maintain'd, whereof a long discourse might be made to shew the particular manage of this important business. Our Fishing plantation likewise in *New-England, Virginia, Groenland,* the *Summer Islands* and the *New-found-land,* are of the like nature, affording much wealth and employments to maintain a great number of poor, and to encrease our decaying trade.

7] A Staple or Magazin for forraign Corn, Indico, Spices, Raw-silks, Cotton wool or any other commodity whatsoever, to be imported will encrease Shipping, Trade, Treasure, and the Kings customes, by exporting them again where need shall require, which course of Trading, hath been the chief means to raise *Venice, Genoa,* the *low-Countreys,* with some others; and for such a purpose *England* stands most commodiously, wanting nothing to this performance but our own diligence and endeavour.

8] Also wee ought to esteem and cherish those trades which have in remote or far Countreys, for besides the encrease of Shipping and Mariners thereby, the wares also sent thither and receiv'd from thence are far more profitable unto the kingdom than by our trades neer at hand; As for example; suppose Pepper to be worth here two Shillings the pound constantly, if then it be brought from the *Dutch* at *Amsterdam,* the Merchant may give there twenty pence the pound, and gain well by the bargain; but if he fetch this Pepper from the *East-indies,* he must not give above three pence the pound at the most, which is a mighty advantage, not only in the part which serveth for our own use, but also for that great quantity which (from hence) we transport yearly unto divers other Nations to be sold at a higher price: whereby it is plain, that we make a far greater stock by gain upon these *Indian* Commodities, than those Nations doe where they grow, and to whom they properly appertain, being the natural wealth of the Countries. But for the better understanding of this particular, we must ever distinguish between the gain of the Kingdom, and the profit of the Merchant; for although the Kingdom payeth no more for this Pepper than is before supposed, nor for any other commodity bought in forraign parts more than the stranger receiveth from us for the same, yet the Merchant payeth not only that price, but also the fraight, ensurance, customes and other charges which are exceeding great in these long voyages; but yet all these in the Kingdoms accompt are but commutations among our selves, and no Privation of the Kingdoms stock, which being duly considered, together with the support also of our other trades in our best Shipping to *Italy, France, Turkey,* the *East Countreys* and other places, by transporting and venting the wares which we bring yearly from the *East Indies;* It may well stir up our utmost endeavours to maintain and enlarge this great and noble business, so much importing the Publique wealth, Strength, and Happiness. Neither is there less honour and judgment by growing rich (in this manner) upon the stock of other Nations, than by an industrious encrease of our own means, especially when this later is advanced by the benefit of the former, as we have found in the *East Indies* by sale of much of our Tin, Cloth, Lead and other Commodities, the vent whereof doth daily encrease in those Countreys which formerly had no use of our wares.

9] It would be very beneficial to export money as well as wares, being done in trade only, it would encrease our Treasure; but of this I write more largely in the next Chapter to prove it plainly.

10] It were policie and profit for the State to suffer manufactures made of forraign Materials to be exported custome-free, as Velvets and all other wrought Silks, Fustians, thrown Silks and the like, it would employ very many poor people, and much encrease the value of our stock yearly issued into other Countreys, and it would (for this purpose) cause the more forraign Materials to be brought in, to the improvement of His Majesties Customes. I will here remember a notable increase in our manufacture of winding and twisting only of forraign raw Silk, which within 35 years to my knowledge did not employ more than 300. people in the City and suburbs of London, where at this present time it doth set on work above four-teen thousand souls, as upon diligent enquiry hath been credibly reported unto His Majesties Commissioners for Trade. And it is certain, that if the said forraign Commodities might be exported from hence, free of custome, this manufacture would yet encrease very much, and decrease as fast in *Italy* and in the *Netherlands*. But if any man allege the *Dutch* proverb, *Live and let others live;* I answer, that the Dutchmen notwithstanding their own Proverb, doe not onely in these Kingdoms, encroach upon our livings, but also in other forraign parts of our trade (where they have power) they do hinder and destroy us in our lawful course of living, hereby taking the bread out of our mouth, which we shall never prevent by pluck-ing the pot from their nose, as of late years too many of us do practise to the great hurt and dishonour of this famous Nation; We ought rather to imitate former times in taking sober and worthy courses more pleasing to God and suitable to our ancient reputation.

11] It is needful also not to charge the native commodities with too great customes, lest by indearing them to the strangers use, it hinder their vent. And especially forraign wares brought in to be trans-ported again should be favoured, for otherwise that manner of trad-ing (so much importing the good of the Commonwealth) cannot prosper nor subsist. But the Consumption of such forraign wares in the Realm may be the more charged, which will turn to the profit of the kingdom in the *Ballance of the Trade*, and thereby also enable the King to lay up the more Treasure out of his yearly incomes, as of this particular I intend to write more fully in his proper place, where I shall shew how much money a Prince may conveniently lay up without the hurt of his subjects.

12] Lastly, in all things we must endeavour to make the most we can of our own, whether it be *Natural* or *Artificial;* And forasmuch as the people which live by the Arts are far more in number than they who are masters of the fruits, we ought the more carefully to maintain those endeavours of the multitude, in whom doth consist the greatest strength and riches both of King and Kingdom: for where the people are many, and the arts good, there the traffique must be great, and the Countrey rich. The *Italians* employ a greater number of people, and get more money by their industry and manufactures of the raw Silks of the Kingdom of *Cicilia,* than the King of *Spain* and his Subjects have by the revenue of this rich commodity. But what need we fetch the example so far, when we know that our own natural wares doe not yield us so much profit as our industry? For Iron oar in the Mines is of no great worth, when it is compared with the employment and advantage it yields being digged, tried, transported, bought, sold, cast into Ordnance, Muskets, and many other instruments of war for offence and defence, wrought into Anchors, bolts, spikes, nayles and the like, for the use of Ships, Houses, Carts, Coaches, Ploughs, and other instruments for Tillage. Compare our Fleece-wools with our Cloth, which requires shearing, washing, carding, spinning, Weaving, fulling, dying, dressing and other trimmings, and we shall find these Arts more profitable than the natural wealth, whereof I might instance other examples, but I will not be more tedious, for if I would amplify upon this and the other particulars before written, I might find matter sufficient to make a large volume, but my desire in all is only to prove what I propound with brevity and plainness.

Chapter iv, the exportation of our moneys in trade of merchandize is a means to encrease our treasure

This position is so contrary to the common opinion, that it will require many and strong arguments to prove it before it can be accepted of the Multitude, who bitterly exclaim when they see any monies carried out of the Realm; affirming thereupon that wee have absolutely lost so much Treasure, and that this is an act directly against the long continued laws made and confirmed by the wisdom of this Kingdom in the High Court of Parliament, and that many places, nay *Spain* it self which is the Fountain of Mony, forbids the exportation thereof, some cases only excepted. To all which I might answer, that *Venice, Florence, Genoa,* the *Low Countreys* and divers other places permit it, their people applaud it, and find great benefit by it; but all this makes a noise and proves nothing, we must therefore come to those reasons which concern the business in question.

First, I will take that for granted which no man of judgment will deny, that we have no other means to get Treasure but by forraign trade, for Mines wee have none which do afford it, and how this mony is gotten in the managing of our said Trade I have already shewed, that it is done by making our commodities which are exported yearly to over ballance in value the forraign wares which we consume; so that it resteth only to shew how our monyes may be added to our commodities, and being jointly exported may so much the more encrease our Treasure.

Wee have already supposed our yearly consumptions of forraign wares to be for the value of twenty hundred thousand pounds, and our exportations to exceed that two hundred thousand pounds, which sum wee have thereupon affirmed is brought to us in treasure to ballance the accompt. But now if we add three hundred thousand pounds more in ready mony unto our former exportations in wares, what profit can we have (will some men say) although by this means we should bring in so much ready mony more than wee did before, seeing that wee have carried out the like value.

To this the answer is, that when wee have prepared our exportations of wares, and sent out as much of every thing as wee can spare or vent abroad: It is not therefore said that then we should add our money thereunto to fetch in the more mony immediately, but rather first to enlarge our trade by enabling us to bring in more forraign wares, which being sent out again will in due time much encrease our Treasure.

For although in this manner wee do yearly multiply our importations to the maintenance of more Shipping and Mariners, improvment of His Majesties Customs and other benefits: yet our consumption of those forraign wares is no more than it was before; so that all the said encrease of commodities brought in by the means of our ready mony sent out as is afore written, doth in the end become an exportation unto us of a far greater value than our said moneys were, which is proved by three several examples following.

1] For I suppose that 100000. *l.* being sent in our Shipping to the East Countreys, will buy there one hundred thousand quarters of wheat cleer aboard the Ships, which being after brought into *England* and housed, to export the same at the best time for vent thereof in *Spain* or *Italy,* it cannot yield less in those parts than two hundred thousand pounds to make the Merchant but a saver, yet by this reckning wee see the Kingdom hath doubled that Treasure.

2] Again this profit will be far greater when wee trade thus in remote Countreys, as for example, if wee send one hundred thousand pounds into the *East-Indies* to buy Pepper there, and bring it hither, and from hence send it for *Italy* or *Turkey,* it must yield seven hundred thousand pounds at least in those places, in regard of the excessive charge which the Merchant disburseth in those long voyages in Shipping, Wages, Victuals, Insurance, Interest, Customes, Imposts, and the like, all which notwithstanding the King and the Kingdom gets.

3] But where the voyages are short & the wares rich, which therefore will not employ much Shipping, the profit will be far less. As when another hundred thousand pounds shall be employed in *Turkey* in raw Silks, and brought hither to be after transported from hence into *France*, the *Low Countreys,* or *Germany,* the Merchant shall have good gain, although he sell it there but for one hundred and fifty thousand pounds: and thus take the voyages altogether in their *Medium,* the moneys exported will be returned unto us more than Trebled. But if any man will yet object, that these returns come to us in wares, and not really in mony as they were issued out.

The answer is (keeping our first ground) that if our consumption of forraign wares be no more yearly than is already supposed, and that our exportations be so mightily encreased by this manner of Trading with ready money as is before declared: It is not then possible but that all the over-ballance or difference should return either in mony or in such wares as we must export again, which, as is already plainly shewed will be still a greater means to encrease our Treasure.

For it is in the stock of the Kingdom as in the estates of private men, who having store of wares, doe not therefore say that they will not venture out or trade with their mony (for this were ridiculous) but do also turn that into wares, whereby they multiply their Mony, and so by a continual and orderly change of one into the other grow rich, and when they please turn all their estates into Treasure; for they that have Wares cannot want money.

Neither is it said that Mony is the Life of Trade, as if it could not subsist without the same; for we know that there was great trading by way of commutation or barter when there was little mony stirring in the world. The *Italians* and some other Nations have such remedies against this want, that it can neither decay nor hinder their trade, for they transfer bills of debt, and have Banks both publick and private, wherein they do assign their credits from one to another daily for very great sums with ease and satisfaction by writings only, whilst in the mean time the Mass of Treasure which gave foundation to these credits is employed in Forraign Trade as a Merchandize, and by the said means they have little other use of money in those countreys more than for their ordinary expences. It is not therefore the keeping of our mony in the Kingdom, but the necessity and use of our wares in forraign Countries, and our want of their commodities that causeth the vent and consumption on all sides, which makes a quick and ample Trade. If wee were once poor, and now having gained some store of mony by trade with resolution to keep it still in the Realm; shall this cause other Nations to spend more of our commodities than formerly they have done, whereby we might say that our trade is Quickned and Enlarged? no verily, it will produce no such good effect: but rather according to the alteration of times by their true causes wee may expect the contrary; for all men do consent that plenty of mony in a Kingdom doth make the native commodities dearer, which as it is to the profit of some private men in their revenues, so it is directly against the benefit of the Publique in the quantity of the trade; for as plenty of mony makes wares dearer, so dear wares decline their use and consumption, as hath been already plainly shewed in the last Chapter upon that particular of our cloth; And although this is a very hard lesson for some great landed men to learn, yet I am sure it is a true lesson for all the land to observe, lest when wee have gained some store of mony by trade, wee lose it again by not trading with our mony. I knew a Prince in *Italy* (of famous memory) *Ferdinando the first,* great Duke of *Tuscanie,* who being very rich in Treasure, endevoured therewith to enlarge his trade by issuing out to his Merchants great sums of money for very small profit; I my self had forty thousand crowns of him *gratis* for a whole year, although he knew that I would presently send it away in *Specie* for the parts of *Turkey* to be employed in wares for his Countries, he being well assured that in this course of trade it would return again (according to the old saying) with a Duck in the mouth. This noble and industrious Prince by his care and diligence to countenance and favour Merchants in their affairs, did so encrease the practice thereof, that there is scarce a Nobleman or Gentleman in all his dominions that doth not Merchandize either by himself or in partnership with others, whereby within these thirty years the trade to his port of *Leghorn* is so much encreased, that of a poor little town (as I my self knew it) it is now become a fair and strong City, being one of the most famous places for trade in all Christendom. And yet it is worthy our observation, that the multitude of Ships and wares which come thither from *England,* the *Low Countreys,* and other places, have little or no means to make their returns from thence but only in ready mony, which they may and do carry away freely at all times, to the incredible advantage of the said great Duke of *Tuscanie* and his subjects, who are much enriched by the continual great concourse of Merchants for all the States of the neighbour Princes, bringing them plenty of mony daily to supply their wants of the said wares. And thus we see that the current of Merchandize which carries away their Treasure, becomes a flowing stream to fill them again in a greater measure with mony.

There is yet an objection or two as weak as all the rest: that is, if wee trade with our Mony wee shall issue out the less wares; as if a man should say, those Countreys which heretofore had occasion to consume our Cloth, Lead, Tin, Iron, Fish, and the like, shall now make use of our monies in the place of those necessaries, which were most absurd to affirm, or that the Merchant had not rather carry out wares by which there is ever some gains expected, than to export mony which is still but the same without any encrease.

But on the contrary there are many Countreys which may yield us very profitable trade for our mony, which otherwise afford us no trade at all, because they have no use of our wares, as namely the *East-Indies* for one in the first beginning thereof, although since by industry in our commerce with those Nations we have brought them into the use of much of our Lead, Cloth, Tin, and other things, which is a good addition to the former vent of our commodities.

Again, some men have alleged that those Countries which permit mony to be carried out, do it because they have few or no wares to trade withall: but wee have great store of commodities, and therefore their action ought not to be our example.

To this the answer is briefly, that if we have such a quantity of wares as doth fully provide us of all things needful from beyond the seas: why should we then doubt that our monys sent out in trade, must not necessarily come back again in treasure; together with the great gains which it may procure in such manner as is before set down? And on the other side, if those Nations which send out their monies do it because they have but few wares of their own, how come they then to have so much Treasure as we ever see in those places which suffer it freely to be exported at all times and by whomsoever? I answer, *Even by trading with their Moneys;* for by what other means can they get it, having no Mines of Gold or Silver?

Thus may we plainly see, that when this weighty business is duly considered in his end, as all our humane actions ought well to be weighed, it is found much contrary to that which most men esteem thereof, because they search no further than the beginning of the work, which mis-informs their judgments, and leads them into error: For if we only behold the actions of the husbandmen in the seed-time when he casteth away much good corn into the ground, we will rather accompt him a mad man than a husbandman: but when we consider his labours in the harvest which is the end of his endeavours, we find the worth and plentiful encrease of his actions.

Chapter v, forraign trade is the only means to improve the price of our lands

It is a common saying, that plenty or scarcity of mony makes all things dear or good or cheap; and this mony is either gotten or lost in forraign trade by the over or underballancing of the same, as I have already shewed. It resteth now that I distinguish the seeming plenties of mony from that which is only substantial and able to perform the work: For there are divers ways and means whereby to procure plenty of mony into a Kingdom, which do not enrich but rather empoverish the same by the several inconveniences which ever accompany such alterations.

As first, if we melt down our plate into Coyn (which suits not with the Majesty of so great a Kingdom, except in cases of extremity) it would cause Plenty of mony for a time, yet should we be nothing the richer, but rather this treasure being thus altered is made the more apt to be carried out of the Kingdom, if we exceed our means by excess in forraign wares, or maintain a war by Sea or Land, where we do not feed and cloath the Souldier and supply the armies with our native provisions, by which disorders our treasure will soon be exhausted.

Again, if we think to bring in store of money by suffering forraign Coins to pass current at higher rates than their intrinsick value compared with our Standard, or by debasing or by enhancing our own moneys, all these have their several inconveniences and difficulties, (which hereafter I will declare) but admitting that by this means plenty of money might be brought into the Realm, yet should we be nothing the richer, neither can such treasure so gotten long remain with us. For if the stranger or the English Merchants bring in this money, it must be done upon a valuable consideration, either for wares carried out already, or after to be exported, which helps us nothing except the evil occasions of excess or war aforenamed be removed which do exhaust our treasure: for otherwise, what one man bringeth for gain, another man shall be forced to carry out for necessity; because there shall ever be a necessity to ballance our Accounts with strangers, although it should be done with loss upon the rate of the money, and Confiscation also if it be intercepted by the Law.

The conclusion of this business is briefly thus. That as the treasure which is brought into the Realm by the ballance of our forraign trade is that money which onely doth abide with us, and by which we are enriched: so by this plenty of money thus gotten (and no otherwise) do our Lands improve. For when the Merchant hath a good dispatch beyond the Seas for his Cloth and other wares, he doth presently return to buy up the greater quantity, which raiseth the price of our Woolls and other commodities, and consequently doth improve the Landlords Rents as the Leases expire daily: And also by this means money being gained, and brought more abundantly into the Kingdom, it doth enable many men to buy Lands, which will make them the dearer. But if our forraign trade come to a stop or declination by neglect at home or injuries abroad, whereby the Merchants are impoverished, and thereby the wares of the Realm less issued, then do all the said benefits cease, and our Lands fall of price daily.

Chapter vi, the Spanish treasure cannot be kept from other kingdoms by any prohibition made in Spain

All the Mines of Gold and Silver which are as yet discovered in the sundry places of the world, are not of so great value as those of the *West-Indies* which are in the possession of the King of *Spain;* who thereby is enabled not onely to keep in subjection many goodly States and Provinces in *Italy* and elsewhere, (which otherwise would soon fall from his obeisance) but also by a continual war taking his advantages doth still enlarge his Dominions, ambitiously aiming at a Monarchy by the power of his Moneys, which are the very sinews of his strength, that lies so far dispersed into so many Countreys, yet hereby united, and his wants supplied both for war and peace in a plentiful manner from all the parts of Christendom, which are therefore partakers of his treasure by a Necessity of Commerce; wherein the Spanish policy hath ever endeavoured to prevent all other Nations the most it could: For finding *Spain* to be too poor and barren to supply it self and the *West Indies* with those varieties of forraign wares whereof they stand in need, they knew well that when their Native Commodities come short to this purpose, their Moneys must serve to make up the reckoning; whereupon they found an incredible advantage to adde the traffick of the *East-Indies* to the treasure of the *West:* for the last of these being employed in the first, they stored themselves infinitely with rich wares to barter with all the parts of Christendom for their Commodities, and so furnishing their own necessities, prevented others for carrying away their moneys: which in point of state they hold less dangerous to impart to the remote Indians, than to their neighbour Princes, lest it should too much enable them to resist (if not offend) their enemies. And this Spanish policy against others is the more remarkable, being done likewise so much to their own advantage; for every Ryal of Eight which they sent to the *East-Indies* brought home so much wares as saved them the disbursing of five Ryals of Eight here in *Europe* (at the least) to their Neighbours, especially in those times when that trade was only in their hands: but now this great profit is failed, and the mischief removed by the English, Dutch, and others which partake in those *East-India* trades as ample as the Spanish Subjects.

It is further to be considered, that besides the disability of the *Spaniards* by their native commodities to provide forraign wares for their necessities, (whereby they are forced to supply the want with mony) they have likewise that canker of war, which doth infinitely exhaust their treasure, and disperse it into Christendom even to their enemies, part by reprisal, but especially through a necessary mainte- nance of those armies which are composed of strangers, and lie so far remote, that they cannot feed, clothe, or otherwise provide them out of their own native means and provisions, but must receive this relief from other Nations: which kind of war is far different to that which a Prince maketh upon his own confines, or in his Navies by Sea, where the Souldier receiving money for his wages, must every day deliver it out again for his necessities, whereby the treasure remains still in the Kingdom, although it be exhausted from the King: But we see that the *Spaniard* (trusting in the power of his Treasure) undertakes wars in *Germany,* and in other remote places, which would soon begger the richest Kingdom in Christendom of all their mony; the want whereof would presently disorder and bring the armies to confusion, as it falleth out sometimes with *Spain* it self, who have the Fountain of mony, when either it is stopt in the passage by the force of their enemies, or drawn out faster than it flows by their own occasions; whereby also we often see that Gold and silver is so scant in *Spain,* that they are forced to use base copper money, to the great confusion of their Trade, and not without the undoing also of many of their own people.

But now that we have seen the occasions by which the Spanish treasure is dispersed into so many places of the world, let us likewise discover how and in what proportion each Countrey doth enjoy these Moneys, for we find that *Turkey* and divers other Nations have great plenty thereof, although they drive no trade with *Spain,* which seems to contradict the former reason, where we say that this treasure is obtained by a Necessity of Commerce. But to clear this point, we must know that all Nations (who have no Mines of their own) are enriched with Gold and Silver by one and the same means, which is already shewed to be the ballance of their forraign Trade: And this is not strictly tyed to be done in those Countries where the fountain of treasure is, but rather with such order and observations as are prescribed. For suppose *England* by trade with *Spain* may gain and bring home five hundred thousand Ryals of 8. yearly, if we lose as much by our trade in *Turkey,* and therefore carry the mony thither, it is not then the *English,* but the *Turks* which have got this treasure, although they have no trade with *Spain* from whence it was first brought. Again, if *England* having thus lost with *Turkey,* do notwithstanding gain twice as much by *France, Italy,* and other members of her general trade, then will there remain five hundred thousand Ryals of eight cleer gains by the ballance of this trade: and this comparison holds between all other Nations, both for the manner of getting, and the proportion that is yearly gotten.

But if yet a question should be made, whether all Nations get treasure and *Spain* only lose it? I answer no; for some Countreys by war or by excess do lose that which they had gotten, as well as *Spain* by war and want of wares doth lose that which was its own.